W9-CNP-804

# BODY CARE

Books by Andrea Wells Miller

*A Choir Director's Handbook* (compiled and edited by)

*The Single Experience* (with Keith Miller)


Study Courses by Andrea Wells Miller

*Faith, Intimacy, and Risk in the Single Life* (with Keith
 Miller)

*BodyCare: Studies in Nutrition and Exercise for God's
 Body of Believers* (with exercise tapes by Bobbie
 Wolgemuth and Judy Moser, Vickie Hanson, Cathi
 Stout, and Jamie Warren)

A Proven Program for Successful
Diet, Fitness and Health

# BODY
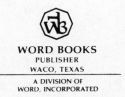
# CARE

Featuring Ten Weeks of Devotions to
Help You Achieve God's Plan for
Your Body, Mind and Spirit

# Andrea Wells Miller

WORD BOOKS
PUBLISHER
WACO, TEXAS

A DIVISION OF
WORD, INCORPORATED

*BodyCare: A Proven Program for Successful*
*Diet, Fitness, and Health*

Copyright © 1984 by Andrea Wells Miller.
All rights reserved. No part of this book may be reproduced
in any form whatsoever, except for brief quotations in reviews,
without the written permission of the publisher.

Scripture quotations in this book are from the
Revised Standard Version of the Bible, copyrighted 1946, 1952,
© 1971, 1973 by the Division of Christian Education of the
National Council of the Churches of Christ in the U.S.A.,
and are used by permission

Library of Congress cataloging in publication data:

Miller, Andrea Wells.
    Bodycare: a proven program for successful diet,
fitness, and health.

    Bibliography: p.
    1. Women—Health and hygiene.   2. Physical fitness for
women.   3. Christian life—1960–      .  I. Title.
RA778.M59      1984      613'.04244      84-7298
ISBN 0-8499-0289-3

*Printed in the United States of America*

TO KEITH MILLER,
my husband, friend, and co-adventurer in life,
who believed in me enough to put up with all the strain
of having another writer in the house!

# PLEASE READ CAREFULLY

The exercise instructions and diet plans contained in this book have been reviewed with medical specialists in the appropriate fields and have been found to be safe for use by the ordinary user in physically sound condition. However, if you have had any medical or physical difficulties that are related to your diet or that may affect your ability to perform these exercises, we advise that you consult with your physician before following any of the instructions or plans contained in this book. In addition, should you experience any physical problems while following any of the instructions or plans contained in this book, *you should consult your physician immediately.*

Because every person's body is different, NO WARRANTIES, EXPRESS OR IMPLIED, ARE GIVEN WITH REGARD TO THE INSTRUCTIONS AND PLANS CONTAINED IN THIS BOOK, AND NEITHER WORD, INC. NOR ANDREA WELLS MILLER WILL BE LIABLE FOR ANY INJURIES OR HARM THAT MAY RESULT TO YOU FROM FOLLOWING THE DIET OR THE WORKOUT INSTRUCTIONS.

# Contents

# CONTENTS

# Contents

## CONTENTS

# Acknowledgments

I want to express my gratitude to the medical and fitness staff of the Houstonian, who "talked straight" to us at our first physical examination and lovingly guided us through the first phases of adjustment to a healthier way of life. In particular I wish to thank Joleen Schovee Graf, whose advice and guidance about the fitness segments of this book were invaluable, and also Elizabeth R. (Betsy) Manis, who supervised the section on foods and helped clarify many details. Also I am grateful to Bill Day, who granted me permission to use *The Houstonian Preventive Medicine Center Nutritional Advice* booklet, and who answered many, many questions.

I also owe thanks to Joseph Paul at Word, Inc., who first envisioned the project and believed it could come to pass. And I am indebted to Anne Christian Buchanan, whose inquisitive mind and energetic spirit, along with sharp editorial skills, helped shape and clarify some occasionally murky passages.

Bobbie Wolgemuth and Judy Moser, creators of the *Firm Believer* exercise records and tapes, have proven to be especially supportive friends, with both their spiritual presence and concrete help. Bobbie's letters of encouragement always seemed to come at low times for me and helped carry me through. I owe thanks to Judy for her presence at the photo session for the exercise section as hairdresser and makeup artist. She and Bobbie together coached me through each pose, and without their critical eyes I would have been lost.

Others who screened the manuscript and offered valuable suggestions are Dr. J. H. Lindsey, gynocologist; The Reverend Kristin Miller-Provence, minister, friend, and stepdaughter; Carolyn Huffman, author and minister's wife; and Margo Piper, Weight Watchers teacher. Since final responsibility for the content of this manuscript rests with me, however, I must also take responsibility for any mistakes or misunderstandings.

The majority of the recipes in the recipe section were used with permission from Judith Fatjo, co-founder of The Phoenix Spa, a health and fitness spa for women and men in Houston, and I am very grateful to her for that.

Special appreciation goes to three friends—Helene Mora, Della Scalan, and Sherrill Spink, who joined me in my "Tom Sawyer" exercise sessions and provided much-needed moral support.

## ACKNOWLEDGMENTS

I also wish to thank the writers whose publishers have graciously granted permission for use of various charts to help clarify some parts of some chapters.

As I think back over the past four years, I can see in my mind the faces of many others who have offered support, information, guidance along the way. I regret that there is not room to mention them all.

Most of all, my heartfelt love and thanks go to my husband, Keith, to whom this book is dedicated. He bravely tested strange new recipes and learned to cook marvelous lowfat soups and make exciting salads. Without his support and cooperation this project could not have happened.

ANDREA WELLS MILLER

# How *Bodycare* Began

It was a cold bright day in January. My husband, Keith, and I tumbled out of bed in our hotel room and pulled on our exercise clothes. Taking a change of clothes with us, we left the room and made our way out in the early morning to the front of the hotel. Hailing a cab, Keith said to me, "Well, here we go. It's scary, but we might as well find out the truth." We were on our way to our first physical examination at the Houstonian Preventive Medicine Center in Houston, Texas.

That was four years ago, and that morning changed our lives. We found out that, while we were basically in good health that day, some things were happening inside our bodies that could lead to problems down the road. And since we love life and want to spend our time on earth as healthy, energetic people, available to do God's will, we decided to do what we could to reverse the trends toward illness we saw happening in each of us.

We'd both had physical exams by other kinds of doctors. But a preventive-medicine doctor is different from other doctors in that he or she looks for things which might lead to *future* health problems. Preventive medicine seeks to put more responsibility for health into the hands of each individual. Rather than waiting until something goes wrong and going to a doctor for a cure, people can do a lot to help keep themselves out of the doctor's office in the first place.

The doctors at the Preventive Medicine Center found that Keith had symptoms which could lead to heart disease and colon cancer. My basic problems were that I was about ten pounds overweight (left over from when I had brought my weight down almost 15 years earlier) and . . . I don't have a better way to put it . . . I was "addicted" to laxatives. We got some good advice from the doctors and nutritionists at the Center and started our own search for ways we could improve our health and prevent future problems. I started reading extensively about health, exercise, and nutrition, and together Keith and I tried to put what I was learning into practice in our lives. During the next three years, guided by the people at the Houstonian, we were able to reverse our direction and improve our health.

I'm now convinced that we'll never stop learning and doing all we can about cooking methods, food, exercise, vitamins, and—for me—

permanent, long-lasting weight control. During these past few years of change, we've tried lots of eating plans—meatless meals, high-fiber recipes, and lowfat and low-sugar cooking—as well as several different forms of regular exercise. Keith cheerfully (for the most part) went along with me as I tried out new exercises, new recipes, new ways of doing things. He gave me honest feedback, too, and once in a while, when I tried something really unusual, he would say, "Honey, that's just too 'far out' for me."

Gradually we worked out an eating plan and exercise routine that works for us, fits into our schedule, and meets our specific health needs.

### The Book Is Born

One of the results of our four-year learning experience is this book. In it, I'd like to share some of the things I've learned about healthy living. I'm not an expert, but I've read many books and research papers by experts. I've had a lot of help from the people at the Houstonian Preventive Medicine Center and from other doctors, nutritionists, and fitness experts who have read what I've written to be sure that what I was putting in the book was both sound and helpful. And I know from Keith's and my own experience that the principles shared here are principles that have moved us toward health rather than away from it.

### Healthy Living and Weight Control: Two Important Factors

One of the two major emphases in this book will be healthy living. More and more researchers are finding that proper exercise and good eating habits can go a long way toward preventing major fatal diseases such as heart disease and cancer. (In fact, the more I read, the more it seems that these are two kinds of illness we may actually contribute to, sometimes unknowingly, by having flabby, weak muscles and by eating too many high-fat, vitamin-poor foods.) Exercise and proper eating can also increase our energy levels, counteract depression, anxiety, and bad disposition and help our creativity and thinking processes immensely.

The other major emphasis will be weight control. God designed our skeletons and muscles to carry a certain amount of weight, and when we get too far above the top range of that certain amount, the muscles and bones are stressed. While nothing may show up for years, as we age the added wear and tear on joints and muscles can lead to arthritis, bursitis, backache, foot problems and other strain-related problems.

Being *underweight* can also lead to physical difficulties, although in our overweight-conscious society these are seldom mentioned. In this book, when I say "weight control," I usually mean *losing* weight, because that's been my particular struggle. But I think the principles of exercise and good nutrition, and of *gradual* change, that we'll be talking about can also apply to people who would like to gain some weight.

## Why Talk about Exercise First? ( . . . or at All!)

Everything I have read indicates that the bottom line concerning health and weight loss is exercise. Now, I don't mean we should become a church full of people in training for a marathon. But moderate daily exercise can gently but firmly improve the body and move us toward health.

The most current books I've studied emphasize that without exercise there is no cure for being overweight (or underweight). A diet alone simply is not enough. So whether you have a few pounds or more to lose (or gain), the best lifetime, permanent approach seems to be putting moderate exercise into your routine as regularly and naturally as getting dressed in the morning or brushing your teeth.

So I will begin by discussing the three basic kinds of exercise, what they do for the body and how to get started on an exercise program that is right for you, whatever your fitness level is now.

I can already see some faces with wrinkled noses saying, "But I *hate* exercise!" Before you get too discouraged, I want to say that we'll be concentrating on finding a form of exercise that is fun—or if not fun, at least pleasant. Of course a grinding drudgery is harder to keep up than one that provides some moments of pleasure. The things I believe are needed when approaching this subject are an open mind, a willingness to try different things, and at least the *desire* to *want* to like to exercise.

## Since Eating Is Here to Stay, What's a Healthy Approach to It?

After the section on exercise, I'll go on to discuss food. We'll look at how food and other substances affect our health, and also at some healthy ways to develop good eating habits without giving up good taste.

Most cooks I know seem to fall into two general categories: those who love to experiment with food and taste it and enjoy it—almost as a hobby—and those who don't want to have to do much to prepare it, because they are always in a hurry to do something else. For both kinds of cooks there is good news.

There are enough interesting taste varieties in *healthy* food to keep creative cooks experimenting for years, and to keep gourmet cooks like Craig Claiborne and Helen Corbitt busy writing books forever! Instead of dreaming up creamy white sauces and fat-and-sugar-loaded desserts, many people are finding that experimenting with herbs, spices, broths, soups, and low-oil or no-oil salad dressings can be enjoyable and rewarding. And baking whole-grain breads and spice cakes sweetened with vanilla, cinnamon, and fruit juices is a wonderful culinary experience. Some of the rest of us would love to benefit from the creativity of such cooks.

Yet, delicious, healthful food can be prepared quickly, too. Baking or broiling meats is a simple approach. Steaming vegetables and eating them raw in salads doesn't take a lot of time. A box of raisins or an apple makes an excellent snack choice at the office or on the run in the car doing errands or carpool chores. And grocery stores are providing better and better whole-grain products from which to choose, so baking at home isn't necessary.

The overall approach to health presented here is a combination of good eating habits and sound exercises to gradually bring our bodies to a healthy, stable, fit state.

## What about Eating to Lose Weight?

There is no "miracle diet" given in this book, although an outline of how to lose weight is given. There are also several other diet programs on the market which do a good, safe job, and you may prefer to follow one of them. But I'll be discussing what constitutes a safe, healthy, and long-lasting approach to weight loss. I'll also discuss what's not so safe, and why. And I'll give you some examples of how I've begun to put this into my life in a way that is realistic for me.

## Can All This Make a Difference?

At the beginning of Keith's and my experience with healthy living my main goal was to help both of us avoid diseases and/or disabilities that we'd found out could be in our future if we did nothing to change the way we were living. I also cared about my appearance and wanted to finish the weight loss I'd started in college 15 years earlier.

I had never been more than 30 pounds overweight. But while the first 20 pounds had come off reasonably fast, I had found that losing the last few pounds was difficult and frustrating.

In these four years I have lost those ten pounds and am now in phase two—learning to keep them off! And I'm happy to say that my laxative addiction is over. If I had known what I know now about food and exercise the whole 30 pounds might have been dealt with all at once—or I might not have gotten into that situation in the first place.

Keith's colon condition has cleared up and remained clear. He has lowered his cholesterol level by 40 points and has greatly reduced other risk factors linked to heart attack.

But to my surprise the benefits from these changes have reached beyond my initial goals. I am reminded every now and then, sometimes in dramatic ways, how much improving our health has meant in concrete ways in our everyday life.

For example, one night last January, four years after that first physical exam in Houston, Keith and I were returning from a speaking trip and had to change planes in Dallas. We were strolling calmly past gate 24, when we noticed on the television screen monitor near us that our flight was scheduled to leave in five minutes—not an hour and five minutes as we had thought. We had misread our tickets.

Our plane had been boarded at gate 39, 15 gates away! I had my coat over my arm, and Keith had a cart with our carry-on luggage on it. We both took off running as fast as we could.

After about four minutes of running in my low-heeled pumps and skirted business suit I felt my second wind kick in, and the feeling reminded me of jogging on the beach. People looked at me strangely as I whipped past them, taking in great gasping breaths through my open mouth. I kept on running and felt a light layer of sweat on my face and around my neck.

In about five more minutes I came to the ramp leading to the plane. It was deserted! I started running down the ramp and I called out, "Wait! Don't go!" I raced around the corner, not knowing whether I would see a great gaping hole at the end of the ramp or a plane with the door open.

To my relief, there I saw two flight attendants staring up at me through the open door of the plane. They had paused in the act of closing the door when they heard me yell. Keith arrived about 30 seconds later, having pushed that cart successfully around people as he was running.

Calculating by the amount of time I ran, I realized that the gate must have been almost a mile from where we started running. (I usually jog a mile in ten and a half minutes, but I was running full speed ahead at the airport!)

Now, it's one thing to be awed by the fact that I can go out on a trail of some kind and run for three miles without stopping. I never thought I'd be able to do that. But to make the connection between having enough health to run three miles in a jogging suit and running shoes and having enough health to make a difference in some other area of my life is exciting.

Four years ago there was no way I could have run all-out for nine straight minutes! And I thought back to the day Keith's doctors had worried about the condition of his heart and was thankful that we both were in so much better shape than we had been! And because of that, we caught our plane!

### Where Does God Fit In?

An important part for me in applying to my own life all the information I've gained has been a strong sense that God is in charge of the earth and all that's in it. He made you and he made me, and he knows what we need in order to be fit and healthy to do his will. He has given us everything we need for health—physical as well as mental, emotional, and spiritual. But our society has gotten further and further away from natural, wholesome foods. And, with all our "labor-saving devices," we don't use our muscles in healthy ways in a day's work. So in the book we're going to deal with ways we can bring our bodies to a healthy state according to what I consider to be "God's natural laws" of nutrition and exercise.

Now, it's tempting to think we can easily change our lives in the area of food and exercise all by ourselves, or that this is not a big enough problem with which to "bother" God. But I've come to believe that God cares about every aspect of our lives, not just the "spiritual" one. And I've discovered that it is only through a relationship to God that I can have the strength to make such dramatic changes. I have not been able to make deep and lasting changes of any kind without regular prayer time and awareness that I cannot do these things alone.

That is the reason for the scriptures and devotions that begin every chapter of *BodyCare.* It is my hope that they will motivate, inspire, and help you, as they have me, to be more aware of God's love for us, his plan for our lives, and his awareness that we are human—sinners in need of his forgiveness and strength.

### Will Being Healthy Make Me a Better Christian?

One thing I want to say here (and I'll also say it elsewhere in these pages) is that I don't believe getting healthy will bring us any more of God's love than we have right now. There are no exercises or jogging trails we can conquer to earn his love; there is no slender body or healthful glow we can achieve to earn it. I believe that he's giving us all the love he has right now, whether we ever lift a finger to move toward health or not. For me, realizing that truth is a wonderful feeling.

And I believe God created the world, nature, and people to interact with each other in harmony. And we who have given our lives to God, to try to be his people, are seekers of ways to live in harmony as he dreamed when he created us. Part of that harmony is to live within a healthy body. Part of it is to try to have a healthy relationship to him in which we surrender one thing after another to his control. He created hearts, arteries, lungs, muscles, appetites, stomachs, and food. And if we can begin to learn about how they all work together as he planned, we can come closer to being all that he has in mind for us to be.

But even if the physical condition of our bodies does not make us more or less lovable in God's eyes, better health *can* lead to a better quality of life. So as we begin this adventure together into *BodyCare*, let us go with the *assurance* of God's love whether we succeed instantly or after some struggles or not at all. Let's try to remember the *promise* of his presence during the process, and let's try to have the *faith* that with God we can grow, change, and become closer and closer to the ideal person he saw when he "knit [each one of us] together in [our] mother's womb" (Ps. 139:13).

# How to Use This Book

*BodyCare* is designed to be read and put into practice over a period of ten weeks. Part One consists of 32 chapters—each containing a scripture, a devotion, and a short lesson on fitness or nutrition. The lessons are designed to take you step by step toward an exercise program and an eating plan that are right for you. I suggest reading a chapter a day the first week (five days), to help you get started, then one every other day from then on (three a week). At the beginning of each week there is a list of "Aims and Activities" to help you check your progress.

The "spaces" between lessons are intended to give you time for planning your own strategy, putting what you are learning into practice, developing new habits. On the days where no devotion and lesson are provided, you might want to spend the time reading your Bible and talking to God about your health needs, asking him to help you understand his will for you in this area of your life.

The other four parts of *BodyCare* contain resources to help you put the information from Part One into practice. Part Two consists of an illustrated exercise routine designed to help you develop better muscle tone. Part Three contains materials to help you work out your own eating plan—food lists, tips on planning a diet, sample menus. Part Four is a mini-cookbook containing recipes that are both healthful and delicious—definitely not "diet food" in the usual sense. And Part Five contains miscellaneous helps—reading lists, suggestions for materials you can send for, tips for planning your schedule, and more.

But all this is not to say that you have to follow a strict ten-week schedule, or follow the exercise routine exactly as planned, or stick to the menus and recipes given. You may prefer to read one lesson a day for a month, or read the whole book at one sitting, or study it with a group. You may decide to go to a health club or join a class instead of following the workout in the book. And you will probably want to adapt your own recipes and menus according to the principles in this book rather than simply following the ones given. I would encourage you to use *BodyCare* in whatever way is most helpful to you, and to make the *BodyCare* program just the beginning of an ongoing adventure of health and fitness.

# Part One

# THE
# BODYCARE
# ADVENTURE

*Ten Weeks of Studies and
Devotions to Help You Get Started on
the Road to Better Health*

# Week One
## (Five Days)

## *Aims and Activities*

(1)  To prepare yourself mentally for the BodyCare program.

(2)  To understand the importance of exercise in weight loss and good health, and to obtain an overview of the kinds of exercise necessary for fitness.

(3)  To see a doctor, if you haven't already, and obtain his or her assurance that you are sound and healthy enough to proceed with a program of sensible exercise and diet. (This is especially important if you are over 35, if you have more than 10 or 15 pounds to lose or gain, or if you have a history of high blood pressure, heart disease, diabetes, or some other chronic disorder.)

(4)  To choose a good 30- to 45-minute muscle-tone workout and to begin doing it three times a week.

# 1

## *Does God Care about My Health?*

### Scripture and Devotion

I first began to realize that God cares about my physical well-being as well as my mind and soul when I came across this verse in the Bible. It is 1 Thessalonians 5:23:

> "May the God of peace himself sanctify you wholly; and may your spirit and soul and body be kept sound and blameless at the coming of our Lord Jesus Christ."

This passage means so much to me because it refers to God's ministering to us "wholly"—to our minds, spirits *and* bodies.

By attending Bible study and prayer groups, I had begun to nurture my soul and grow in my faith by learning more about how to pray and read the Scriptures. I'd also begun to take my emotional concerns to God and pray for the faith to let him help me with my worries and fears. I had begun studying to develop my mind, too, trying to better understand who I am under God and how I can begin to do his will.

But until recently, the idea of seeking God's will concerning my physical fitness and my health never entered my mind. I've always felt that things like how much I weighed and what shape I was in were up to me, and that God was mostly concerned with my spiritual well-being.

And yet, when I read this scripture, I seem to hear Paul asking for a blessing of peace for the Thessalonians "wholly"—for their spirits, souls, *and* bodies. So I'm now beginning to talk to God about my health, too, asking him for the patience, the grace, the discipline, and the desire to make the changes I need to make in order to be healthy.

Resisting the "temptations" of unhealthy foods and getting over being too lazy to exercise have been recurring battles for me. They still are. But trying to develop the *desire* to make these changes has been

29

even more challenging! As Thomas à Kempis pointed out in *The Imitation of Christ*, "He [or she] who merely flees the outward occasions [of temptation] and does not cut away the inordinate desires hidden inwardly in his [or her] heart shall gain little; temptation will easily come again and grieve him [or her] more than it did at first."[1]

It seems to me that my *desire* for unhealthy foods is what makes it so hard to resist them. If I didn't *want* ice cream so much, I wouldn't care about eating it. I'm certainly never bothered with temptations to eat raw oysters! Ugh! (Pardon me if you're an oyster lover.) So until my desires change, patience, grace and discipline seem very hard to come by.

So I have decided this time to invite God into my struggle to become fit for him—to be ready to do his will, to see how God might want me to approach this problem in my life. I am learning to pray for help and to try to be specific about the areas which give me the most trouble. I'll share some of those prayers with you as we go along.

> DEAR LORD, you know I have *wanted* to keep my body healthy, but I haven't always been willing to pay the price. I want to be sound in spirit, mind, *and* body. I ask you now to come into my life and to be present as I study how you made my body and what it takes to keep it fit.
>
> When I read Paul's words to the Thessalonians, I am thankful that you are a God of peace, and that you care about my health as much as you do about my soul. Help me to remember this as I try to learn what you would have me to learn during this time. In Jesus' name we pray, AMEN.

### Exercise: The Neglected "Twin" in the Fitness Formula

To take good care of our bodies, we need to know about two things: exercise and proper eating. But for most of my life, whenever I thought about getting in shape, I usually thought first about losing weight, which led me to think about what I ate. Now, I have never been a chronic overeater who stuffed myself way past full at every opportunity. I ate three meals a day, a snack here and there, and that was about it, except for occasional splurges on birthdays, holidays, or other special times. Yet whenever I would become unhappy about the way I looked or the way my clothes fit, my answer was to "go on a diet."

---

1. Thomas à Kempis, *The Imitation of Christ* (Garden City, NY: Image Books, div. Doubleday & Co., 1955), 45.

The trouble was, I found I could successfully diet down to a certain weight (which was still about six pounds higher than I wanted to be), but then my weight loss stopped. And while I was dieting I felt run-down and tired; I had to eat so little in order to lose weight that I couldn't stay healthy. I really thought I had a serious metabolism problem.

(Before I go on, I want to say that many women *do* have metabolism problems, caused by an ineffective thyroid gland, blood-sugar irregularities, or other difficulties. If you have trouble losing weight and keeping it off, it's a good idea to let a doctor do a blood test to make sure you're not having one of these problems. My checkup at the Houstonian confirmed that I don't have any disorders of this kind.)

Then I read some studies that really changed my approach to fitness (and weight loss). These studies indicated that women who did not change the number of calories they ate, but who began to move around more—doing exercises, walking a greater distance in the parking lots of the stores in which they shopped, taking the stairs instead of the elevator when going up only a flight or two—lost weight. "Hmmmm," I thought. "Maybe this is something I should pay attention to." And paying attention to exercise has turned out to be very helpful.

Another thing that influenced my thinking about exercise was a book by William Bennett and Joel Gurin called *The Dieter's Dilemma.* In it, the authors talk about recent studies that indicate a human body tends to have a "favorite" weight. Bennett and Gurin refer to this weight, which varies from individual to individual and is influenced by many factors, as "setpoint."

Researchers have found that people can diet and move their weight lower than their setpoint, but that as soon as they stop dieting their weight returns to setpoint. If they do manage to stay at a weight lower than the setpoint, they are hungry, miserable, and tense almost the whole time. Their rate of metabolism (which is the speed at which the body burns calories) even drops, so that it takes fewer calories to put on weight. In other words, our bodies do everything they can to entice us back up to that setpoint.[2]

According to Bennett and Gurin, however, there are three things that seem to help a person lower her or his setpoint. Two of them are definitely unhealthy: amphetamines (as found in diet pills) and nicotine (as found in cigarettes). But the third one is very healthy, and it

---

2. William Bennett, M.D. and Joel Gurin, *The Dieter's Dilemma: Eating Less and Weighing More* (New York: Basic Books, 1982), 62.

is physical activity.[3] Apparently certain kinds of exercise raise the rate of metabolism—not only during the time of exercise, which may be very brief, but for six to eight hours *after* the exercise!

All this is not to say that what we eat is not important. Most of the studies I've read stress that a *combination* of exercise and good eating habits is the best strategy for healthy weight loss—as well as for good health in general. But since it's psychologically difficult to start making a lot of changes at once, I'm going to suggest that you concentrate on exercise first, without worrying too much about changing what you're eating. (Of course, that means not eating *more*, either!)

As you begin to exercise, you may very well see some pounds drop off—without eating less. Or even if you don't lose any weight right away, you will probably notice that you lose inches and that your clothes begin to fit better as your muscles are toned and your weight redistributed. But exercise does more for us than just help us lose weight and look better. So before we start talking about *how* to exercise, let's talk for just a little while about how exercise can improve and maintain our health.

## *Everyday Bodily Functions*

I've found that just weighing the right amount doesn't necessarily mean I'm really healthy. Not only should I weigh within 10% of my ideal weight, but my body should also have only a certain amount of fat on it. I need strong, firm muscles to support my weight properly—both my bones and my internal organs. And I need a strong heart to make sure enough blood circulates throughout my system. Good circulation in turn helps keep the other bodily systems functioning properly (including the digestive system, which makes sure my body gets what it needs for energy, for keeping wear and tear repaired, and for flushing out waste materials). It keeps our minds alert, our emotions more stable, and our outer limbs, hands, and feet warm and healthy. It even affects the quality of our skin, hair, and nails by getting important nutrients to those areas. Eyesight, hearing, taste, touch, and smell are all affected by the efficiency of the circulatory system.

For all these bodily needs—weight control, reduced body fat, and good circulation—to be met, regular exercise is a necessity. A well-exercised body with firm muscles and flexible joints is more fit for having babies and keeping up with them while they are growing up. It

---

3. Ibid., 101.

is more able to handle the stress of the workplace. And many kinds of recreation can't be enjoyed as much without good muscle tone and quick reflexes. Good hard play is an emotional and psychological release which contributes to our overall balance—another important part of fitness. And, of course, a trim, well-toned body *looks* better than a flabby one.

## Preventing Medical Problems

In addition to these normal, everyday bodily functions, I've learned that there are medical problems which can be reduced or prevented by exercise. In fact, most of the books I've read about exercise or weight control include chapters which give researched evidence of the value of exercise. My research leads me to the conclusion that we can possibly contribute to our own health problems by *not* exercising.

There are many good research studies related to health problems mentioned in these books, but I won't include all the research data here. (I've included the names of some of the books I read in a reading list in the back of this book.) Instead, I'll list just a few of the disabilities which are thought by some doctors and researchers to be connected with lack of exercise. We'll talk about medical problems related to being overweight later on. The following are health problems having to do with lack of exercise only.

Research has shown that exercise can play a big part in preventing heart attack and strokes. In fact, after some kinds of heart attacks, patients can resume a normal life only if they start exercising according to their doctor's instructions. Also, hypertension (high blood pressure), diabetes, upper-respiratory infections,[4] depression, anxiety, and high cholesterol tend to improve with exercise.

Other ailments such as loss of sexual sensations in both men and women, minor headaches, hangovers, upset stomachs, lack of energy, ulcers, and arthritis have been reduced in people who began to exercise. Other conditions which can be helped by exercise include low back pain and aging.

Now before you get excited because I mentioned aging, it's *not* proven that we live longer if we exercise. But we do know that by improving health and fitness, we can slow down the physical *signs* of aging and give our bodies the abilities and conditions typical of a body that is much younger. In other words, we may not live longer

---

4. Kenneth H. Cooper, M.D., M.P.H., *Aerobics* (New York: Bantam Books, 1968), 5.

because of exercise, but exercise helps us feel better while we are living.

So, people who already have any of these conditions might improve if they start a sensible exercise program. And I believe exercising can go a long way toward helping other people avoid such problems.

The more I read, the more I began to see how I could improve my health by exercising. But before I could convince myself to start investing any amount of time in it, I wanted to learn a little more. We'll be talking about some of the things I learned in the next chapter.

# 2

## *Choosing an Exercise Program— Muscle Tone*

### *Scripture and Devotion*

As I started out learning about exercise, I found out that our bodies don't need just any old exercise. They need three different types of exercise: muscle tone, flexibility, and aerobic exercise. All three work together like members of a well-rehearsed musical trio to give us the best kind of physical fitness. In this chapter we will begin talking about the first kind—exercise that helps build muscle tone. And since this chapter is about getting stronger muscles, here's a scripture which has helped me through difficult times. It is Philippians 4:13:

> "I can do all things in him who strengthens me."

This scripture is a heartening message, and it describes how I feel on days when I am well and strong, when my body is beginning to respond to exercise. But then, like a sudden cloudburst out of nowhere, discouragement and boredom can appear to banish my enthusiasm. Suddenly I'm no longer the least bit interested in even getting out of bed—much less doing any more sit-ups, jogging any more miles, or looking at one more bowl of whole-wheat cereal.

At times like these I remember the way I felt a few days before— springy, cheerful, and in tune with God and the world—and I wonder, can I really "do all things in him who strengthens me"? What was Paul talking about? And I begin to suspect that Paul probably wrote that on a day when he, too, felt springy and cheerful and didn't have any blisters from his sandals or tired muscles from walking all day.

One such day, when I wasn't feeling at all energetic, I read in *The Imitation of Christ,* "one thing withholds many from growing in virtue and from an amendment of life, and that is a horror and a false worldly fear that they may not be able to stand the pain and labor needed to win virtue."

"Boy, that's me," I thought. I don't even want to *mention* to anybody that I'm trying to get in shape, because then, if the pain is too much and I decide to quit, they'll know I blew it.

I read on: "But they will profit most in virtue who force themselves vigorously to overcome those things that are most grievous and irksome to them. A woman [my editorial change] profits most and wins most grace in those things in which she has most overcome herself, and in which she has most subjected her body to her soul."[1]

Wow! That was a new idea for me, and somewhat threatening. What if I couldn't overcome myself? What if I couldn't subject my body to my soul? By letting sluggish physical feelings or my emotional lows give me an excuse to lie around instead of going out to exercise, was I letting my body rule my soul?

I read again Paul's claim: "I can do all things through him who strengthens me." I decided to believe that if Paul could do it, so could I. And I began to pray silently at difficult times during the day for the strength to do the things I knew I had to do to get in shape.

On days when I feel I can do all things with or without God, I forget easily that I need to rely on him. But there are more days when I know I'd never make it if I didn't have Jesus as player-coach on my team!

> DEAR LORD, you are my strength, and when I'm in touch with you I can do more than I can without you. Even the last three sit-ups. Even exercising when I'd rather be doing something else. Help me to remember that when I'm feeling inadequate and lazy. Forgive me when I forget you're there. And thank you for loving me so much that you'll patiently watch me go through all my struggles and failures, knowing that, when I finally stop and ask you to help me, together we can do what seemed impossible for me to do alone.
>
> Be with me today and in the days ahead as I try to learn to remember to call on you for strength. In Jesus' name, AMEN.

## Why Good Muscle Tone Is Important

Although muscles *improve* with use, rather than wear out like machinery, I sometimes catch myself thinking and acting as if I'd

---

1. Thomas à Kempis, *Imitation of Christ*, 70.

better "take it easy" so I won't wear out my body. But although joints and bones and teeth may wear out, muscles need daily movement and light stress to keep their tone and to get stronger. In fact, there is no way to keep muscles firm except to exercise them. And there are so many good reasons to keep them in shape.

In the first place, when certain muscles get weak, just normal movement can put too much stress on the spine, foot bones, and knees, possibly causing injuries to them. If the muscles were strong and able to absorb the minor shock of walking or running, as they were intended to do, these bones and joints would be protected. Also, as strange as it sounds, one of the most common causes of lower-back pain is weak stomach muscles. Doing exercises which strengthen the stomach muscles can help alleviate an aching lower back.

The next fact is exciting if you're trying to lose weight or keep it off. Researchers have found that it takes a lot more energy to maintain muscle tissue than it does to maintain fatty tissue. Muscles are made of a type of tissue which requires more calories than fatty tissue every time it moves.[2]

That means that a person with well-toned muscles burns more calories just by walking across a room than a person with fat-loaded flabby muscles would burn by taking the same walk. Muscle toning creates within the body the kind of tissue that is hungry for fuel and will burn more calories in daily movements.

## How Muscle Tone Can Be Improved

Muscle tone improves when the muscles are used in constructive ways. But it's easy to get everyday housework and walking around an office confused with real exercise. Though these things may leave you exhausted, they do not necessarily build muscle tone. You may find that after doing exercises which do improve your muscles, housework and walking around the office don't leave you quite so exhausted! But what kind of movements *are* constructive and build muscle tone?

## Exercise Classes

One way to improve muscle tone is to join an exercise class, and they've become more and more available. I have found I am more likely

---

2. Ted L. Edwards, Jr., *From Weight Loss to Super Wellness* (Austin, TX: The Hills Medical/Sports Complex, 1983), 9.

to exercise regularly when I make a commitment to show up at a specific place and time. Also, I like sharing the exercise time with other women who are committed to the same goal of getting in shape. Another advantage is that I have an instructor to guide me and encourage me along the way.[3]

## Working Out Alone

But there are times when I must do without the luxury of a class. In the small town where I now live on the Gulf coast, there isn't an exercise class. So I've found that having an exercise tape with instructions is helpful. (There are many excellent and enjoyable tapes available, including tapes that feature good Christian music. I've included a list of possibilities in Part Five of this book.) I can set aside a certain time each day, turn on the tape, and get a good workout without ever having to leave home! This is when I need lots of motivation from inside, however, and I often ask for this motivation in my prayer time.

Also, there are times when I don't even have access to a tape player, and I just have to think up exercises on my own. I usually turn on the radio, then do whatever I can remember from all the exercise classes and tapes I've been through. I warm up, then exercise each body part from the head down—arms, waist, abdomen, legs, hips, and buttocks—ending up with a cool-down period.

Part Two of this book contains an exercise program I've outlined for times like this. You can follow it if you can't get to a class or don't have a tape. Or you can use a routine from several excellent books on the market.

## No Class? Start a "Tom Sawyer" Group!

When we first moved to our small Gulf-Coast town, I started out just fine—exercising to my exercise tape. But then I ran into a problem. I found I had trouble making myself turn on the tape player and exercise. After missing about three weeks of exercise, I mentioned to a new friend of mine that I really wanted to exercise, but that I couldn't seem to make myself do it. She said she had the same problem. So I said, "Why don't we meet together somewhere and do this tape together?"

---

3. Editor's note: Andrea Wells Miller has helped create an exercise and nutrition course for group use, including five outstanding exercise tapes by Christian exercise leaders. The course is also called *BodyCare* and is available through your local bookstore or by contacting Word, Inc., Waco, TX 76796.

I got permission to use a room at my church, and one morning the two of us went over there with an exercise tape called *Firm Believer*.[4] We met together three mornings a week. Then some other women found out that we were meeting regularly, and they joined us.

The whole process reminded me a little bit of Tom Sawyer's technique of getting a fence painted. He pretended that painting that fence was fun, and soon his friends lined up to paint with him. Well, the difference for me is exercising with friends *is* fun. But how to get other people to want to exercise with me was a challenge. So I said to them, in effect, "I'm going to do these exercises because I want to be in shape, and if you want to do them at the same time—great!" I worked hard to avoid any comments or speeches about whether *they* "needed" to be in shape. And I think it's very important in getting a group going to make it clear that you as a beginning leader are doing exercises because you need them, and not because you want to straighten out other people's lives.

Now, after two months, there are four of us. I started the whole thing to help me stay motivated. And so far it's working!

## Equipment with Weights

Another popular way to build muscle tone besides going to an exercise class or working out alone at home is to go to a fitness club which has various pieces of equipment with weights on them. These machines are designed to give different sets of muscles a good workout.

But if you go to a place like this, it's a good idea to get the club's fitness director to show you what to do, because the amount of weight you need for your level of fitness is probably different from what someone else would need. And the amount of weight for you should be determined by a trained person. The instructor can also show you the precise physical movement required to correctly exercise each muscle, as well as how fast or slow to do each one.

When used properly, this type of equipment can be very helpful. But if not used correctly, it is at best a waste of time, and at worst can cause injury.

I'm usually not interested in a club that claims the machines will do the work of muscle toning for me. I've learned that vibrating belts and rollers do not improve muscle tone. And the belts can cause

---

4. Judy Moser and Bobbie Wolgemuth, *Firm Believer: A Complete Exercise Program Featuring Today's Christian Music* (Waco, TX: DaySpring Records, div. Word Inc., 1982).

injury to internal organs. Herbal wraps, saunas, and whirlpools are pleasant, and good for relieving stress and tension. But they are not effective muscle toners or fat reducers.

## "Free Weights"

It is also possible to improve muscle tone with hand-held weights not attached to machines, often referred to as "free weights." These are available at many health clubs, or they can be bought at a sporting goods store and have instruction booklets with them. It's amazing how much harder one has to work with only a half-pound weight in each hand! But be careful about trying to start with weights that are too heavy. You can hurt your back or damage the muscle itself this way. Follow the instruction booklet carefully, or ask your health club's fitness instructor for help.

I sometimes use cans of soup as weights when I work on arm exercises. Also, tube socks with a little buckshot, some BBs, or a small plastic bag of sand or gravel make good adjustable weights. Put the amount of weight you want to use in the sock, then tie the top in a tight knot. When you're ready to increase the weight, just untie the knot and add more!

There are some other important things to remember as you set out to strengthen your muscles—like warming up, cooling down, form, speed, breathing and how hard to push yourself for improvement. We'll look at these in the next chapter.

# 3

## *More about Muscle Tone*

### *Scripture and Devotion*

Strengthening our muscles is very important. But since it is also possible to injure, tear or strain muscles, I want to spend this chapter talking about a few fine points which will help make your muscle-tone activities more effective. But before I do, let's talk about Romans 12:1:

> "I appeal to you therefore . . . by the mercies of God, to present your bodies as a living sacrifice, holy and acceptable to God, which is your spiritual worship."

When I first read this scripture in the light of Keith's and my new commitment to go on the adventure of discovering how to get in shape, I imagined a scene, an encounter between Jesus Christ and me. It seems kind of corny, in a way, but it helped me start thinking about how God might view my physical condition.

The scene opens in a large hall, such as I imagine the old Roman courts of law might have been. Christ is sitting at one end, and I can see him far away as I enter the building. There are two rows of columns, one on my left and the other on my right, and I am supposed to walk across this room between the two rows of columns until I reach the place where Christ is seated, waiting for me.

He looks friendly enough, so I take a deep breath and start walking. As I go, I become conscious of my body. I'm aware that my untoned muscles are jiggling as I walk, my tummy sticks out too much, and my thighs brush each other with each step I take. I try to stand up straighter, hoping I can diminish some of these uncomfortable feelings.

Before I even get to the end of the room, I push the image from my mind. "Wait a minute!" I think. I'm not ready to do this. The full meaning of "presenting my body as a living sacrifice" isn't clear yet, but it's beginning to be. If I "sacrifice" my body to Christ, what does he want with it?

I am told that the Hebrews believed that the body and soul were wrapped up together somehow. This would mean that to offer my body to God would be to give my whole self to him, to dedicate myself to doing whatever he wants me to do with my life.

God has created the human body with certain capacities. But these capacities can be lessened by lack of care—by nonactions as well as actions. Nonactions include things like not thinking of good health as a vital part of a spiritual life, not exercising, and not knowing how foods and their nutrients work together to bring health. Actions would include doing harmful things to the body—things like putting fat-loaded foods into the digestive system, putting cigarette smoke and alcohol into our circulatory systems, staying up too late, and taking on too many responsibilities for one person to reasonably handle.

As I followed this line of thinking, the concept of "BodyCare" came to mean learning about the capacities of my body for health, energy, and vitality, and trying to do the things I need to do to fulfill those capacities, just as I try to develop my soul through spiritual activities like prayer, Bible study and participation in the church's life and worship. While I live on this earth, I have the opportunity to achieve and maintain a level of fitness which will allow me the energy, strength, and endurance to do a lot more for God than I could if I'm not in shape.

Now a quick look around any room full of people tells me that God didn't give all people the kind of body that fits our current standard of "beautiful." We must deal with various physical dimensions like height, nose length, facial shape, skeletal structure, and fat distribution. In fact, I've read that there are almost no people who really like the way they look—even models and movie stars who "set the standard" for what is considered fashionably beautiful.

But that "beautiful" standard is not what I'm talking about. Each of us has a maximum potential. Each of us can move toward that potential—improving our muscle tone, the distribution of our body fat, and the condition of our hair, complexion, nails, and overall skin tone. And we can add much to our lives by enjoying the maximum energy levels possible. To me, that is the goal of BodyCare—not just losing weight or looking good or being stronger (although these things are important to me), but becoming as fit as I can be to do God's will.

With these things in mind I return to my visualized encounter with Christ. But things are different this time. Now I am sitting at the table with him. My body is the same body I'd felt embarrassed about before. Only now I can feel that Christ loves me any way I come to him, regardless of whether I'm up to my best potential. Now that I'm aware of how far away from my potential I am, I want to talk to him about it.

I tell him, "Lord, I want to dedicate myself to you, to being the woman you meant for me to be. I am beginning to see the ways I am missing out on the full potential you gave me by not being in shape. Will you help me as I learn about how to exercise and nourish my body properly so that it can be the best possible sacrifice to you?"

And in my vision Christ smiles and says, "Of course I'll help."

> DEAR LORD, I am becoming so aware of how much potential I have in my physical body for energy, for health, for strength. I want very much to present my body as a living sacrifice to you, and I want to begin now to improve my knowledge of how to do this. Help me as I read and study to begin to see concrete ways in which I can put exercise and good nutrition into my life, not as a temporary thing just to help me look prettier, but as a permanent, lasting way of living.
>
> As Paul says in the passage above, "by the mercies of God" I am to present my body as a living sacrifice. Grant me your mercies, your love, your patience, and your forgiveness as I begin, falter, and begin again to care for my body. In Jesus' name, AMEN.

## Warm-Up and Cool-Down

Although I never took this seriously when I was growing up, I've come to realize that it's important to prepare my body for exercise by warming up just before I begin and by cooling down right afterward.

Until recently it was believed that we should prepare our bodies for exercise by first gently stretching our arms, legs, back, neck, and torso. But now exercise experts are saying that to begin by stretching a "cold" muscle is not good.

The best kind of beginning warm-up consists of doing something that involves the entire body's major muscle groups, like walking briskly for three or four minutes. This can be done outdoors or just by walking in a big circle around a room. Gradually adding other body movements like arm circles or punching fists into the air brings your body slowly alive and helps prepare the heart, lungs and muscles for some hard work. This holds true no matter what physical activity you're about to do, whether it be muscle toning, aerobic exercise, tennis or anything else.[1] Once your body has been prepared in this way, begin to exercise.

## How an Exercise Is Done Is Important

Whatever you do to improve muscle tone, this next point is one I consider to be essential. Whenever I am following an exercise tape, an instructor in a class, or doing my own exercise program with weights, I try to pay attention to the way I do each movement, the exact position of all my body parts, and the speed with which I do an exercise.

When I can, I like to work out in front of a mirror to be sure I am putting my elbow, knee, or arm in the proper place. If an exercise isn't done correctly, it will not develop muscle tone in the correct muscle, and all that energy and sweat can be wasted!

When I find, after a few weeks or months, that I can finish a particular workout easily, I then try concentrating on form—lifting my arms straighter, keeping my knee higher on leg lifts and holding each sit-up for an instant in picture-pose position. I've found that by adding these extra touches I can keep on getting a good workout for my muscles without having to change to a "harder" tape as often.

When I first started exercising, it sometimes seemed as if an exercise were going at a speed which was too slow for me. The reason, I later learned, was that my muscles were so out of shape that it was hard for me to move them in a slow, controlled manner through the exercise. When I started to concentrate on controlling my leg or arm, I saw how much more strength was needed to do an exercise slowly. I can now see that if I continue to hurry through a particular exercise, I won't get that muscle in shape as well as I could.

At other times, the pace seemed much too fast for me. Some muscles need muscle tone in order to move quickly. In those cases, I tried to do the exercise as fast as I could, *while still concentrating on form*, until I noticed that, as the weeks went by, I could gradually pick up my speed and keep up with the class. I can't emphasize enough the fact that if you will do an exercise the best you can for *three or four weeks*, you will be amazed at how much easier it is—which will be a kind of unseen evidence that you are stronger and more flexible. I mention this because once I can do things easily I tend to forget how hard they were.

---

1. If you're using an exercise tape or going to a class that begins with a "stretching" warm-up, try to do this other kind of warm-up I'm recommending *first*. And then, as you begin the tape or the class, be sure you do the stretches gently—without bouncing or jerking.

## How Often to Work on Muscle Tone

As good for you as muscle-tone exercises are, muscles should not be toned daily. I learned that three times a week is about the right amount, because during a workout one's muscles are "torn down" just a little bit by the strain put on them. This is normal, and is not considered harmful if one rests a day in between workouts. As a matter of fact, this is the normal way muscles are strengthened.

During the time between workouts, a period of 36–48 hours, the muscles repair themselves and are then stronger than they were! It is the healing period *between workouts* that does the strengthening.

For this reason, working out for muscle tone two days in a row is not as good for our muscles as working out every other day.

## Breathing

There is another thing I discovered which, when I remember to do it, really helps me have a better workout, and that is breathing deeply.

When we move, our muscles need more oxygen in order to release energy. Oxygen is carried to the muscles by the blood, which is pumped through our entire bodies by our hearts. As we breathe, we get oxygen into our lungs so the blood can pick it up and deliver it to the muscles.

The more we move as we exercise, the more oxygen we need. So, breathing deeply and regularly during exercise is especially important. Sometimes I catch myself holding my breath while doing the harder exercises like sit-ups, and many friends have said they do the same thing! But try not to do that! Holding your breath keeps the oxygen from getting to your muscles. I've found that breathing regularly (rather than holding my breath and then "catching up") lets me last longer or do more repetitions with less muscle pain, because there is more oxygen circulating around.

Another interesting thing I learned is that, while I am exercising, waste materials left over from the burning of fuel are released into the muscles to be flushed out of the system. This waste is picked up by the blood as it goes through the muscle. If these chemicals aren't flushed away, muscles are more likely to be sore. By breathing deeply I am providing oxygen to the heart, which is a muscle, too! The heart can then pump blood even better, and this in turn helps wash away the waste materials, making it less likely that I'll have sore muscles.

One way I've found to train myself to remember to breathe while doing hard exercise is to breathe in a rhythm with the exercise. I breathe out when the muscle is *stressed* and in when it is being *relaxed.* This would mean that I would exhale when coming *up* during a sit-up, and inhale while lying back *down.* Or I would exhale when lifting a leg, and inhale while lowering it. To make sure I'm completely blowing out all the "bad air," I often make a little noise which sounds like whispering the word "choo" each time I breathe out.

If you can remember to breathe in the same rhythm and tempo as the exercise you're doing, I think you'll find your body responding to the exercise faster and more comfortably.

As I began doing good exercises for muscle tone, I began to notice that, even though the muscles in my legs, stomach, and arms were getting stronger, I still couldn't touch my toes with my knees straight. I've never been very flexible, and I wondered if I was a hopeless case. So I kept on reading, and I learned some things about how exercise can improve flexibility. I'll be talking about that in the next chapter.

# 4

## *Flexibility*

### Scripture and Devotion

Before we get started on a discussion of flexibility, one of the three kinds of exercise which our bodies need, let's take a look at 1 Timothy 4:7–10:

> "Train yourself in godliness; for while bodily training is of some value, godliness is of value in every way, as it holds promise for the present life and also for the life to come. The saying is sure and worthy of full acceptance. For to this end we toil and strive, because we have our hope set on the living God, who is the Savior of all . . . especially of those who believe."

When I first read this I thought, "Wait a minute! Is Paul saying that bodily training isn't important?" But then I realized that this scripture is making a point about the relative value of bodily training as compared to training in godliness. And that hits me right between the eyes with a reminder I need to hear.

As I continue learning about how to take care of my body, I can easily get so concerned with how much I weigh, how many sit-ups I can do, and how far I ran this week, that I can forget all about the main emphasis in my life—to learn how to be God's person. I can easily concentrate so hard on weighing the right amount that my weight becomes what I think about most—instead of who God would have me to be. I can shut out other people by not making time to bake a casserole for someone who is sick or to spend an afternoon talking with a friend who really needs someone to listen.

The reminder I read in this passage is that godliness is of value in *every* way, since it holds the promise for the present life and also the life to come. My physical well-being is important, and Paul seems to agree when he writes that bodily training is of some value. But getting in shape just for the sake of feeling or looking good is not the goal of my Christian quest; getting to know Jesus Christ and learning what he wants me to do is the goal. The reason for fitness is to have the health and energy I need to do God's will.

The struggle to become fit is the means by which I can come closer to this goal. And through the struggle I am learning how set I am in my own ways—and not in the ways of the Lord. Through the struggle I learn that alone I am weak, but with Christ I can more often solve problems and overcome emotional desires that lead to destruction. And these godly lessons can carry over into all areas of my life. Turning my will about food and exercise over to God is a good place to begin. But what about my will concerning money, clothes, loving my husband, my friends, spending time in prayer with God, and on and on and on?

Over and over I have had to confess that in my enthusiasm to get healthy I have begun to pay less attention to the other things in my life about which God may want to teach me. And I saw that only through the process of learning to give all my thoughts, desires, and will to God can the rest of wholeness come—physical, emotional, and mental.

> DEAR LORD, thank you for this reminder of the whole meaning of giving my life to you. Thank you that I am learning about how you keep your promises through the improvements I am finding in my health. Help me to remember that you can teach me so much in every area of my life. And help me to keep on training myself as Paul says, "in godliness; for . . . godliness is of value in every way, as it holds promise for the present life and also for the life to come." In Jesus' name, AMEN.

## Why Do We Need Flexibility?

Of the three kinds of exercise our bodies need, flexibility is perhaps the most overlooked. Many people who cannot reach past their knees believe that they were just "born that way" and that nothing really can be done about it. I was one of these people.

It is true that some people are naturally more flexible than others. But flexibility is a key part of the overall fitness picture for everyone—even "stiff customers" like me. If we don't regularly stretch our muscles and tendons, they get even more stiff as time goes on. And the resulting stiffness can lead to problems.

Our bones are held together by a combination of muscles, tendons and ligaments. Muscles are amazingly elastic, but without regular stretching they tend to draw up and become shorter than the bones to which they are attached, especially around joints which stay bent a lot—like the knee joint. The large muscle in the back of the thigh is a good example of this kind of shortening. Muscle-toning exercises and aerobic exercises like jogging shorten this muscle, and many people who are very fit and can run long distances still find it hard to bend over and reach their toes. Their hearts may be in great shape, and they may have great strength in their muscles, but without flexibility they don't have overall physical fitness.

Also, the tendons and ligaments must be stretched gently so that they'll stay elastic and be able to absorb minor shocks from walking as well as the more major shocks from accidental falls or bumps. This elastic quality can help prevent broken bones and dislocations, and can help protect people from the brittle bone condition that often comes with aging.

I mentioned before that one common cause of lower-back pain is weak stomach muscles. A second common cause is inflexibility. Stretching exercises develop flexibility in the lower back, hips and thighs, which can relieve many kinds of lower-back pain.

## Slow and Gentle Is Best

Having read all these good things that flexibility can do for our bodies, I decided to see if I could "loosen up" any. And as I've begun to work on stretching, I've learned that there are good and bad ways to stretch.

When I was in high-school gym classes, we used to stretch by leaning over to touch our toes and "bouncing" up and down—which was supposed to help us get closer and closer to the floor. Now, twenty years of research later, physical therapists are finding that this bouncing can cause tiny tears, pulls, and strains in the muscles and tendons which, though not noticeable at the time, can lead to injuries later on. These tiny tears heal into very small scars, which cause the muscle to be less elastic.

Not only that, but when a muscle is suddenly jerked, its normal reaction is to tighten up to protect the joints from being torn apart. So when we stretch by bouncing and jerking, the muscle doesn't get longer and more elastic; it becomes shorter and tighter—in self-defense!

Experts now say that we should gently move into a stretch position until we are barely beyond the point of comfort (*not* in extreme pain), and hold that stretch while breathing steadily. Stretches should be held from five to thirty seconds.

When it seems that a stretch is hurting too much while I'm holding it, I ease up a little bit until I find the point at which I'm still stretching the muscle, but not hurting it. I've learned that there is a difference between "feeling a stretch" and holding a painful stretch.

So remember two things about stretches: (1) Move gently into them without bouncing, and (2) stay away from the point of pain.

## A Really Rigid Body Can Limber Up

In most good workouts, there is usually a set of exercises in which you sit on the floor with your legs straight out in front or out to each side. The instructions are to lean to the left, right or forward, and the instructor sometimes says something like "touch your nose to your knee."

When I first began exercising, I could hardly keep my balance sitting this way! As I mentioned before, my lower back and the backs of my legs were so stiff I could barely sit up straight, much less lean forward. After two years, however, I can lean forward a little. From the time I began doing stretching exercises up to now, I can see and feel a lot of progress. But sometimes the progress is so slow I want to quit, especially when I see somebody who seems to be actually bumping her nose on her knees! But now I know that if I keep on doing these stretches, gently but firmly, with warmed-up muscles, I will gradually continue to improve. And what a difference this new flexibility is making in so many other areas of my daily life—a difference in everything from just walking around to sitting on the floor at a party!

Since I began working on this project, I've run across some people whose flexibility problem is the opposite of mine; they are *too* limber. It is possible to have tendons and ligaments that are too loose. People with these "loose connections" need to be careful that they do not over-stretch during exercise—that they do not stretch as far as they can. Over-stretching for someone like this might cause a joint to become dislocated. So if you're extremely limber, be careful not to go too far with stretching exercises.

Doing exercises to make us stronger and more flexible is an important start in any fitness program. But it is the third kind of exercise—aerobic exercise—that really makes the difference. We will begin discussing this third kind of exercise in the next chapter.

# 5

## *Aerobic Exercise*

### Scripture and Devotion

The more I studied about how my body responds to exercise, and about how God's natural laws can help me improve my fitness level and health, the more I began to see that many of the principles for living life in general also seem to apply to getting in shape. For example, 2 Corinthians 9:6–7 gave me some clues:

> "He [or she] who sows sparingly will also reap sparingly, and he [or she] who sows bountifully will also reap bountifully. Each one must do as he [or she] has made up his [or her] mind, not reluctantly or under compulsion, for God loves a cheerful giver."

This scripture has two different messages for me when I think of it in relation to getting in shape. The first sentence, "[She] who sows sparingly will also reap sparingly, and [she] who sows bountifully will also reap bountifully," says to me that I can become fit only in proportion to the amount of effort I'm willing to put into it. I've seen that the amount of work I need to do to learn about exercise, dieting, and cooking is a lot. How faithfully and vigorously I'm willing to exercise will also determine how fit I can become. So, being a very competitive person who is anxious to jump right in and get busy, I started pushing myself to learn quickly and exercise hard in a hurry!

After a few weeks, I was feeling burned out and ready to quit. About that time I reread Paul's words from 2 Corinthians. And this time the second sentence jumped out at me in a new way: "Each one must do as [she] has made up [her own] mind, *not reluctantly or under compulsion,* for God loves a *cheerful* giver" (italics mine). I saw then that my enthusiastic attack was mostly due to my *compulsion* for doing the most, the best, and the fastest. And part of my compulsion was due to my desire to get it all over with faster so I could forget about it and go back to my familiar, though unhealthy, habits. And I was definitely not feeling *cheerful* about what I was doing!

I reevaluated my approach. I thought about some of the pleasurable things I had squeezed out of my schedule so I could begin this massive reeducation process. And I decided I really wanted to become the "cheerful giver" God wants me to be, not to fake it any more. I needed to take a new look at the way I was going about making these changes. Instead of rushing, like I had to get it all done immediately, I needed to develop a realistic, gradual plan.

My thinking began to go like this: "I've got the rest of my life to live, which is plenty of time (unless I have an unusual accident along the way). I've spent years learning these old habits, so why do I need to relearn everything in three months, six months, or even a year? And why the hurry to get it over with if I've decided I'm not going back to my old, unhealthy habits? As long as I've made a commitment inside myself to change, and do something every day—however small it may be—toward making that change, then eventually I'll make it. Over the years, I *can* improve my health—rather than continue to make it worse." And I won't be so constantly frustrated. After all, as a doctor pointed out to me, we don't usually gain weight at a rate of twenty pounds a month, so there's no point in trying to lose it that fast.

Again, I was reading *The Imitation of Christ*, by Thomas à Kempis. I noticed that he spent a lot of time writing about changing habits. One paragraph stuck in my mind as I was wrestling with the problem of compulsion and how it led me to be unhappy and resentful. The paragraph was, "If we would every year overcome one vice, we should soon come to perfection, but I fear rather to the contrary, that we were better and more pure at the beginning of our conversion than we were many years after we were converted."[1] I realized I had been much more enthusiastic and optimistic about getting in shape when I had first gotten started than I was now after weeks of knocking myself out trying to do it all at once.

So I made up my mind to back up and try to do what Thomas à Kempis recommended—to overcome one vice each year. It seems like this has left me more time to have a balanced life. Having room for friendships, recreation, meaningful work, and prayer time gives me a more cheerful and less impatient attitude.

Four years later, I find that not everything I need to change is changed. But when I look back over that time, I can see some major changes that are now a part of my routine life. And I feel genuinely cheerful a lot more of the time.

---

1. Thomas à Kempis, *Imitation of Christ*, 43.

DEAR LORD, I realize that the effort I'm willing to put into making the changes to become your person directly affects the results I can expect. But I also know that these changes must become a part of my life—as much a part as breathing is, or as sleeping at night.

Help me to make these changes one by one, and to learn how to give you more and more control over this area of my life, without losing my cheerful attitude which I know you love so much. And help me to learn balance as I develop a plan for growth. I see so much I need to change. Lead me one step at a time through this learning and adjusting period. In Jesus' name, AMEN.

## Aerobic Exercise

In addition to flexibility and muscle tone, the third kind of exercise our bodies need is aerobic exercise. Aerobic exercise is any physical activity that requires a steady, uninterrupted output from the muscles. There are many forms of it, including walking, jogging, bicycling, running in place, jumping rope, swimming, aerobic dancing, cross-country skiing, rowing, roller skating, ice skating, and racketball—to name a few.

Aerobic exercise strengthens the muscles of the heart and lungs and improves their performance. This form of exercise also gives us more energy, makes us more alert, helps with emotional problems like anxiety and depression, and raises our metabolism so that we can burn more calories. In fact, this kind of exercise has often been cited as the most important one for overall fitness.

## The Source of Our Physical Energy

The energy our bodies need is supplied by burning fuel (glucose and fat) from the food we eat. Burning the fuel requires oxygen. While the body can store food, it cannot store oxygen. Without food, the body can keep going for over a month. But without oxygen, the body will die in less than fifteen minutes.

Even if a normal day's work doesn't require a lot of energy, many people find that they are often too tired at the end of the day to give time to their children, to their husband or wife, or to friends. They often feel like lounging in front of the TV set instead of playing with the children or going out with their mate or with friends. And many of them often wonder, "Why am I so tired? I haven't done that much today!"

On the other hand, even when a day takes a lot of energy, people who do aerobic exercise often find that they have some energy to spare at the end of the day.

The energy which comes from aerobic exercise is not just physical energy. Studies by Dr. Kenneth Cooper, Dr. Charles Kuntzleman, Dr. Ted Edwards, Jr., and Dr. Covert Bailey, as well as other exercise researchers, have shown that doing aerobic exercise can also increase mental and emotional energy.

## Stoking the Furnace to Burn More Fuel

If one is overweight, there is visible fat on the body under the skin. But there is also unseen fat within the muscle tissue itself. Even people who appear to be at a normal weight can have fat hidden in their muscles, which is unhealthy.

Aerobic exercise, which demands an increased amount of energy from the body, burns up fat, and therefore helps bring weight levels down. Of course, eating properly is also necessary, and we'll talk more about that later. But the most recent findings are that a diet alone cannot guarantee that you have lost *fat*—internally or externally— and cannot promise you lasting results.

Not only does aerobic exercise burn calories while we are doing it, but it raises our metabolic rate, which is the speed with which we use up calories, so that we keep on burning calories *after* the exercise period is over! Dr. Ted Edwards, Jr., says that the metabolism remains above normal for up to six hours after aerobic exercise.[2] We can actually burn up extra calories all that time!

## What's Effective and What's Not

To be effective aerobically an exercise must be continuous, must keep your heartbeat at 70% to 85% of its maximum, and must last a minimum of seventeen minutes (give or take a few minutes, depending on which book you refer to) not including warm-up and cooldown.

As a result of reading various books on aerobic exercise, I find that different writers answer the question of how often to do aerobic exercises and what the minimum workout time is in different ways.

---

2. Edwards, *Weight Loss to Super Wellness*, 9.

## Week One, Day Five: *Aerobic Exercise*

Dr. Covert Bailey urges a 12—14 minute exercise period six days a week.[3] Dr. Ted Edwards, Jr., says that "to change our bodies from fat-storing machines to ones that burn fat and stay trim, we must do aerobic exercise "at least 30 to 45 minutes every day."[4] I found no one who recommended less than five times a week, however. So I try to do aerobic exercise for at least 20 minutes a day, six times a week—or five during weeks in which some unforeseen conflict comes up.

But when one imagines going out and slowly running around a track for 17 minutes, it's easy to see that muscle tone and flexibility are needed in order to be able to run (or walk, cycle, or swim) without hurting ourselves or getting too tired. And I began having much more fun when jogging *after* I'd done muscle-tone and flexibility exercises for a couple of weeks. I try to do a good 45-minute muscle-tone exercise session three or four times a week. It makes a lot of difference!

---

3. Covert Bailey, *Fit or Fat?* (Boston: Houghton Mifflin Co., 1977), 22.
4. Edwards, *Weight Loss to Super Wellness*, 5.

# Week Two
## (Three Days)

## *Aims and Activities*

(1) To continue on your chosen muscle-tone exercise program three times a week.

(2) To gain an understanding of how to pace yourself and deal with soreness.

(3) To take and record your resting pulse rate and to calculate your working heart rate in preparation for beginning a program of aerobic exercise.

# 6

## *How Hard Is Hard Enough?*

### Scripture and Devotion

One of the unpleasant byproducts of beginning an exercise program is sore muscles. While I was suffering through a bad case of them, I ran across this scripture, which relates to some of the feelings I have when I've really overdone my exercises. The reference is Romans 5:3–5:

> "We rejoice in our sufferings, knowing that suffering produces endurance, and endurance produces character, and character produces hope, and hope does not disappoint us, because God's love has been poured into our hearts through the Holy Spirit which has been given to us."

When I wake up in the morning after a really hard day's exercise and feel the aches and pains in my muscles, I try to remember these words. To me, my sore muscles indicate several things.

First of all, the soreness means I have been lazy for too long. Just doing a normal workout was too much for me, and I'm now suffering for it.

But then, I realize that I'm suffering because I'm going to stop being lazy. In three or four days, depending on how bad the sore muscles are, I'll feel fine again. And after I'm over the pain, I'll be stronger and have more endurance.

When I think of endurance, I think of being able to walk up a flight of stairs more easily, carry two bags of groceries at a time without almost dropping them, sit and write longer without getting a backache. I'll also be able to do more of the exercises instead of dropping out so often to rest. So I begin to feel that the sore muscles are "worth it," especially since I know they're only temporary.

Being aware of the good things exercise is doing for my health inspires me to keep on exercising, in spite of the pain. That's a form of building character. I learn, too, that I can endure pain and still perform, which gives me courage in other painful areas of my life.

The *hope* of becoming fit begins to enter my mind, and every time I move a sore muscle I am reminded that I'm getting closer to my goal. The soreness is a source of both pain and hope at the same time!

So I come full circle, lying there in the bed dreading the pain that will come when I try to sit up and swing my legs over to the side. I suffer, I rejoice, I endure, I grow and I have hope . . . most of the time!

DEAR LORD, sometimes it hurts to grow. I don't like to hurt, and so avoiding pain becomes an excuse that keeps me from doing what I know I must do to grow as you would have me to. Help me to find the courage and endurance and hope I need to keep going. I know that through the Holy Spirit I can be filled with a sense of your presence and love for me. Your caring spirit helps me face the pain. Forgive me when I duck out of my responsibilities because of pain—or my fear of it. Help me to trust in you when the going gets rough. In Jesus' name, AMEN.

## The Competition Trap

When I'm in an exercise class, I often catch myself looking around the room to see how everyone else is doing. Then I try to be sure I do at least as well as the best woman in the class. When I reach the end of my endurance on an exercise, I find I am willing to push my body beyond what is good for it to make sure I look good to the women near me.

I don't know where I learned this habit, but I have paid dearly in terms of sore muscles and the strong temptation to drop out of the class because I can't do "as well as" Laurie, who can bend over and swish her forearms on the carpet without bending her knees or even groaning!

One day a few years ago I joined an exercise class at a health club in Houston. The leader, Joleen Schovee Graf, said a very meaningful thing to me. She told our class that each one of us is responsible for her own level of fitness. Therefore, we should listen to the pain thresholds of our own bodies to decide how many repetitions of a given exercise we should be doing or how high we should be jumping when we do aerobics. She said, "Each class I have taught is filled with people who are at different levels of fitness. I try to lead you in a workout which will be enough for fit people, but I expect you to avoid hurting yourself and to drop out of an exercise whenever you feel that you have done all your level of fitness will allow."

When I heard that, I was able to relax and do the exercises without trying so hard to compete with others in the class who were in better shape. I looked around the class and realized the other women were probably so busy working on their own exercises that they weren't paying much attention to me anyway. How self-centered it was for me to think that they were all waiting to see me fail to do the last few sit-ups or leg lifts!

I decided to try to pay more attention to the music, the leader, and the way I was doing the movements, and less attention to the women around me. The result was much better than I had expected. I began to relax and let my body flow with the movements, sometimes pretending I was a great ballerina in rehearsal for opening night. I would get caught up in these fantasies and find that I could do more repetitions with less pain because I would *forget about how well I was doing*, especially in relation to the other women. I started looking forward to each class and feeling very good at the end, tired and sweaty though I was. And I could actually begin to say (after a few weeks) that the exercising was *fun*.

My fear in saying this is that I might be giving someone the idea that she should stop exercising at the first sign of a small ache. So I want to add that, in order to improve, each time we exercise we must demand from each muscle a little more than it has ever done before. If we don't ask our muscles to do this, they don't get stronger. So we must put up with some sweat and discomfort.

When I suggest dropping out of an exercise before the class or tape instructor finishes counting, or before you have finished the repetitions recommended in a book, I am referring to stopping because of an extra deep *pain* that could damage a muscle or cause you to be so sore that you won't want to keep going to class. If you experienced so much pain that you constantly avoided exercising, then it's very unlikely that you would improve much physically in any case!

When I find I can't do all the sit-ups, I try to say to myself something like "Hmmm, I can see I've got some work to do." And I resolve to do at least one or two more the next time I exercise. This, in place of the old "look-how-bad-you-are" lectures I used to give myself, has often kept me from dropping out of class.

## Sore Muscles: An Ounce of Prevention . . .

Being sensible about what we can do when we begin an exercise program can help prevent sore muscles, too. Often I push myself a little too hard at first, hoping that starting with a very strenuous workout will speed up the process of getting fit. And sometimes I'm trying to convince myself that I'm really serious this time. But, unfortunately, the result of all this enthusiasm is often negative, because I wind up too sore to be very interested in going back to class or turning on my tape the next time.

So now when I start to exercise, I try to remember to go just past the point of real discomfort, but not to the deep kind of pain which takes all my courage to endure. The phrase "No pain, no glory" certainly has some validity, but I've learned it can be carried too far. I know I've got to sweat and push myself beyond what my muscles are used to doing. (My research tells me I should feel a "burn" in the muscles.) But at the same time, being aware that I could easily do too much has helped me keep from getting such sore muscles.

Being careful to do the exercises correctly can also do a lot toward reducing soreness. As we discussed earlier, breathing regularly while exercising helps wash away waste materials in the muscles left over from burning fuel. If these wastes are left to settle in after a good workout, they will tend to make us sore. So will neglecting to warm up and cool down properly—I try to always warm up by walking briskly before exercising and to stretch gently afterward, while I cool down.

Letting exercised muscles cool too fast can make them sore. If you're at home or at a health club, remembering to jump right into a hot shower can help prevent soreness. Putting on a warm-up suit before going outside to get in your car after class on a cold winter's day is another good idea.

## A Pound of Cure . . .

But let's say that I've done all of the above and I'm still sore. I used to stay away from class or stop exercising until I felt better. But I learned that this isn't necessarily the best thing to do. Granted, it's more uncomfortable to come to an exercise class all stiff and sore, but I find that when I gently work those muscles, the soreness heals a little faster.

So, on a day when I'm hurting, I go to class or turn on the tape player anyway. Before I start, however, I gently walk around the room a few times, then do a few gentle stretches. Slowly stretching toward the floor or bending to the side helps those muscles begin to loosen up. Then, as the class or tape begins, I start out slowly and pamper the muscles, but also move them. And when it hurts too much, I just lie back and breathe deeply, stretching my toes and hands toward opposite walls in the room, and let the others go on with the exercises without me. It's usually easier to get through the exercise sssion than I think it will be.

My main problem is that I'm afraid people will think I'm being lazy if I don't go all out. It's only my pride, however, and not wisdom. When I can overcome my pride and make myself go to class, sore muscles and all, I generally get over the soreness sooner. So I've learned not to deprive myself of the inspiration and support of the other members of the class, even if I can't do a vigorous workout.

To me, the most important thing to remember is that God created my body, and it's unique. Each body responds to exercise in a way all its own. Our job, it seems to me, is to learn what we can do to improve our own health, and to begin to put into action what we have learned.

## How Far Toward Pain Is Too Far?

But once I had decided to concentrate on my own individual levels of exercise, and to try to prevent sore muscles by being sensible about how hard I work out, I wondered how I can tell when I'm doing too much. Demanding that my muscles do more than they're used to causes feelings I've always considered uncomfortable. Being out of breath, hot, sweaty, and aching are things I've always tried to avoid. But I've also been one of those perfectionists who couldn't be satisfied with just doing a little running or a few repetitions on the weight equipment at the gym. I've thought to myself, "If a little bit will help some, then a lot will really help—and probably faster." And I've gone through what seems to me to be torturous rigors, trying to speed up the process.

Without discipline, dedication to regular workouts, sweat, panting and aches, nothing much will change. But pushing oneself too hard can lead to discouragement or even injury. How can you tell how much is too much?

The secret, it seems to me, is for each person to begin to sense the fine line between "discomfort" and actual "pain," and to realize that getting in shape *will* take time, no matter how fast *I* am prepared to go.

So I began to try to pay attention to the physical feelings I experienced during exercise and to classify them according to whether they were "discomfort" or "pain." By continually doing this, I learned some things about how much pain I can stand.

For a long time, I had been very sensitive to pain. I didn't like to be hugged too tightly; I hated having my back "scratched" even gently with fingernails and would only cautiously kiss my husband when he hadn't shaved. But as I got in touch with the physical feelings I had during exercising, I began to notice that there really is a difference between discomfort and pain. Instead of backing away from discomfort as soon as I felt it, I began to try staying uncomfortable a while.

And I discovered that, contrary to my fear, the discomfort often doesn't become pain at all. In fact, I began to see that the discomforts of an aching muscle, shortness of breath, and perspiration are signs that I'm getting better, and that all is going as it should go.

The tired, relaxed ache in my muscles which I felt while lying on the floor after a good workout was evidence to me that I had done well and would soon see the benefits. I would think to myself, "While I don't like exercising all that much, I sure do like *having exercised*." And now, as I've gotten less fearful of pain, I find that I really enjoy having my back scratched.

And what I learned about physical pain could be transferred to other areas of my life. I began pushing myself little by little beyond what I had thought I could stand, and I found that I was tougher than I had thought. As I became physically stronger, I noticed that I felt more confident emotionally, more able to make tough decisions or face disappointments or disagreements in other areas of my life. I felt more sure I could survive the aftermath of fearful situations.

On the other hand, as I learned to curb my excessive enthusiasm and prevent myself from overdoing, I learned a new kind of self-control that also added to my confidence. Instead of throwing myself into new things impulsively, I was able sometimes to evaluate them with a more realistic idea of what they were likely to cost me in time and energy. Then, if I decided to go ahead, I was not suddenly overwhelmed with the thought, "What have I gotten myself into?" This new awareness of my boundaries and limitations added to my sense of emotional and spiritual well-being, too.

So I'd like to suggest that you try not to think of a fitness program as a race or a competition to see who can get in shape first. In a race, everyone lines up at the same place on a starting line. But when it comes to health and fitness, we all start from different places.

I hope that as you begin doing exercises, you will be aware that your own physical fitness level is where you must begin. Feeling guilty or ashamed about that level is, to me, just wasting time. No matter how out of shape you are, the fact that you are reading this now, may be a part of a fresh commitment to do something to change.

Sorting out the differences between feelings of physical discomfort and real pain is a very helpful and important way to measure how hard we are working when we exercise. But when it comes to aerobic exercise, which will be the subject of the next five chapters, it is also important accurately to monitor the pulse rate. In the next chapter we will be looking at why pulse rate is important and learning to use pulse rate to determine how hard to exercise.

# 7

## *The Importance of the Pulse*

### Scripture and Devotion

Here are a couple of verses which inspire me as I keep on trying to improve my fitness level. They are Psalm 121:1—2:

> "I lift up my eyes to the hills. From whence does my help come? My help comes from the Lord, who made heaven and earth."

In addition to physical exercises, there is another discipline I try to do at the beginning of each day. I try to spend some time in a kind of quiet time with God. When I do this, it is remarkable to me how much better the things in my day seem to fit together. And surprisingly, there is usually enough time to do the important things.

In this quiet time, I usually read for a few minutes, then pray. This kind of prayer reminds me of "lifting my eyes unto the hills." I usually sit relaxed, close my eyes and ask, "Lord, is there anything you want to tell me now? I'm listening." Then I breathe deeply a couple of times and relax again, imagining that Jesus is in the room trying to speak to me.

What often happens is that very mundane things start coming to mind, like "Write mom," or "Call about the air conditioner." At first these thoughts irritated me and I felt they were cluttering up my quiet time with God. I wanted the inspiring, holy, life-changing thoughts to have room to come to my mind! But then I heard of an idea from Dr. Paul Tournier, a Swiss psychiatrist and a Christian. He suggests keeping a pencil and paper handy to jot down thoughts that come to mind. That way, they are safely in a place where they won't be lost or forgotten, and we can go back to the listening.

Every once in a while during this time I'll see something about myself, and I'll understand a little better why I'm struggling so hard.

One thing that keeps coming to me is my lack of patience. As I go along learning about exercise and nutrition and trying to put what I'm learning into practice, I often get discouraged because nothing seems to happen very fast. But one morning when I was feeling this way I was reading *The Imitation of Christ*, and I got another insight which helped me with my problem of impatience: "If you can be quiet and suffer for a while, you will, without doubt, see the help of God come in your need."[1]

When I first read this, it was as if I could see myself rushing frantically around trying to think of quick solutions to all the new problems I was running into: "How can I make myself exercise every day? What am I going to do about all this new information about food? How will I ever change these old habits permanently?"

I saw that if I can just sit quietly without all these questions clanging around in my head, if I can just listen for a while, sooner or later God will point out answers to my questions. I saw that I need to learn to live without instant answers to everything. And I also realized with relief that I am not responsible for solving all the problems by myself. In fact, the more I try to solve them without God, the worse they seem to get!

> DEAR LORD, help me to remember to sit quietly and listen for your guidance each day. Help me to know when to ask questions, when to talk, and when to just be quiet.
>
> Lord, I need to trust you more. Sometimes I act as if I really don't believe you could make any difference. Forgive me. I love you very much and I want to be all you had in mind when you made me.
>
> Thank you that you give me help. When the hills of problems surround me and I lift up my eyes, you are there. I ask for your peace and guidance, today and always. In Jesus' name, AMEN.

## How to Take Your Own Pulse

The more fit I become, the better my heart can pump blood around inside my body to carry oxygen to my muscles, flush out wastes, and so on. When my heart muscle is strong, my heart can pump more slowly, because the stronger muscle is able to pump more

---

1. Thomas à Kempis, *Imitation of Christ*, 78.

blood with each pulse beat. So, checking my pulse rate when my heart is resting is one measure of how fit I am.

The easiest way I have found to take my pulse is to place the first two fingers of one hand (not a finger and thumb) on the opposite side of my neck below my jaw. In other words, if I'm using my right hand, I place the first two fingers on the left side of my neck. There is a major pulse point there in front of the muscle that runs from behind the ear to the shoulder. By pressing lightly on that pulse point, I can feel my own heart beat. It is important not to press too hard, however; it is possible to actually make the pulse seem slower than it is by putting too much pressure on the neck. Another place to take a pulse is on the wrist, just below the thumb.

Here is the procedure for taking a pulse: First, put your wrist watch or a clock with a second hand in a place where you can see it, either on the table or wall or on the wrist of the hand you aren't using to feel your pulse point. Next, find your pulse point on your own neck or wrist. Then, while you keep your fingers on the spot, count the number of beats you feel for a period of ten seconds.

You counted your pulse for only ten seconds, but we want to know how many times your heart beats in a full minute. To find this out, multiply the number of beats you counted by six. This is your basic heart rate:

$$\underline{\hspace{3cm}} \times 6 = \underline{\hspace{3cm}}$$
(*number of beats*)　　　　　　　(*heart rate*)

## Resting Pulse Rate

Taking your pulse at various key times will help you keep track of your own progress. One of the pulse rates is called a "resting pulse rate." The best time to take a resting pulse rate is first thing in the morning, before you get out of bed. Since even the slight activity of getting out of bed, having breakfast, and sitting down to read will raise your pulse rate slightly, the rate you take now won't be the same as your pulse would be right after you wake up.

Tomorrow morning after you wake up, use a clock or watch with a second hand, and count your heartbeats for ten seconds. Then, using the formula above, calculate your resting heart rate. Write this number on the space provided on the chart on p. 71 along with the date on which you counted this pulse. (For ease of reference, this chart is also printed as a worksheet in the back of the book on p. 359.)

As you begin doing aerobic exercise, your heart muscle will get stronger and it won't need to beat as often to do the job it's doing now.

So by recording your resting pulse rate now and then comparing it to a resting pulse rate taken one month, two months, and so on from now, you can watch your resting pulse rate get lower and lower as your body gets more and more fit.

## Working Heart Rate (WHR)

Each person has a maximum heart rate which is the top rate the heart is capable of beating without damage. But no one should push her heart rate this high, even when exercising. The maximum is reserved for emergency action only.

But on the other hand, if we don't work hard enough to make our hearts beat harder than normal, we don't strengthen them. There is a range of pulse rate called the "working heart rate" (WHR) range. It is the ideal range within which a particular heart should beat when exercising if the exercise is to do any good. If your heartbeat is lower than the lowest end of the range, your heart is not working hard enough to improve much. If your heartbeat is too high, you risk damaging your heart, and you've passed the point where your body can provide oxygen needed to burn fat. So your body burns muscle tissue instead, just to keep up with the extreme demand. That will work for a while, and can be helpful in emergencies—such as running from a band of cannibals in the jungle. But for everyday exercise it's dangerous, and also not helpful for reaching the goal of burning fat. (An important note: People who are just beginning to exercise should try to stay at the lower end of their working heart rate range. As the body adjusts to exercising, it is safer to work out at the higher end of the WHR range.)

There are several ways to figure the WHR range. I like to use the method recommended by Kenneth Cooper in his book *The Aerobic Way*. Dr. Cooper recommends that we keep our heart rate within 70% to 85% of its maximum when exercising. To figure your WHR range, follow the steps below and fill in the results on the chart on p. 71.

## How to Calculate Your Working Heart Rate Range

To find out your WHR range, it is necessary first to find out what your maximum heart rate is. To do this, subtract your age from the number 220. The answer is approximately your maximum heart rate, give or take a beat or two. For example, a 30-year-old would have an approximate maximum heart rate of 220 minus 30, or 190.

With this number, you can figure out your working heart rate range. First, multiply your maximum heart rate by 70%, (or .7); this will give you the *minimum* rate at which your heart needs to work to benefit from exercise. Then multiply that same maximum heart rate by 85%, (or .85). This will give you the highest heart rate you should allow yourself during exercise.

If during exercise you should take your pulse and find that your heart rate is higher than the top of your range, (85% of your maximum) that means you should ease up (but not stop completely) and let your heart get back down to a rate within your ideal range. Also, remember to "listen to your body" for other signs that you may be pushing too hard, regardless of your pulse rate. Such indicators would include feeling light-headed or nauseated or dizzy or very hot and flushed.

Be sure to take your pulse as quickly as possible after you stop exercising, so it won't have time to start slowing down. (Even a few seconds can change the results considerably.) Then compare your exercising rate to your WHR range to find out if you're working hard enough or too hard.

## Recovery Heart Rate

It's also a good idea to check your pulse rate again after you cool down to be sure your heart has recovered enough for you to stop exercising or sit down. Your heart rate should drop to 120 or below before you stop moving around. Most exercise tapes or classes end with a slow cool-down exercise designed to help your heart rate slow down gradually. If you're exercising on your own, take a few minutes to walk around slowly, do a few stretches, and take some long deep breaths to allow your heart to slow down. Never sit down or lie down immediately after strenuous exercise. This puts an extra load on your heart which can be dangerous.

It is a good idea to get in the habit of taking these two pulse rates (the WHR and the recovery heart rate) each time you exercise. You'll soon get the feel for how hard is hard enough for your own level of fitness. This may sound complex, but, once you have tried it a few times, taking your pulse after exercising will be second nature. And after some months your after-exercise rate will probably be pretty close to the same number each time.

## Not All Exercises Are for the Heart and Lungs

Some kinds of workouts are not designed for exercising the heart and lungs. When you're doing muscle-tone or stretching exercises, you can't really expect to have heart rates in the WHR range. The goal of this kind of exercise is to develop strength and flexibility in other muscles besides the heart muscles. Some people do such exercises vigorously enough, without stopping in between exercises, to raise their pulse considerably. But most people find it works better to have a separate time in which they concentrate on aerobics—working specifically on reaching the WHR and maintaining it long enough to give the heart and lungs a good workout.

One thing I've really enjoyed about getting in shape is trying to do various kinds of aerobic exercise. I've tried swimming, walking, jumping rope, aerobic dance, and jogging. There are things I like about each one, and things that aren't so pleasant. But the variety has kept me interested and involved, which I believe has helped me continue to improve my physical fitness level. There are a few facts about doing each of these kinds of aerobic exercise in the following four chapters.

## PULSE RATE

Resting heart rate at beginning of exercise
commitment: _____

Date taken: _____

Resting heart rate after _____ months: _____

Date taken: _____

MAXIMUM HEART RATE: _____
*(subtract your age from 220)*

WORKING HEART RATE RANGE:

(1) .70 × _____ = _____ (lower)

(2) .85 × _____ = _____ (upper)

(3) Working heart rate range is: _____ to _____$^2$
*(lower)*   *(upper)*

---

2. After aerobic exercise, pulse rate should be between the upper and lower figures.

# 8

## *Beginning Your Own Aerobic Exercise Program*

### *Scripture and Devotion*

In this chapter I want to talk about getting started on an aerobic exercise program. But first, let's think for a few minutes about 2 Corinthians 12:9:

> "My grace is sufficient for you, for my power is made perfect in weakness."

Every time I begin an exercise program after not working out for months at a time, I go through the same series of feelings: Boy, it doesn't take long for my body to get out of shape. Why do I let this happen?

During what is usually a two-week period of readjusting to hard exercise, I feel embarrassed and discouraged that I've let myself slide. I often make silly jokes about being flabby and hope other people around me won't think I'm awful because I haven't kept up with exercising. Exercising just seems like such a drag sometimes!

But in Phillip Keller's book, *Lessons from a Sheep Dog*, there is a passage which really hit me. He writes,

> The greatest delusion any man or woman can ever come under is the idea that it is a "drag" to do God's will. Just the opposite is true! Yet our old natures, our strong, selfish self-interests, our sensual society, our arch-foe Satan—all endeavor to deceive us into believing that it is a bore and bondage to serve the Master, to carry out His commands in glad-hearted cooperation. [1]

---

1. Phillip Keller, *Lessons from a Sheep Dog* (Waco, TX: Word Inc., 1983), 76.

I realized that he was right! I do consider it a bore to exercise every day, and bondage to "restrict" myself from certain foods. Maybe it's my attitude that needs changing.

When I read in 2 Corinthians that "God's power is made perfect in weakness," I realized that my best hope is to admit that I am weak and selfish, and that my old habits are strong. Paul seems to me to be saying that the power of God can work in a person like me, that when I am willing to confess my weakness, God's kind of power has room to come into my life and be perfected. I could see that without my weaknesses I would never have to call on God for anything. These repeated failures to keep myself in shape were what kept driving me to look deeper for answers about myself—answers which I find come from God.

Good ol' Thomas à Kempis said it for me again. He wrote,

> When a good person is troubled or tempted or is disquieted by evil thoughts, then he or she understands and knows that God is most necessary, and that he or she may do nothing that is good without God.[2]

As I continue to try to break my old habits and to wrestle with feelings like "it isn't fair that I have to exercise every day," I am trying to learn to tell Jesus about them. I am trusting a little more each time that he can work through me to bring me to a condition of health which will make me most able to carry out his will.

> DEAR LORD, thank you for your grace to me—that unconditional love that forgives me for my weakness and inspires me to keep on trying to be all I can be for you. Your grace is sufficient for me. And as I learn to trust you with my physical well-being as well as my spiritual health, I find more and more that I need your strength. I ask you to fill me with your grace today and to help me understand clearly what your intentions for my life are. In Jesus' name, AMEN.

## Beginning an Aerobic Program

In an earlier chapter, we said that aerobic exercise is one of the three kinds of exercise our bodies need. I also mentioned that the

---

2. Thomas à Kempis, *Imitation of Christ*, 44.

minimum recommended duration for aerobic exercise to be effective is about 17 minutes, depending on *what kind* of aerobic activity you choose to do.

You might think that when beginning an aerobic program you should start with only a few minutes and work up to the full 17. But I suggest that you start with the full 17 minutes, even though you may not be able to go very fast or very far at first. The idea is to keep moving—however gently—for 17 minutes.

The way to measure the effectiveness of aerobic exercise is to make sure it raises your heart rate to within the WHR range and no higher. So it doesn't matter how fast or slow you go. When you first begin, it won't take as much effort to raise your pulse rate to that level as it will later. And as the weeks go by, your muscles and endurance will develop naturally. So go ahead and use the full time right from the beginning. Just be sure not to overexert yourself and to keep track of your pulse rate to make sure you're not pushing your heart rate too high.

Whatever your chosen aerobic exercise, begin by warming up your muscles as I described in chapter 3. Try to spend at least five minutes warming up before you begin.

## A Test to See How Hard You Can Work

Here's a little test I read about in Covert Bailey's book, *Fit or Fat?*. If you like, you can try it the first day you do your aerobic program. No matter what kind of aerobic exercise you're planning to do, this test can let you know how it feels when you raise your heart rate up to 70% of the maximum.

Go outside and choose an object a half-block or so away—a tree, telephone pole, parked car, etc. Walk or run to and from that object at the speed you think is comfortable. When you get back to where you were standing, take your pulse. If it is within your working heart range, then you have hit your best speed or exercise level. But, chances are, if you haven't been doing anything aerobic, your heart rate will be much higher than your top maximum working heart rate should be. If that is the case, let your heart return to a lower pace by just walking around a few minutes. Then try the distance again, only slower. Take your pulse again. Keep experimenting until you find the pace at which you can go to the object and back without going past your upper limit. Then you'll know how you'll feel when you're doing your full seventeen minutes at the proper level.

Dr. Bailey (in *Fit or Fat?*) tells the story of a woman who started out walking but quit because she quickly got too tired. She found out that all it took to raise her heart rate to her working range was to stand on the floor and alternately raise only her heels. Even walking slowly was too much for her heart/lung system at that point.

As I've said before, we each have our own level of fitness. Comparing what you are doing to what someone else does has nothing to do with getting yourself in shape. If you choose to begin by walking for 17 minutes, try not to let anyone kid you or make you feel guilty because you can't go out and start jogging right away. The fact that you are investing 17 minutes a day, five or six days a week, in working your heart and lungs at the level *they* need says you care for your body's fitness level. And after a few weeks you'll probably be amazed at how much your fitness has improved.

## When to Check Your Pulse Rate

It's hard to take your pulse during exercise. Stopping often to take it interrupts the continuous movement you need to give your heart/lung system a good workout. So once you've found a comfortable pace, don't stop and check your pulse until you are at the end of the entire workout.

In any of the activities we're about to discuss, if your pace seems too tiring, slow down. One rule of thumb to go by is this: If you are too out of breath to chat with someone while you are exercising, you are probably pushing yourself too hard. Pay attention to other body signs that say you're pushing too hard, such as dizziness, nausea, or being flushed and too hot.

# Week Three
## (Three Days)

## *Aims and Activities*

(1)  To continue with a 30–45 minute muscle-tone workout three times a week.

(2)  To become aware of the various kinds of aerobic exercise available.

(3)  By the end of the week, to pick one kind of aerobic exercise and begin doing it, at your own beginning level, for at least 20 minutes, five days a week.

# 9

## *Walking*

### Scripture and Devotion

It's been quite a process for me to find my own pace and know how hard I can work out. I seem to alternate between pushing too hard and not doing enough work. This scripture has really helped me realize how much God knows about my own abilities and limits and, therefore, how much he can help me. It's Psalm 139:1–3, 13–15:

> "O Lord, thou hast searched me and known me! Thou knowest when I sit down and when I rise up; thou discernest my thoughts from afar. Thou searchest out my path and my lying down, and art acquainted with all my ways. . . .
> "For thou didst form my inward parts, thou didst knit me together in my mother's womb. I praise thee, for thou art fearful and wonderful. Wonderful are thy works! Thou knowest me right well; my frame was not hidden from thee, when I was being made in secret, intricately wrought in the depths of the earth."

The first time I remember hearing this Psalm, I was at a women's prayer group meeting in Georgia with 29 others. A woman read the entire Psalm as a morning devotion, and before she had finished I realized I had tears streaming down my face.

I was crying from relief—a mixture of embarrassment and joy which came from the realization that I could admit to myself and to God that I couldn't do everything I needed to do to improve my health. I didn't have to keep on pretending that it was easy for me.

I had been studying nutrition and exercise and trying to fit all I was learning into my life—with much difficulty. I was at a "fed up with it all" stage and was almost ready to throw it out the window. But

I still pretended to be "gung-ho" and enthusiastic. The truth was, I wasn't interested in sweating and hurting and cutting chocolate-chip cookies out of my life. I just wanted to be healthy *without* all that!

Also, I had begun to get the feeling that God would love me better as soon as I lost my ten pounds and ran three miles (every day . . . without skipping any) and had *fun* doing it! It hit me like a bucket of cold water that I was trying to earn some kind of approval from God by getting trim. But that morning I realized, in a way I could really see, that God loves me just because he is God and I am his child. God's grace, as I understand it, means that he loves me. Period. Not because of *anything* I am (trim and fit) or anything I do (run a marathon or even a mile).

The words, "Thou knowest me right well; my frame was not hidden from thee, when I was being made in secret," mean so much to me. God knows about my weak knees, my sluggish metabolism, my pot tummy, my attraction to unhealthy foods. In fact, the reason he knows all this is that he made me. "Thou didst form my inward parts, thou didst knit me together in my mother's womb." If he made this puzzle that is my body, then he knows the answers to the riddles of why I'm not trim and fit.

How many times I've said to myself, "But Lord, if you only knew how easy it is for me to gain weight!" Or, "If you only knew how busy I am. I'll never find time to exercise every day!" "Lord, you know how my knee hurts when I run very far." When I heard this scripture I thought, "Yes, God knows all those things. And he is involved in my process to become fit." The scripture had come to me at a turning point in my struggle, and it means a lot to me today.

DEAR LORD, instead of complaining about all my physical problems, I want to praise you like this psalmist did—because you made me and know me. You even know what I'm thinking, and what I am doing.

Help me to learn to ask you for the patience and faith to keep on my plan even when my body doesn't seem to respond to my efforts to shape it up. Forgive me for quitting so often, and thank you for understanding and taking me back when I return. You are acquainted with all my ways, so you know the answer to the riddles of why my body isn't as healthy as you know it could be. Teach me, Lord, and help me to listen, to recognize your voice, and to learn. In Jesus' name, AMEN.

## Various Choices for Aerobic Exercise

My first experience with aerobic exercise was with a swimming program. I've also enjoyed jumping rope, cycling, and aerobic dance. But right now, my aerobics program centers around jogging, because it's the most convenient form of aerobic exercise for me at this time.

Jogging and walking are two of the most convenient forms of aerobic exercise. The only equipment you need is a good pair of shoes. There are no monthly dues as there probably would be with racketball or swimming. (You're already paying taxes on the city streets.) And it takes the least amount of time to get ready to do either one of these. You can begin and end at your own front door. Also, you don't have to fit your schedule to someone else's. Walking and jogging are activities you can do alone, whereas with racketball you need a partner and with swimming you need someone to watch you. Many people do like to walk or jog with a partner, however, because having someone with whom to share the time makes exercising more interesting.

When I first decided to start doing some kind of aerobic exercise, I looked hard and long at all the options. I was glad to see that jogging isn't the only one.

## Beginning an Aerobic Walking Program

I've found that a hearty walking program provides very good exercise for one's heart and lungs, provided it is done correctly and for a long enough time. So, if walking is to be your choice for aerobic activity, where do you begin?

First of all, I think it is a *must* to buy some good jogging shoes. You don't need any other fancy equipment, but since walking for aerobic exercise puts more strain on the feet than normal walking, it's important to have good foot support.

Just any old rubber-soled shoe is not good enough; neither are tennis shoes or golf shoes. Researchers have designed jogging shoes specifically to protect feet under the strain of walking or jogging. The heel support and padding help prevent blisters, control side-to-side sway, and absorb the shock of vigorous walking (or running). Improper foot support can bring on foot problems, spine problems, and knee problems.

It's not really all that important what you wear on the rest of your body; any clothes that are comfortable and appropriate for the weather will be fine. In cold weather, I usually need fewer clothes than I think because the body heat from the exercise keeps me warm. (Besides, the harder my body has to work to keep me warm, the more calories I burn!) I like to dress in layers, so that when my pulse rate goes up and I get warmer I can take off a layer or so as I go along. But when I get to the end of the walk and start to cool off, I put a jacket or sweater back on to keep from getting chilled, which can lead to stiff and sore muscles.

## Getting Started

Once you're dressed and you've got your shoes on, you're ready to start. It's important to spend five minutes or so warming up. Then simply start walking briskly. Dr. Kenneth Cooper, in *The New Aerobics*, recommends a one-mile walk in 15 to 18½ minutes for the first week in a starter program. The speed he recommends varies with the age of the person. For more details about times and distances to walk for your age group, see *The New Aerobics.*

One way I've found to choose a route is to walk away from the starting point for half the time, then turn around and go back. As your fitness level improves, you'll find you can go a little farther each day before the half-time mark. Or if you live in a neighborhood where you can walk around a block, time yourself as you walk around it once. Then walk whatever number of laps it takes to go 15 to 18½ minutes.

As I've said before, it's all right to walk the full time period beginning the first day, *provided you keep your heart rate within your working heart rate range.* What counts is the *time* you spend encouraging your body to improve, not how far or fast you go.

## How to Walk for Aerobic Exercise Benefits

As you continue to walk, try to keep your arms hanging naturally (not stiff elbows or elevated, "pumping" elbows). Let them swing in rhythm with the walk. Increasing the distance your hands swing will help increase your heart rate if it is too low.

But if you notice that your leg muscles are feeling tired, it's a good idea to slow down, even though your heart rate isn't high enough yet, so you'll be able to walk the full amount of time. As you keep doing these walks every day (as well as doing muscle-tone and flexibility exercises), these muscles will get stronger and more flexible and you can pick up your walking speed.

An especially beneficial form of aerobic walking is racewalking, which is an official sport with certain rules. According to a recent article in *American Health* magazine, when you are racewalking "you must keep unbroken contact with the ground and your knee must be straight or locked when it's on the ground." There can be no bobbing the head or shoulders up and down—a sign that you've broken contact with the ground.[1]

Ron Laird, America's champion racewalker, switched from running to racewalking. He claims that this kind of walking tightened his stomach muscles better than running and slimmed his thighs also. In fact, as *American Health* points out, fast walking is one of the central exercises in Wendy Stehling's best seller, *Thin Thighs in 30 Days.*

Recently I was advised by my doctor not to jog for a while (several months) because of a slipped kneecap. With proper therapy and rest, he said, I should be able to jog again. But in the meantime I've been experimenting with walking. And until I started trying the racewalking methods described in the *American Health* article, my pulse rate stayed at or below 100, which is hardly in my WHR range! But as I've started really walking as fast as I can, keeping my knee locked and one foot in contact with the ground, things have improved. I've found that racewalking gets my heart rate up, even after spending two years as a jogger! So far, I've managed to get my speed up to doing a mile in 13¾ minutes. And when I walk at that speed, my pulse rate is up above 120. *American Health* indicates that speeds up to 13½ minutes per mile (4.5 miles per hour) are possible.

Another method I've heard of for raising the heart rate while walking is to carry a little extra weight, such as a light backpack or a pair of *small* hand weights. If you're 15 pounds or more overweight, however, I don't recommend adding any weight. The reason is that our bones and joints are built to withstand a certain amount of pressure. When we walk our feet, knees, and hips absorb an amount of weight equal to two times our body weight. (When we jog, the stress is six times our weight!) So any excess body weight compounds the amount of weight our joints must handle. It would be even more of a strain on these weight-bearing joints to add any *more* weight. Moving our arms and legs more vigorously while walking seems to be a better choice.

Before you get carried away with the idea of walking for aerobic exercise, I want to stress that our leg muscles need time to develop the strength for strenuous walking. So if this is the first time you've ever tried a walking program, I'd suggest that you start by walking comfortably for 17 minutes without checking your pulse rate or the dis-

---

1. Gary Yanker, "To Thin Thighs, Tighten Belly, Try Racewalks," *American Health*, September/October 1983, 16.

tance you've gone at all, just to get your legs used to the extra work. Then, after a few weeks, begin to check your pulse to see if your heart rate is getting high enough. Remember to "listen" to your body for signs that you're pushing too hard. Heavy breathing beyond the point at which you can talk, a pounding heart, dizziness, nausea, and severely aching calves are all signs that you need to slow down.

Many people enjoy walking as their aerobic exercise. And there are many others who like to jog. Having spent a few miles on the jogging trail, I'd like to spend the next chapter telling you a few basic things I've learned about that form of aerobic exercise.

# 10

## *Jogging*

### Scripture and Devotion

The more I study, the more amazed I become at the intricate interrelationships between exercise, nutrition, and health. Our bodies and the resources available to us for their nurture are wonderful and complex. And it is awesome to think of how all these things work together for our benefit. The scripture for this chapter gives me even more assurance that God is involved in every area of our lives—especially our health. It is Jeremiah 29:11:

> "For I know the plans I have for you, says the Lord, plans for
> welfare and not for evil, to give you a future and a hope."

If God knows a plan for us, to give us a future and a hope, then what part must I play in his plan for me? This passage triggered some thoughts in me about changing—whether I could change myself, or whether God would change me without my participation. If my participation and cooperation are needed, how do we work together?

A few years ago I read an article in the paper about Burt Lancaster, who claimed he was "living like a saint" in order to avoid some heart surgery. It seemed he had nearly died during a gall bladder operation, and the doctors had told him his problem could be solved by having bypass surgery on his heart.

But he said first he wanted to try to improve his health by other methods. So he says, "I'm not smoking, I'm not drinking, I'm living like an Olympic athlete. I'm getting plenty of exercise, a salt-free diet, walking and jogging."

The doctors were beginning to think, at the time the article was written, that Burt may be able to avoid the surgery.

This reminded me of the way I tend to react when I detect a problem in my life. I'm willing to turn it over to the Lord with a quick,

"Change me, make me what you'd have me to be" attitude. I spiritually lie down on the operating table, grab the ether mask, and get ready for surgery and the healing that will follow, saying "Okay, Lord, here I am . . . 'yielded and still, mold me and make me after thy will.'"

It's as if the Lord says, "First, fold your arms across your chest."

"Great!" I answer.

But then he says, "Now, sit up and lie back down 100 times." That's *not* what I had in mind!

And yet many times I think there are things God would have me do that can improve or even solve my problem without radical surgery—but the problem is, I have to do the work myself, make some sacrifices I'd rather not make. It would be so much easier if God would just "knock me out" and do things to me. When I woke up, there would be pain, of course. But I could shrug and say "I had no choice. I have to be suffering because of God's surgery." The hard part comes when we have to *choose* to put ourselves through some pain.

Do you know how the last ten sit-ups feel? They hurt like the dickens! And yet I know I have to go through this kind of pain, sweat, and effort in order to improve. Sometimes I don't seem to have the courage to do it. I would just as soon skip the workout as go through the pain. In fact, I dislike the feelings of pain and discomfort so much that, even when I'm putting on my tights and turning on the tape recorder and starting the warm-up, there's a certain feeling of dread in the back of my mind.

I've often looked at exercise leaders and said, "I wish I were disciplined like you. Then I could get rid of my pot tummy"—as if being disciplined were something you are or you aren't. But I don't consider myself disciplined at all. I have selfish motivations. What makes me exercise is the desire to have the *results* exercise produces.

Overcoming the dread of putting myself through an uncomfortable workout does not feel like discipline. It feels more like courage . . . the will to go through something, in spite of the fact that it's somewhat painful, in order to grow in ways that I want to grow—need to grow.

And it seems to me to be a similar procedure with spiritual problems and emotional ones. There are some painful exercises that must be attempted if growth is to occur. We can't always just say, "Okay God. I'm yielded. It's up to you." I don't think that this kind of radical surgery is the only way problems were meant to be handled.

The way we (God and I) work together might be that he provides the basic equipment (the design of my body, the foods in nature, etc.) and the information as to how it's supposed to work. He provides the help with motivation, dealing with failures, temptations and so on. I provide the openness to his leadership, the courage to begin, to keep on trying, to come back after failures, and the admission that I need God's help to handle this area of my life.

> DEAR LORD, thank you for your assurance that you know the plans you have for me. Thank you for giving me the clue that the plans are for good and not evil, and that they bring hope. I ask you to come close to me and help me as I keep on trying to work exercise into my life. Help me to find the courage to choose a little pain and discomfort in order to be able to grow into the woman you planned for me to be.
>
> Thanks for the fact that at the end of each workout there's a good, tired feeling. And thanks for the feeling of new energy that comes when I have rested. In Jesus' name, AMEN.

## Jogging

I've learned that there is a difference between jogging and running. The definitions vary, but here they are: According to some sources, jogging is a combination of running gently for a while and walking for a while. Running means that you keep running nonstop the whole time. Another source says that the only difference is the speed. They say that walkers cover a mile in 14 minutes or more, joggers cover it in 9 to 14 minutes, and runners take 9 minutes or less. For the purpose of this book I'm going to use the second definition.

If you haven't been exercising at all, I strongly recommend that before you begin to jog you spend three to four weeks walking to get your leg and hip muscles prepared for the stress. Also, it seems to me that jogging for speed isn't really all that productive just for the purpose of exercise. If you're training for a marathon or race of some kind, that's another issue. But as long as your heart rate is within the proper working heart rate range, it doesn't matter how fast you are jogging. You will probably notice that, as the months go by and you continue to run, your time will improve, simply because your body is in better shape and your heart can handle more work.

## Equipment

If you decide to try jogging for aerobic exercise, I want to say again (at the risk of repeating myself) that I think it is a *must* to buy some good jogging shoes. Jogging puts even more strain on our feet than walking, as much as six times our body weight. So it's very important to have good foot support, and jogging shoes are especially designed to protect feet from the kind of stress that happens when we jog. As I said before, the heel support and padding built into a jogging shoe help prevent blisters, control side-to-side sway (which is hard on ankles and knees) and absorb the shock of jogging. Since the cost of shoes is about the only expense for this type of exercise, I think it's well worth it.

The other things I mentioned in the previous chapter about what to wear and how hard to push oneself also apply to jogging. To choose a route, you can either chart out a route in your neighborhood by driving your car along it and measuring how far it is, or you can use your wristwatch and keep track of the time. I've often been told that jogging on concrete is hard on your body, so if at all possible try to run on a surface that "gives" a little: asphalt, grass, firm sand, cinder track, etc.

## Good Muscle Tone Is Important

I find that when my stomach, back, and hip muscles are not in good shape, the bouncing effect of jogging makes me uncomfortable inside my lower abdomen, and can possibly stress the female organs as well as the bladder. But when I've been working out regularly and have my support muscles in good shape, I rarely have these uncomfortable feelings.

## How to Run for Aerobic Benefit and Endurance

When I first started running, I ran with bent knees and took long and high steps. That's the way I had run in high school track—for speed, as in the 100-yard dash. But Bill Day, Director of the Houstonian Preventive Medicine Center, showed me a smoother, more comfortable way to run. He is in his forties, and runs marathons (26-mile races). He said, "I began to notice that at about the 18- or 20-mile mark, these 65-year-old guys would start passing me up, and the way they run explains how they lasted so well." He told me to take smaller steps, and to keep my feet close to the ground, almost parallel to it. He said, "If you could watch my foot in slow motion, you would see that the heel hits just barely ahead of the toe, but at regular speed it looks like my foot hits all at once." When I watched him, it looked in some ways more like a shuffle. That was quite a change for me, since my foot was hitting in two distinct motions, making a kind of ker-plunk sound as the heel hit followed by the toe. But when I tried running the way Bill showed me, I realized how much body stress and energy I saved.

## How Much Time to Spend Jogging

The minimum daily run which fitness experts say promotes physical fitness is a run of 20 minutes a day (five minutes for your heart
rate to get up to its working level plus 15 minutes at that level), five or
six days a week. Any less than this, the experts indicate, doesn't
*improve* fitness. Once a person is in shape, however, running three
or four days a week will maintain that level. But to *get in shape,* and
to burn calories, you need to jog five to six days every week. It's also
important not to skip two days in a row.

If you want to try jogging, I would suggest you start by walking for
a week. Then try walking and running combined for another week.
The third week, try gently running the whole time. If you're feeling too
uncomfortable at any time, go back to what you did the week before.
You may decide after some experience that you can burn calories and
exercise your heart and lungs without jogging at all. Or you might
begin to enjoy the experience of jogging and go on to expand your
running time.

For some suggestions about exact times and distances, see *The
New Aerobics* by Kenneth H. Cooper.

## Increasing Running Time

After three or four weeks of being able to jog the entire 20 minutes, you may want to begin increasing your time. A good rule of
thumb to follow is to increase about 10% of your distance a week. So if
you're jogging 20 minutes, you could increase your time by two minutes for a week, running 22 minutes. To get up to 30 minutes would
take five weeks:

| | |
|---|---|
| Week 1 | 22 minutes |
| Week 2 | 24.2 minutes |
| Week 3 | 26.6 minutes |
| Week 4 | 29.2 minutes |
| Week 5 | 30 minutes |

Working gradually up to a time of 30 minutes a day is a good goal,
according to Dr. Ted Edwards, Jr., in *From Weight Loss to Super
Wellness,* (p. 5). After this level, extra miles don't add that much
improvement to fitness. For some people, however, they're just plain
fun.

I heard George Sheehan speak at a fitness club I belonged to, and
he said "The first three miles are for our bodies, and the next three are
for our minds."

## Do Not Rush the Adjustment Period

I've read that the body goes through cycles of improvement, and these cycles average out to be about three weeks in duration. At first, a lot of improvement happens, but then it tapers off. The trick is to know when it's time to add a little more stress, since increasing too fast causes injury, and waiting too long causes boredom or discouragement.

In studies done at Washington University's Department of Preventive Medicine, it was found that exercising groups reached a plateau of aerobic improvement at about three weeks. Their cardiovascular improvement leveled off at this point, even though they continued at the same level of exercise for four and five weeks. Also, they achieved half their improvement in less than eleven days, with the other half coming more slowly over the rest of the time. So the suggestion is, if you want to get in shape fast, "be sure to spend at least 11 days at each level. A faster pace may ultimately slow you down. And if you don't increase after three weeks, you're probably just on a maintenance program."[1]

As I've suggested, some people find that running is painful at first. So spending a week or two walking allows your legs to get used to the extra stress of going longer distances. At the same time, it builds up your ability to get oxygen to your muscles.

As you begin a jogging program, your heart and lungs may handle it moderately well, but your ankles, calves, knees and hips might be strained. (It's especially important to be aware of this if you are over 40 years old.)

Unfortunately, the strain is not always something you can feel while you are running. After a few days of running the stress sometimes shows up a few hours after you quit running. You may notice an ache in your knee or a stiff hip joint when you get up from sitting or lying down. By the time you notice it, it's too late to back off and try something milder. So don't give in to the temptation to rush into jogging too quickly. Start out at a safe level of exercise and increase your distance and speed slowly. This will let your muscles develop and adjust to the increases, and the strengthened muscles will help protect your ankles, knees, hips, and spine from the added stress.

If a persistent pain develops, the best prescription is to stop running for a week to six weeks, depending on how bad the pain is. If it is

---

1. E. C. Frederick, "When to Push Your Body," *American Health*, September/October 1983, 16.

strong and consistently uncomfortable, go to a doctor, preferably one who practices sports medicine.

Both walking and jogging provide good aerobic exercise. But in case neither one of these appeals to you, or if you can't do either because of physical problems (like knee or back weaknesses), there are other ways of getting the same aerobic results. We'll talk about four of these in the next chapter.

# 11

## *Four More Aerobic Activities*

### *Scripture and Devotion*

By now, you may be struggling with the process of finding time to fit in 20 minutes of aerobic exercise every day plus 30 to 45 minutes of muscle toning and flexibility three times a week. Doing this is hard, I know, but it's vital to maintaining health and fitness, and to controlling weight. There is a scripture which really doesn't have anything specifically to do with health, but which encourages me when I feel overwhelmed by the many changes I'm trying to make. The scripture is John 14:27:

> "Peace I leave with you; my peace I give to you; not as the world gives do I give to you. Let not your hearts be troubled, neither let them be afraid."

It's funny what thoughts go through my mind when I read this passage through the lens of trying to learn how God can help me overcome the obstacles which keep me from getting in shape. When I first began trying to make a lot of changes in my daily routine to make time in my schedule for exercise, I felt anything but peaceful. All this thinking, planning, and *work* seemed to be disrupting what had been a relatively peaceful, established routine. Somehow, I used to have time to get my work done, be with my family, and have some times for myself. What in the world could Jesus have been talking about when he referred to leaving us with peace when I was going through all this chaos in learning to live a healthy life for God?

Then I thought back over my life, and I remembered other times of chaos. When I first left home and went to college everything seemed to be in chaos. There were weeks of planning my wardrobe, packing, moving everything into a tiny dormitory room built for two but with three girls in it, figuring out how to register for classes. Then when I'd done that there came more chaos . . . finding out where classes met and what books to buy, wondering when I'd have time to study, meeting new people, and learning all the new names. It seemed to go on forever! But gradually the new chaos developed into a routine, and I felt peaceful again.

Other times brought this feeling of chaos, too—the end of college and the change to graduate school, leaving graduate school, setting up my own apartment, getting my first job, moving from place to place. And although I don't have children, I've watched my friends go through times of chaos as each new child is born, and a time of struggle as new routines are developed.

I began to see that while each new change in my life brought with it a feeling of unpeaceful confusion, the resulting growth and improvement in my life which came out of that confusion was better for me after all. And a better kind of peace always seemed to return.

I thought about the phrase, "not as the world gives," and I thought to myself, "The world's peace seems to be finding the easy way to do everything . . . achieving the good life . . . having no worries . . . being free from problems. A lot of people say that in 'the good life' chaos, pain, and problems do not exist. But everything I'm doing now seems to indicate that without some discomfort and pain there is no improvement." With stronger muscles—which came out of the "pain" of exercise—I can do my physical work more easily. And with a stronger heart and lungs I have more energy for everything, even some left over for things I didn't think I could have done before.

And so I decided that the kind of peace Jesus is talking about might be the peace that comes after the chaos, the kind that results from the strengthening which happens when I struggle and challenge myself to do things that are both physically and emotionally difficult.

Growth seems to come from problems. When I resist those problems, not giving in to them but striving to find resolution, I grow. To get stronger muscles I have to overcome the resistance my muscles offer when I try to make them work a little harder than they ever have. And to get stronger spiritually, I have to wrestle with my spiritual weaknesses. Knowing that Jesus has promised to be with me and help me develop the strength to overcome problems brings peace, even in the midst of the struggling.

So I resolved to keep on working out the snags in my chaotic life until I had developed a new routine that was peaceful and smooth. I realized once again that this approach to living is a lifelong project, not a temporary endeavor I'll put up with until I am "in shape." And once I had realized this, I felt a new wave of peace come over me. I was no longer struggling with my discontent about having to go through all this chaos. I was convinced instead that it was out of the *struggle itself* that new strength, health, and God's kind of peace would come.

And then I remembered the last line of that verse: "Let not your hearts be troubled, neither let them be afraid." Now that I was not so busy trying to find an easy way out of this chaos, or a shortcut to good health, but was facing the reality that this is God's way for me to live— struggles, growth and all—my heart *did* feel less troubled, and I was less afraid that I would never be able to make all the changes.

> DEAR LORD, thank you for the promise of peace in my life. Come into my heart and mind where the chaos of making new changes is tumbling all around and give me a sense of your presence as I continue trying to leave enough time in my daily schedule for the exercise I know I need to keep strong, free from injury, and full of energy.
>
> Help me to go on from here into the rest of my life— learning, growing, and getting stronger in body, heart, and my relationship with you. Forgive me when I try to find a shortcut around what I know to be best, and bring my desires back to you. In Jesus' name, AMEN.

## More Kinds of Aerobic Exercise

Now let's consider four other possible choices for aerobic exercise: jumping rope, cycling, swimming, and aerobic dance.

### JUMPING ROPE

Jumping rope is another great aerobic exercise. It takes a lot of energy and raises the heart rate very rapidly, so the minimum time for it is only 12 minutes. In fact, 12 minutes of steadily jumping rope without stopping will give your heart the same amount of work as if you had jogged for 30! For many people, this becomes a favorite method of exercising because it gets results so fast! It is fun to do for variety when other things seem boring, or to be alternated with walking, jogging, or aerobic dance.

But while jumping rope is good for your heart and lungs, it is even harder on knees and ankles than is jogging. A person should jump rope only after she has some pretty good muscle tone and aerobic endurance. Very strong leg and ankle muscles are needed to prevent injury.

Also, it has been recommended that, because of the jarring and strain on legs and ankles, jumping rope should not be done two days in a row, and it should not be the only kind of aerobic exercise one does. (This is especially true for people 40 years old and older.) Also, wear shoes with good support and avoid jumping on concrete. I have jumped rope after exercise class, or in my garage on rainy days when I didn't want to go out and run.

## How Many and What Kind of Jumps Should You Do?

I started by jumping 500 jumps, three times a week. Then I gradually increased by about 50 jumps a week (10%) until I was jumping for about ten minutes (about 1,200 jumps). For variety, I used different foot steps. Sometimes I jump with both feet at once, with a little bounce between jumps. Then I change to jumping with one foot, stepping on the other foot between jumps (sometimes called "Rock the Cradle"). Then, for a high-level workout, I might jump 50 or so jumps at double the speed, jumping with both feet but with no bounce between jumps. There are a number of acrobatic things to do with a jump rope, too, such as crossing your arms, walking forward or back while you jump, and throwing the rope backward to jump.

## CYCLING

For several reasons, many people prefer cycling, which can be done either on a bicycle outdoors around your neighborhood or on a stationary cycle in your house. You need to pedal continuously without interruptions, because any kind of slowdown or stop allows your heart rate to drop.

The main problem people mention when trying to exercise out of doors on a bicycle is finding a long enough route. The best routes seem to be along wide, country roads during times when the traffic is very low. Or, if you're fortunate enough to live near a bicycle trail, these can make good exercise routes.

Exercising with a stationary cycle is good if running hurts or if there isn't a good place to jog or ride a bicycle in your neighborhood. Setting up a cycle in front of the television set or near a radio or tape player can make it possible to get two things done at once. People have told me they cycle during the evening news or while listening to an interesting study tape.

## Getting Comfortable

If you aren't comfortable sitting on the seat of the cycle, it's hard to last the full amount of time necessary for a good workout. The seat should be high enough so that your leg is almost, but not quite, straight when the pedal is in the down position. The handlebars can also be adjusted, and will probably need to be changed if you change the position of the seat.

## Adjusting the Pedal Tension on a Stationary Bike

Finding out what speed and resistance is needed to get your heart rate up to the working heart level requires a little trial-and-error experimenting. There is an adjustment on the front wheel of the cycle which makes it harder or easier for a person to pedal.

Once you have adjusted the cycle and set the resistance control at the lowest setting, try pedaling for three or four minutes, then stop and take your pulse. If your pulse isn't high enough, tighten the resistance control. If your pulse is too high, pedal more slowly. Watch the speedometer and note your speed. Try again for another three or four minutes, and take your pulse again. Keep experimenting like this until you know how to pedal to get your heart working in the right range. Then finish your 17 minutes, taking your pulse once again at the end to be sure you are at the right place.

Be sure to warm up before you begin. One way to warm up is to pedal slowly for two or three minutes before moving up into your workout speed. Also, make sure you walk around or pedal slowly again when you've finished—until your pulse rate has dropped below 120—before you sit down or lie down.

## SWIMMING

Another excellent aerobic activity is swimming. The advantages are that there is no pounding strain on any body joints as in running. Finding a pool with lanes marked off in it for swimming laps is ideal. But swimming in a backyard pool can offer a lot of aerobic exercise, too.

## Getting Comfortable

Getting comfortable with being in the water is important. I used to have trouble with water getting in my ears. Swimming would keep my ear stopped for hours and sometimes for several days. So I bought a pair of earplugs. Also, the water ran up my nose and irritated my sinuses. So a nose clip fixed that. Last of all, my eyes burned because I kept opening them to make sure I was swimming in a straight line and to see where the end of the pool was. Now a comfortable pair of swimming goggles not only protects my eyes from the chlorine in the water, but also allows me to see the stripes painted on the bottom of the pool very clearly, so I can swim in a straight line.

## Which Stroke Is Most Effective?

For the first year of my fitness program, I preferred swimming because my legs hurt too much when I ran even a mile. My favorite stroke was the breaststroke, but when I swam this way my heart rate didn't get up high enough. I had read that the most effective stroke to use for aerobic exercise is the American overhand crawl. So I decided to change to the crawl stroke.

The first day I swam using the crawl stroke, I could barely do eight laps! My arms hurt so much I thought they would fall off, and I was panting so hard I couldn't keep my head in the water. I got out of the pool very discouraged. The next day I barely managed to get through eight laps again. But by the end of the week, I had gotten up to ten, and swimming with the crawl stroke felt easier than when I'd first started. Within a month, I had worked up to a full 24 laps. After a year of daily swimming five days a week, I found I could swim a mile (88 laps) comfortably and enjoy the restful, quiet atmosphere of the water.

If you're not a good swimmer but have access to a pool, there is an excellent aerobic exercise which you can do in the deep end of the pool. Hold on to something which will help you float, like a volleyball, beach ball, or kickboard. Run in place, moving your legs under water. You can get your heart rate up just fine and there is no wear and tear on your legs and feet! I've heard of people who do this for a full thirty minutes. It's nice to listen to music or a study tape while doing this. (Be very careful to remember to start the radio or tape player *before* you're in the water—to avoid electric shock!)

Dr. Ted Edwards, Jr. provides a detailed description of two kinds of aerobic exercise you can do in a pool.[1] One is a set of exercises with a beach ball which will give you muscle strength and elevate your heart rate, and the other is a lap-swimming routine, using the crawl and the breaststroke or doing laps by kicking only, holding on to a kickboard.

## AEROBIC DANCE

Aerobic dance is possibly the most enjoyable aerobic activity I have ever done. It combines music, movement, muscle-tone[2] and

---

1. Edwards, *Weight Loss to Super Wellness*, 71–92.
2. I want to add here that while aerobic dance will lightly tone some muscles, it is no substitute for a workout which concentrates on muscle tone alone.

aerobic exercise. If you've never done it before, it's probably best to find a class and join it. The instructor teaches as the class goes along. But if you're familiar with how some of the steps are done (or quick to catch on to written instructions) there are aerobic dance tapes available, so you can do aerobic dance at home. This is handy in case there is not a class meeting at a convenient time for you.

The main problem is the temptation to stop between dances and stand around, which lets the heart rate drop. If you join an aerobic dance class or use a tape at home, try to remember to keep walking, jumping lightly in place, and swinging your arms between dances.

Now that you have some choices about exercising your heart and lungs, I hope you'll soon be enjoying the increased energy and endurance (and calorie usage!) that are the products of regular aerobic exercise. But as you get into the full swing of things, you may begin to realize, as I did, just how important it is to make sure you balance the energy spent on exercise with the repair-and-healing time spent in rest. That will be the subject of the next chapter.

# Week Four
### (Three Days)

## Aims and Activities

(1)  To continue with muscle-tone workouts.

(2)  To begin to settle into a routine of aerobic exercise—20 minutes a day, five days a week. (Continue to take it easy, but exercise the full time and monitor your pulse rate.)

(3)  To gain an understanding of your body's need for rest. (Try to make sure you get at least eight hours of sleep a night for the duration of the course.)

(4)  To weigh yourself and record your present weight.

(5)  To calculate your ideal weight, taking into account your body frame and your activity levels.

# 12

## *The Importance of Rest*

### Scripture and Devotion

Life can't be all work and no relief! Without adequate rest, we can't become healthy and fit to do God's will. So I was pleased to find that God is interested in giving us rest and helping us with the loads we must carry in life. Here is Matthew 11:28—30:

> "Come to me, all who labor and are heavy laden, and I will give you rest. Take my yoke upon you, and learn from me; for I am gentle and lowly of heart, and you will find rest for your souls. For my yoke is easy, and my burden is light."

Resting, even for health reasons, has always been difficult for me to do. I am an active, "attack" kind of person who wants to *do* all the right things to bring myself to and maintain a state of health. I want to get all I can out of each day, and I often shortchange myself when it comes to rest.

When I came across this passage recently, I wondered what it might mean in terms of learning how God made our bodies and what keeps them healthy. I was reading the *Communicator's Commentary*—the volume on Matthew by Dr. Myron S. Augsburger, who is a teacher, preacher, and scholar. According to Dr. Augsburger, there is a legend that Jesus made the best yokes in all of Galilee in his carpenter's shop. They were tailor-made to fit the animals who would wear them. In this scripture for today, Jesus could have been using an illustration from his work, saying something like this (I'm using Dr. Augsburger's words): "Yoke yourself with me, for my task for you is shared and made easy and the burden is light."[1]

---

1. Myron S. Augsburger, *Matthew*, The Communicator's Commentary Series, ed. Lloyd John Ogilvie, Vol. 1 (Waco, TX: Word Books, 1982), 50.

I'm beginning to see that God made our bodies to function in a certain way, fueled by certain foods and toned by certain kinds of movement. When we don't follow those natural laws, our bodies fall below the level of fitness which God designed. Yet I'm also aware that I am often unhappy and unwilling to follow good health practices. I find myself wishing I could stay healthy without all that. I wonder, "Why did God set things up this way?"

And so my thoughts turn to other of God's natural laws that I can easily accept and live by without all this resistance and questioning.

One of the natural laws I thought of is the law of gravity. With this law, as with other laws, God has left me free to decide what my own behavior will be. If I want to, I can choose to climb up on a tall building, walk over to the edge of the roof, and step off. But what happens after that is out of my hands. God's natural law of gravity takes over and I am pulled to the ground with such force that I am sure to be injured or killed. Everybody seems to know that will happen, and anyone who attempts to jump off a building is considered suicidal or temporarily insane, or is thought to have accidently "fallen" off.

Now, gravity is a law with which I can easily live. I may occasionally lose my balance and fall, or drop a glass dish and see it break on the floor, but I don't get mad at God about it! I just feel clumsy. I recognize the fall as a natural result of the law of gravity.

Imagine my trying to bargain with God about walking off the edge of the tall building! I might say, "Well, I'll just step out here for a minute and then go right back." Do you think I'd get away with it?

And yet, when I'm dealing with the natural laws of nutrition and exercise, I react differently. I want to be free to put too much fat or sugar into my system, or to stop exercising without becoming out of shape, or to go without sleep in order to fit as much as I can into each 24-hour period. Doing those things is like choosing to jump off a roof, only the physical damage is more subtle and gradual. So why do I feel irritated, cheated, and angry because I gain weight or get flabby and tired? These are just natural laws God created, I reason, like the law of gravity.

The law of gravity is a good thing. It holds everything in place on the surface of the earth. The laws of nutrition and exercise are good things, too. Only I've gotten everything so bent out of shape that I don't recognize the value in those laws. It's as if somebody sneaked into a department store at night and switched all the price tags on the merchandise. When I go in to shop, all the things that were made to be really valuable appear to be cheap and worthless, while the things that are actually of little value or are harmful appear to be valuable and appealing. I pay a high price for them, but they do not bring me happiness and health.

As I thought about these natural laws, I decided that what I need to learn is to pay attention to the way God intended for me to use food. I need to concentrate on finding his will and not on what special yummy snack I can have before bed (or on my birthday, or to celebrate losing weight, or at any time). Learning to be God's person includes learning to follow the natural laws he made.

And when I take this yoke upon me and learn about health, I will be healthier and more at peace. When I don't, I'll still be battling the bulges and the flab.

> DEAR LORD, forgive me for taking so many liberties with your natural laws of how to keep my body in shape. Today's world seems like a department store with all the price tags changed. It seems so attractive to enjoy rich foods, and there are so many good reasons not to exercise, to stay up late to get my reading done, or to rely on fast, convenient foods.
>
> Help me learn to respect your laws. Help me to turn to you for wisdom and rest, and to trust you when you say your yoke is easy and your burden is light. Thank you for your love, patience, and firmness during my learning time. In Jesus' name, AMEN.

## Rest

I have not found much written about resting. I think, knowing human nature, most writers of fitness books concentrate on telling us about the benefits of exercise and trying to get us out of our chairs and out there moving! In the beginning stages, it's almost as if we are guilty of having *too much rest* from exercise.

But Dr. George Sheehan, in his book, *Dr. Sheehan on Running*, includes a chapter on rest and stress, and the long-distance runners I know personally have told me that adequate rest is just as crucial to their performance as is sound training and good nutrition. They also say that resting is perhaps the hardest thing to remember to do! When exercise starts being fun, it is sometimes hard to pull back and rest.

There are two kinds of rest that I think are important. One is sleep, and the other is taking "time out" from exercise and the business of life in general.

## The Importance of Sleep

Our bodies use the time we spend in sleep to rebuild energy and repair tissue. Every other body function that takes energy, except for basic survival functions like breathing and heartbeat, is shut down during sleep. So when we add any amount of exercise to our lives, it's important to get an adequate amount of sleep (usually about eight hours) so our bodies can rebuild the energy we spent and repair any damage that might have happened. Athletes in training for the Olympics often sleep nine hours a night. And professional athletes sometimes sleep up to 18 hours before a game!

Dr. Sheehan explains that there are two kinds of sleep. The first is called REM (Rapid Eye Movement) sleep—the kind of sleep during which dreams occur. The other kind is deep, non-dreaming sleep, called "S" (Slow Wave) sleep because the brain waves, as measured on an electroencephalogram, slow down. Most of our sleep time is made up of "S" sleep, with REM sleep occurring at intervals for relatively short periods.

Each of these two different kinds of sleep has a different job to do. REM sleep apparently is concerned with our psychological function. Without it, we soon start having serious emotional and intellectual problems. A person who is irritable or forgetful after staying up too late is possibly suffering from a lack of REM sleep.

"S" sleep is necessary for physical performance and health, and it is during this kind of sleep that tissue repair is believed to take place. A person who consistently fails to get enough "S" sleep will probably be physically fatigued and more susceptible to illness and injury.

Because people vary in the amount of sleep they need, each person must listen to her own body to determine how much is right for her. But in today's high-pressure society the call of our bodies and minds toward sleep often gets drowned out by the call of undone chores, unwritten letters, unread books, and husbands and children who need attention. Many adults feel compelled to push themselves beyond their endurance levels. I know that I, in my pride, often refuse to admit what my real endurance levels are and to make sure I get the rest I need.

When this happens, I eventually pay the price. I become "run down" and tired, less effective in my work, less able to enjoy play. I may even become ill. Dr. Sheehan points out, "Nature . . . makes no allowances for such mistakes. Her penalties for violating curfew are a lot more substantial than any coach's. And nature's bedchecks occur every night."[2]

One form of sleep that can be extremely valuable is the nap. Many people think that only children need to take naps. But I have found that just lying down briefly in the afternoon (or any other time of day when energy levels run low) can pay enormous dividends in terms of decreased fatigue and restored energy. Naps can be especially helpful during times of unusual stress or times when we can't get enough sleep at night—when there's a crisis at work, for instance, or a new baby in the house.

## The Importance of "Time-Outs"

Besides sleep, there's another kind of rest I have found to be very important as I progress toward the goal of fitness. I have learned that sometimes, during periods when I'm trying to increase my exercise levels, I feel more tired and have less energy than usual. At other times the *fun* of aerobic exercise clicks in and it's easy to become somewhat compulsive about my running or swimming or whatever else I am doing. I have found that, in either case, it is helpful to remember to take occasional "time-outs."

By "time-outs" I mean any one of several things. One kind of time-out could be a day of exercise in which I go easy on myself. For instance, if I'm trying to increase my distance in running, I'll be following the general rule of thumb, which is to increase my distance by about 10% each week. So, to go easy on myself, one day I might relax and run my regular old distance. Or I might run a little more slowly than usual, being satisfied to run at the bottom (70%) of my WHR range instead of pushing for the top (85%). These letups provide relief from the feeling that I always have to push as hard as I can every time I exercise.

In the past, on days when I felt tired or "down," I would sometimes skip exercise because I didn't feel ready to push hard. Now, instead of skipping, I try to go on out there but just have an easy walk or run. When I allow myself this kind of time-out, I'm not as tempted to skip a day of exercise.

There is another kind of time-out which involves taking periods of time and spending them entirely on myself—not exercising at all, but perhaps just watching the sun go down from the back porch. It might be a whole evening, an hour, or a minute. But taking that time

---

2. George Sheehan, *Dr. Sheehan on Running* (New York: Bantam Books, in cooperation with World Publications, 1975), 108.

revives me; I can go back to my job or the things I am doing for others refreshed and more alert.

I can't tell you how much these time-outs have meant as I've gone along the road to getting in shape. It's a relief to realize that rest is something I *need* as a part of my fitness program, not something I indulge in because I'm too lazy or too weak to go out and exercise hard every day!

I mentioned at the beginning of this book that a large part of my struggle to become fit has involved losing weight. That was one of my goals from the start, and I suspect that many people reading this book are concerned with weight—either taking it off or putting it on. But up to this point in the BodyCare course I've said very little specifically about weight, other than to point out the fact that I believe exercise is the key to permanent weight control as well as to other aspects of fitness and health. I think it's important to take major changes in our lives one step at a time. But in the next few chapters we will begin looking at how our weight (too much or too little) affects our health. Then we will look at what our weight *should* be, and begin to look at some sensible methods for keeping our weight within the healthy range.

The exercise guidelines we've already looked at and the food guidelines we'll talk about later also apply to people who weigh the right amount but who want to improve their energy levels, resistance to colds or extreme mood swings, and general health.

# 13

## *How Maintaining Healthy Weight Benefits the Body*

### *Scripture and Devotion*

I think it's fair to say that most of us want to lose or gain weight because we want to *look* better. But there are other reasons for keeping ourselves at the proper weight. Studies have shown that how much we weigh has a direct connection with how healthy we are. And for that reason I believe weight control is an important aspect of my call to be as fit as I can be in order to be more available to do God's will.

Today's scripture is one that helped me see that my taking care of my health—and keeping my weight under control—means a lot to God. It is 1 Corinthians 6:19–20:

> "Do you not know that your body is a temple of the Holy Spirit within you, which you have from God? You are not your own; you were bought with a price. So glorify God in your body."

Many thoughts and feelings tumble around in me as I think about this passage. Without studying any scholarly commentaries, I first thought that Paul was referring to keeping free from immoral sexual activities. And I still think he is. But I think he is also referring to *other* sins which make our bodies less than they were created to be, such as being overweight or physically out of shape.

I don't want to concentrate on trying to decide whether overeating or not exercising are sins. From one perspective, I think they are, if they separate us from God by becoming the focus of our lives, or if they lead to poor health which disables us with sickness so that we aren't able to do his will. Another way to think of excess fat and weak muscles is to regard them as "encumbrances" which prevent us from being our best for God.

Whichever it is, I think it's clear that my physical body is all I have with which to serve God while I am in this life. Out of love for him and gratitude for all he has done for me, I want to do everything I know to keep healthy and free from illness.

When I compare my body to a building which was built for a rare and special guest (the Holy Spirit), I get an interesting picture of what I might look like from God's perspective when I let myself get out of shape.

"Out of shape" could mean I am overweight, bogged down with cholesterol and layers of fat on the internal organs or within muscle tissue, lungs wheezing along at minimum capacity, kidneys overworked with trying to flush out waste materials. Or it could mean that I catch every cold that comes along, get knocked off my feet regularly by the flu, and am chronically too tired to do anything but the minimum each day.

Either way, it's as if I am a building whose floors are never mopped or dusted, whose furniture is buried under mounds of garbage, whose plumbing is clogged with things not meant to be flushed down the drains! It's as if the air conditioner filters are never cleaned so that fresh air can circulate, as if mildew and mold are allowed to accumulate inside, making the atmosphere unhealthy.

If I am weak, sick, or cause my own premature death by not keeping my internal systems clean and efficient, then it seems to me that I am not "glorifying God in my body" as Paul suggests we should. By exercising and eating properly, I can "clean house" within my body and help keep it operating smoothly and efficiently.

> DEAR LORD, I know that my body is a temple of your Holy Spirit within me, and I want to glorify you. I am so grateful to you for paying the price you paid for me.
>
> Help me to be willing to pay a price to honor you. As I learn to trust you with control of this part of my life, help me to begin to see what changes I can make to become more healthy. In Jesus' name, AMEN.

## Being at Ideal Weight Is Important to All Areas of Health

In an earlier chapter we discussed some of the ways exercise can help overcome or prevent certain health problems. In a similar way, the fact that a body weighs more than it was designed to weigh can bring on or heighten other health problems.

There are three kinds of fat in the body—fat found just below the surface of the skin (the kind that shows up as bulges), fat within the fibers of our muscles (which doesn't show at all), and fats found in the bloodstream.

A person who is overweight and looks fat knows that she has too much fat. But even people who seem to weigh a normal amount, if they are not in good shape, can have excess fat within the tissues of the muscles themselves or in the bloodstream. Too much of any of the three kinds of fat can lead to health problems in several ways.

## Strain on Muscles and Joints Built for a Lighter Load

Carrying extra weight on bones and joints built for a normal load strains all the muscles and joints, especially the ones called the "weight-bearing" joints: hips, knees, and ankles. This daily strain can lead to diseases of the joints such as arthritis.

When I imagine that I am a person of normal weight who has to carry a ten-pound sack of sand with me everywhere I go, I can easily see that there will be a lot of extra wear and tear on my joints, as well as extra energy needed to move this weight as I walk, sit down, and get up from sitting or lying down.

## Heart Disease and Heart Attacks

Extra fat in the blood system (known as cholesterol) is now known to be a major contributing factor in heart disease and heart attacks. This kind of fat builds up within the blood vessels, leaving less and less room for blood to flow in and out of the heart properly. Finally, when a major vessel near the heart becomes too clogged with fat, the blood is blocked from its proper rate of flow, and a heart attack or stroke can occur. In these cases, surgery (called bypass surgery) is often performed. A blood vessel from another part of the body, usually the leg, is used to bypass the blocked part of the clogged vessel. The blocked vessel is not removed. One end of the new vessel is inserted into the artery above the blockage, and the other end of it into the heart. This surgery is so refined that in a very high percentage of the cases the patient not only survives, but can recover and resume a normal life. But the survival and recovery *always* depend on the patient's permanently changing the eating and exercise habits which led to the problem.

## Internal Organs Burdened

Another problem caused by too much fat is that organs inside our bodies become surrounded by layers of extra fat which make them have to work harder to do their job. This creates problems for the liver, the bladder, the lungs, and other organs. The extra work created for these organs can cause them to wear out or break down sooner than they would otherwise.

## Surgery More Complex and Risky

In addition, if surgery were to be required for any reason, the surgeon would have a harder time getting to the place that needed surgery, creating more risk for the patient. And recovery for a patient whose body has too much fat is slower and more risky because of such potential problems as: infection, hemorrhage, breakdown of the wound (or incision), collapse of small sections of the lung, or thrombophlebitis, which is the forming of blood clots in the veins deep within the muscles in the leg or pelvic area.

Medical research has linked being overweight with increased risk of diabetes, blood clots, varicose veins, respiratory disease, gout, gastrointestinal disorders, gall bladder disease, and liver disease. Studies have also shown that overweight women are more likely to suffer from toxemia during pregnancy and to develop cancer of the womb's lining and of the breast. Being overweight has been linked to disorders of the menstrual cycle, including infertility because of failure to ovulate.

In addition, too many pounds can make any other health problem we may encounter worse—even though that problem isn't directly related to being overweight. Excess weight is often caused by lack of exercise and by unhealthy eating. These same two things can also make the body more susceptible to allergies and infectious diseases such as colds and the flu.

## Emotional and Mental Effects

There is also evidence that having too much fat in proportion to what we need for normal living can lead to chemical imbalances in the body. These imbalances can contribute to being tired and mentally slow, and to having emotional conditions like depression and anxiety. I'm not saying that being overweight *causes* depression and anxiety, but research seems to indicate that certain chemicals in our bodies *promote* these two conditions, and that these chemicals are related to being overweight. Overweight people may tend to think that they are depressed because they don't like being overweight. But in actuality their depression could be partly due to the effect of the excess fat on the chemical balances in the body which regulate our moods.

## Fit to Do God's Will

I've tried to outline some medical findings which can serve as motivation for keeping our weight within a healthy range. And I want to mention another thing which has become a strong motivation for me. I believe that everything I have is a gift from God—the fact that I was born in this generation to my family, in this country, and at this particular point in history. Also, another gift to me is that I'm saved by God's grace and will be his child forever.

Along with that, I believe that God has saved me *for a purpose*, and that as I live my life seeking his will he will show it to me step by step. So that I can be ready to be all that he has in mind for me, I believe I must try to bring my body to a healthy level of fitness, both in weight and in strength, through eating properly and exercising.

To me this means that the body I have been given is also a gift from him. He *knows* what its strengths and weaknesses are, how my metabolism works, how my willpower fails me, and what all my problems with being fit are. If I can find information about how to care for my body so that I can have more strength, energy, and emotional stability, and if I do not use that information to care for my body, then I am not being a good steward of the things God has given to me.

## The Man Who Hid His Talent

In some ways, we are like the man who was given ten talents, and who invested them and made them grow (see Luke 19:11–27). I believe our physical bodies are part of God's gift to us, and when we invest in caring for them, our investment will cause our good health to increase. And like the man who took his one talent and, because he was afraid to risk, hid the talent for safekeeping, we can lose our health by not applying what we know to our daily lives. I have noticed that when I don't do the exercises and eat the foods I know will improve my health and fitness, I am in effect losing the full use of my body which God intended for me to have.

Therefore, when I put time in my "busy" day to tend to these bodily needs, I know I am contributing to my overall preparation for doing God's will. Bible study, prayer, contact with other Christians, and supporting God's church are vital to becoming a strong Christian spiritually. In much the same way, I believe taking care of our own health and the health of those people who depend on us for nourishment and nutritional guidance is vital to become a strong, healthy person, available to do God's will.

Therefore, losing weight and getting in shape is now no longer just a "vanity trip" for me. I *do* care about how I look. But I am also trying to be a good steward of one of God's best gifts to me, a body which is a "tool" for God in the most personal sense. For wherever I may live in this world, in one sense this body will always be my home.

So now that we've talked about a few of the health reasons for keeping our bodies free of excess fat, let's talk about how much we should weigh. What weight is a healthy weight for each individual?

# 14

## *The Right Weight for You*

### Scripture and Devotion

As I have thought about weight control, I have realized that a lot of my problem has to do with my feelings and attitudes. This passage in Jeremiah seems to illustrate what I was seeing about myself:

"The heart is deceitful above all things, and desperately corrupt; who can understand it?" (Jer. 17:9).

I realize I've written a lot in this book about how I wrestle with problems. But I've never read much about people who struggle like this. Most people who write about the subject of fitness and weight control seem to get involved with exercise programs and go on diets with good results and the greatest of ease. That simply hasn't been the case for me. So I hope you'll be patient with me as I talk about my struggles, because this is really the way I've had to come to terms with what it takes to have good health. And since I believe good health is a part of my response to the call to be God's person, I think talking about this part of the process is important. Perhaps it will be helpful to someone else to know that struggling, failing, recovering, and struggling some more can be part of a "successful" approach to fitness and health.

The problem I think of when I read this passage in Jeremiah is that of wanting my own way. I want to be trim and healthy, but I don't want to have to jog, sweat, try to touch my toes in exercise class, and count every slice of bread that goes into my mouth.

From my reading, the way to get in shape is now clear to me: exercise, eat properly, get enough rest. I know my pleasure should begin to come from having a healthy body rather than from certain unhealthy foods. So I go for a few days or even several weeks doing everything right.

But then I begin to let up a little. I don't measure everything I eat—I just eyeball it and figure it's probably close enough (when it's almost half again what I should eat). I add an extra pat of butter and don't count it in my daily allowance. Or something comes up and I skip exercise "just this once"—only I do it the next day, too! I can go for days or weeks like this, thinking I am working at getting fit but not really making any headway. I am just kidding myself—or as Jeremiah puts it, my heart is deceitful and desperately corrupt.

Thomas à Kempis explained it to me when he wrote,

> Many persons, through a secret love that they have for themselves, work indiscreetly according to their own will and not according to the will of God, yet they do not know it. They seem to stand in great inward peace when things go according to their own mind, but if anything happens contrary to their mind, they are soon moved with impatience and are quite downcast and melancholy. [1]

As I thought about how I sometimes act, I realized, "It's true." When I step on the scale in the morning and my weight has stayed the same or gone down, I am happy and optimistic all day long. But let that scale show me a half-pound or pound *gained*, and I am upset for hours! Especially if I *think* I didn't "cheat," and therefore don't "deserve" to gain!

I now know that I may not lose a pound every day, and that fluctuations in the amount of water in my system may show an extra pound gained some mornings, even when I didn't go off my diet. But even knowing this, I still feel impatient and angry when the scales don't go my way. And I often make myself miserable the rest of the day.

The only hope I have found for coping with this is to recognize that I am likely to be dishonest with myself, that in a sneaky way I am probably trying to get something for nothing by not keeping my diet commitments. There's no way to really "understand" why I do it. But the miracle is that by turning to God and asking him to help me I can begin, and *am* beginning, to do a better job of following good health practices more consistently.

> DEAR LORD, help me to recognize when I am kidding myself and to face it. Thank you that you forgive me for my failures. That inspires me to try harder and gives me hope that I can succeed. When I feel angry, help me to look be-

---

1. Thomas à Kempis, *Imitation of Christ*, 47.

yond that anger to ask the question, "Am I angry because things aren't going my way?" Help me to know the answer, to see how I'm working against your natural laws of nutrition and exercise. And help me to know what to do about my anger. In Jesus' name, AMEN.

## What We Should Weigh

Several factors determine what we should weigh. Two of them are our height and bone size. Since we can't go inside our bodies to measure our bones, here's a little test I learned from a lecture by Nancy Fong, the nutritionist for the Houstonian Preventive Medicine Center. You can do it on your own body to get an approximate idea of what a healthy weight might be for you.

First, you must determine if you have a small, medium, or large frame. Use the thumb and baby finger of your left hand to make a circle around the wrist of your right arm. If the tips of your fingers touch, then you probably have a medium-sized bone structure. If they do not meet, then your bones are large, and if they overlap, then your bones are small.

Now here's a formula by which we can tell how much we should weigh. For the first five feet of your height, allow 100 pounds. Then add five pounds for every inch of height over five feet. If you are 5'4" inches tall, this formula would mean you should weigh around 120 pounds—100 pounds plus twenty more for the four inches over five feet of height. (Men should add 6 pounds per inch of height over five feet.)

If you have a small frame, subtract five pounds from the total and, if you have a large frame, add five. If you have a medium frame, add or subtract nothing. This formula gives you your approximate healthy weight range: a ten-pound range with that number as the center.

I am 5'8" tall, with a small frame, which means that my healthy weight range centers at 135, with 130–140 being the correct range. You can use the worksheets at the end of this chapter and the back of this book (pp. 120, 361) to calculate your own ideal weight range.

## There's More to Fitness Than What the Scales Say

But there is more to being in shape than just seeing the right number on the scale. I took you through this little test because I think one of the first things to do in evaluating whether or not you're at a good weight is to take a realistic look at what you should weigh. I found out that I had a completely unrealistic idea about my weight. I had felt that any "decent-sized" woman should weigh under 120 pounds. And I kept reading the statistics on Miss America contestants and seeing 116, 117, 113 for women who were often as tall as I am. When I weighed 140, I looked pretty good, especially if I dressed right and kept my muscles in shape. But I hated myself for being what I thought was almost twenty pounds overweight.

In *The Dieter's Dilemma*, however, William Bennett and Joel Gurin point out that our idea of "normal weight" is usually set arbitrarily by society, not by what is healthy.[2] A hundred years ago, many of us would be considered scrawny and underweight and too bony to be attractive—fashion models and movie actresses too! Today, it's considered fashionable to be very thin. But research shows that being underweight is as unhealthy as being overweight in terms of being susceptible to illness and fatal diseases!

So I began to tell myself, "If movie actresses need to weigh ten pounds under their ideal weight range in order to be successful professionally, let them. It's their job. But my job is not acting or modeling, and all I want is a healthy life, energy, and the freedom from illness to do God's will." So I know my healthy weight range is 130–140, and I'm trying to learn to be satisfied to weigh within those two numbers.

The authors also point out that a third factor (besides height and bone size) which can affect a person's "natural" healthy weight is genetic predisposition. Some people are tall, some are short. Some have blue eyes, others brown. And some people have a propensity to being heavy while others do not. So for these people moderate heaviness (within 10% of the ideal weight we just calculated) is not necessarily unhealthy.

Provided a person eats balanced meals, has normal blood pressure and pulse rate, and has well-toned muscles and good cardiovascular fitness, what that person weighs is not all that crucial. The only reason some people become committed to weighing a certain number on the bathroom scale is what current society makes us think we should weigh.[3]

This is harder to accept than it is to understand. I still feel ashamed when I weigh in at the doctor's office and the scale reads 138. I want to make excuses for myself all the time, even though the

---

2. Bennett and Gurin, *The Dieter's Dilemma*, 71–76.
3. Ibid., 168–209.

doctor doesn't ever criticize me for it. But I'm trying to realize that while I try to stay at the lower end of my ideal range—130 pounds— 138 is a perfectly healthy weight for someone who is 5'8" tall and has small bones—especially fully dressed. And it is whether I have good muscle tone (muscle weighs more than fat) or just a bunch of flabby fat that determines whether I'm really healthy.

So as I'm thinking this through, I'm learning to like my body a little more each week—and to concentrate on keeping it firm, energetic, and free from illness instead of trying to reach some arbitrary point on the scale. I believe that loving ourselves is very important if we are going to be free to do God's will. So many things about life are better if we can learn to love ourselves, or at least like our physical bodies a little better. And I believe that we have *God's* love, no matter what we weigh.

There is one more factor which relates to how much we should weigh. To be really healthy we should have the proper ratio of body fat to lean muscle mass. When we don't exercise, we can have a higher percentage of body fat than we should, even if our weight is "normal." Muscle mass weighs more than fat. So when the proper balance is achieved our physical size will be trim, but our weight may be a little higher than it would be if we were not exercising. Weighing 130 pounds without muscle tone would leave me at a bigger dress size than weighing 130 pounds with muscle tone and the correct ratio of body fat. Or in other words, if I weigh 125 pounds with high body fat and little muscle tone, I may be the same size I would be if I weighed 130 but had low body fat, but I would not be as healthy.

The first year I took a physical examination at the Preventive Medicine Center, I weighed 134 pounds, but my body fat was measured at 26%. Since a percentage of 22% is ideal for women (19% for men), I was advised to lose 4% of my weight—or five pounds. That would make my "prescribed weight" 129 pounds.

That whole year I swam laps, jogged a little, and jumped rope. The next year I weighed in again, and the scale still said 134! I was shattered—I had worked so hard! But then they measured my body fat and found it was 17.9%. I didn't need to lose any more weight at all! That explained to me why my clothes fit so much more loosely and I "felt skinnier." I had shed fat and built muscle.

It has been helpful to me to know what my "ideal weight" is. The test you just gave yourself is only an estimate—and it is a little high according to some sources I have read. Another chart to go by is one I've seen in *Jane Brody's Nutrition Book*; it is printed on the next page:

## IDEAL WEIGHT IN POUNDS[4]

### Women

| Height | Age | | | | |
|--------|-------|-------|-------|-------|-------|
|        | 20—29 | 30—39 | 40—49 | 50—59 | 60—69 |
| 4'10"  | 97    | 102   | 106   | 109   | 111   |
| 5'1"   | 106   | 109   | 114   | 118   | 120   |
| 5'4"   | 114   | 118   | 122   | 127   | 129   |
| 5'7"   | 123   | 127   | 132   | 137   | 140   |
| 5'10"  | 134   | 138   | 142   | 146   | 147   |

### Men

| Height | Age | | | | |
|--------|-------|-------|-------|-------|-------|
|        | 20—29 | 30—39 | 40—49 | 50—59 | 60—69 |
| 5'3"   | 125   | 129   | 130   | 131   | 130   |
| 5'6"   | 135   | 140   | 142   | 143   | 142   |
| 5'9"   | 149   | 153   | 155   | 156   | 155   |
| 6'0"   | 161   | 166   | 167   | 168   | 167   |
| 6'3"   | 176   | 181   | 183   | 184   | 180   |

From this chart I can see that the "healthy weight range" prescribed for me at 5'8" (age category 30—39) is about 131. So my goal of 130 is fairly realistic until I reach the age of 40—which isn't that far away! Then I'll be considered healthy according to this chart, even if I weigh around 135.

As you begin to eat more balanced meals and exercise to burn off excess fat and develop muscle tone, your actual body weight may not change much, unless you are quite a bit overweight. As fat dissolves, we lose weight. As muscle develops, we gain weight. And muscle tissue weighs more than fat. So even though you may lose more square inches of fat than you gain muscle, your weight could stay almost the same. But when you get to the ideal percentage of body fat, you may be a dress size or two smaller. And if you're like me, that will really feel *good*!

---

4. Jane Brody, *Jane Brody's Nutrition Book: A Lifetime Guide to Good Eating for Better Health and Weight Control by the Personal Health Columnist for the New York Times* (New York: W. W. Norton Co., 1981), 287.

## Large Weight Loss Goals Can Be Met in Stages

I hope you won't feel too discouraged if you've just found out you've got a lot of weight to lose. One approach that helped me is to lose weight in several stages. You might spend a month losing eight or ten pounds, then two months learning how to keep your weight at that new level. Then, go for eight or ten more pounds in a month, and spend two more keeping it there. By going in a pattern like that, you can have relief from being on a long, long diet. At the same time, you'll be learning what it's going to take to keep your weight down when you do reach your goal. And in a year, a person could go through four such cycles and lose 30 to 40 pounds.

As I have said many times in this book, studies have shown that regular exercise seems to be the key to permanent weight control. But that doesn't mean that what we eat is unimportant! A nutritious, balanced eating plan plays an important role in keeping us healthy and keeping our weight where it should be. So in the next chapter we will begin talking about food. We will be asking, "*How much* food is needed to maintain proper body weight?"

## MY IDEAL WEIGHT

Height: _____

Frame Size: _____(S, M, L)

First 5', allow 100 pounds:                    100

Add 5 pounds per inch over 5':                 ___

Add or subtract 5 pounds if L or S frame:      ___

                              TOTAL: ___

Ideal range is: _____ to _____
              *(total minus 5)*      *(total plus 5)*

# Week Five
## (Three Days)

## *Aims and Activities*

(1)   To continue with muscle tone and aerobic workouts. At this point you may want to concentrate harder on getting your pulse rate into the proper range. Or, if the aerobic program you've been doing isn't satisfactory for some reason, try another one. Many people alternate among several kinds of aerobic exercise.

(2)   To learn to calculate the calories needed to maintain your ideal weight.

(3)   To gain a general understanding of what the four basic food groups are, how each contributes to the body's health, and what percentage of the day's calorie needs should come from each group.

# 15

## *How Many Calories Do You Need?*

### *Scripture and Devotion*

I've wondered for a long time about how much I should eat just to maintain a proper weight, once I lose down to what I should weigh. So I did a little investigating about that. But before I go into it, here is Isaiah 55:8:

> "For my thoughts are not your thoughts, neither are your ways my ways, says the Lord."

I sailed into exercise group this morning with my tape recorder, my exercise mat, and lots of enthusiasm. But when it came time to begin, no one else was there. I had dragged myself out of bed and gotten myself over to the church on time. I had moved the furniture, turned on the lights and ceiling fans, and prepared the room for my friends. Where were they???

Then I remembered why I started this group. I started it for me. I'd asked some other women to exercise with me. "That way," I thought, "I'll be sure to do it myself." And it had worked. Here I was, dressed and ready to go.

"It doesn't really matter if anyone else shows up," I told myself, "because my purpose is not to have a big group, but just to get motivated to exercise."

I tried to console myself, but the nagging question came into my mind anyway: "So why am I so mad?"

It seemed to me then that perhaps I had secretly wanted to be the leader of an exercise class. But I reminded myself that the whole purpose of starting the group was simply for me to do my exercise and take care of my own health. "Okay, God," I said, turned on the tape, and started exercising. I made it through the entire tape alone, and didn't mind half as much as I'd been afraid I would.

As I drove home, I remembered other things about getting in shape that sometimes make me angry. For example, if my husband decides to have something for dinner that I "can't" have, I feel angry at him. But from God's perspective that's not reasonable. My husband's metabolism is his, and my metabolism is mine. And what he "can" eat may be different from what I can. And even if it's not the best choice for him either, it's not my job to be angry about his choice. He is in charge of his own life.

At other times I catch myself thinking, "But I don't eat that much. I shouldn't gain weight!" Yet I've never really known how much I do eat. I've had to face seriously just how much (or little) I *need* to eat for the sake of good nourishment and maintaining health. When I compare what I actually need with what I've always thought I *should* eat, what I *need* seems so small. But my careful studies of nutrition have convinced me that this smaller amount is enough.

Then I thought about cars and the kind of fuel they need. Our Honda has a 14-gallon tank, and it takes unleaded fuel. If I were to treat it as if it were a large Pontiac, which could hold 21 gallons of regular fuel, and try to put all 21 gallons of gas in the 14-gallon tank, I would waste a lot of gas. Also, if I tried to substitute regular gas for unleaded, I would risk messing up the Honda's engine. I don't even consider doing that!

My husband needs more food than I do because he has more muscle tissue and he is physically bigger. But *I* want *him* to eat like our Honda . . . little bitty servings like those I need for good health. Or I expect him not to eat things that I know would put fat on *me*! And I get angry at *him* when what he eats doesn't make him fat!

I reasoned this time that the amount of food *I* should eat is for *me* to deal with. My husband has to deal with *his* own body and what *he* should eat. And when I get angry at anything having to do with getting myself in shape, I stop and ask myself if it might be because my ways are not God's ways. Am I secretly working according to my own will? And more times than I'd like to admit, I am. It seems to me now that the best way to have my way is to make God's way my way.

> DEAR LORD, I am seeing more and more through this experience that your ways are best, but they sure aren't my ways. I find myself angry at you, at other people, and at myself over this discovery. Help me to begin to be able to relax and change my habits. I see so clearly that I cannot do this without your help. And thank you once again for being there when the going gets rough. In Jesus' name, AMEN.

## How Do Calories Relate to Body Weight?

The energy we receive from food and the energy we use up when we are active is measured in "calories." When we give our bodies more calories than we need for energy, our bodies store up these calories as fat, in case we need them later.

I feel sure this process came in handy when cave men went through periods of having plenty of food and then times of starvation. In fact, there is a theory about human metabolism which holds that the people whose bodies were most efficient at storing extra calories were the ones who survived those prehistoric days. The others did not survive because they lost too much weight and died during times of famine. In today's world, this inherited trait is no longer beneficial in many societies, but there are more people who have this ability to store fat than those who do not.

In order to keep our bodies from storing fat, we need to try to keep from putting in more calories than our bodies can use. There are two ways of approaching this. One is to limit the number of calories we take in (eat less). The other is to increase the number of calories that are burned for energy (exercise more). Most successful weight reduction programs involve both. But in order to know how much to cut back eating or to increase activity, we must know how many calories are required just to *maintain* a given weight.

There are charts available from various sources that show how many calories men, women, and children need each day. One of these charts, prepared by the Food and Nutrition Board of the National Academy of Sciences—National Research Council, shows that females between the ages of 23 and 50 need between 1,600 and 2,400 calories a day. This chart is based on the needs of the *average* person, however. Caloric needs vary from person to person depending on age, height, weight, and level of activity.

Another way to get an idea how many calories are needed to maintain a given weight is to use a formula. It is estimated that we need about 15 calories per pound to maintain a certain weight. So, by multiplying 15 times your ideal weight, you can see what you would have to eat each day. If your weight is to be 125, then you can probably eat 1,875 calories a day without gaining or losing weight. If you weigh 110, then 1,650 calories is what you need. But let's take a look at what men can eat: A man who weighs 175 will need 2,625 calories just to keep his weight at that level. That's 1,000 calories per day more than a 110-pound woman needs.

The problem I have is that I have always thought it's "fair" to give my husband and myself equal servings of food at dinner—especially when it comes to rare delicacies. We share fifty-fifty, right? Wrong! When I learned this formula, I could see that equal sharing when it comes to food is definitely *unfair!* He ate what was right to maintain his weight, but if I ate an equal amount I gained weight!

So I realized that what is really "fair" is for me to eat *less* food than he does. I have to remember that when I am serving our plates for dinner. And when he serves the plates, I ask him to give me smaller servings than his. The new rule at our house is "unequal servings mean equal nutrition." Learning this has been hard for him, too. He says it feels as if he were cheating me or being greedy. But gradually we both are learning that it simply takes less food to keep me healthy than it does him.

Of course, if you are running hard or doing some other kind of aerobic exercise, you're burning up some of those calories and can add them in to your daily allowance without gaining or losing weight. (If you *want* to gain or lose weight, that's another story, and we'll come to that a little later on.)

To get an estimate of how many calories you must eat to maintain your weight if you're exercising, you can use this formula:

| *If you're:* | *You should eat:* |
| --- | --- |
| Extremely inactive | 12 calories per pound |
| Lightly active | 15 calories per pound |
| Moderately active | 20 calories per pound |
| Extremely active | 25 calories per pound |

Now, let's talk about what lightly, moderately and extremely active mean. If you've never exercised before, and you start going to an exercise class three times a week, you may feel as if you're "extremely" active! But the sources I have read say that just going to an exercise class for 45 minutes to an hour three times a week means you are lightly active. I might consider myself moderately active, because I jog two to three miles a day five or six times a week and do muscle-tone exercises for 45 minutes three days a week. Therefore, a woman like me who wants to stay at 130 pounds and is moderately active could eat 2,600 calories a day and still maintain her weight.

## The Exact Number of Calories Is Hard to Pin Down

The charts and formulas mentioned in this chapter can be very helpful in getting an idea of how many calories are needed to maintain weight. But since it's difficult to measure our various metabolic rates, a kind of "trial and error" adjustment is usually necessary.

For instance, I calculated that with my height, frame, and "moderate" level of activity I can maintain my ideal weight with about 2,600 calories. But I have found that in actual practice I *gain* weight at 2,600 calories. That means that, in order to keep my weight stable, I either need to take in fewer than 2,600 calories or increase my level of activity. So I have adjusted my calorie-need level down to 1,950— about 15 calories per pound. (If you *lose* weight at your calculated calorie level, and you don't want to lose weight, you would need to increase your calorie intake. Unless you are *very* active, I wouldn't recommend lowering your activity level, because you need the exercise to keep your body systems functioning well. But you may find it helps to concentrate more on the kinds of exercises that build muscle tone and to limit fat-burning aerobics to the amount needed to keep you healthy.)

In figuring my calorie needs, I'd also have to remember that the number of calories my body requires will change if my level of activity changes. If for some reason I discontinue my running program and therefore drop from being moderately active to being only "lightly active," I will have to refigure my calorie needs according to the formula for the lower level of activity. I have found that the formula for "extremely inactive" people can come in handy if I'm sick for a few days or have to stop exercising for another reason. I just recalculate using the formula (in my case, that means multiplying 130 pounds by 12 calories) and try to stick to the lower calorie count (1,560 calories).

When I kept track of the food I ate in a day, I was amazed at how quickly I could eat 2600 calories. To me, that much food seemed like nothing at all. And yet that is all I need to stay really healthy. Knowing that has helped me during the times I felt deprived or cheated because I "couldn't have" certain kinds of food.

## Not Just Any Old Calories Will Do

But just eating the right number of calories each day is not enough to keep us healthy. In order to get the nutrients our bodies need for energy and building tissue, we need to eat the *right kinds* of foods as well. Our daily calorie intake should include correct ratios of four basic food components in order for our bodies to make use of them properly. (We'll talk about this in the next chapter.) In fact, if too large a percentage of our daily intake is made up of fats or sugars, we may gain weight even on the minimum number of calories.

All this began to fall into place for me when I took the time to study nutrition and the kinds of foods we need to be really healthy. That will be the subject of the next chapter.

# 16

## *The Four Food Components*

### Scripture and Devotion

The food we eat consists of four basic components, and it is how these four components are combined that makes for the most efficient digestion and utilization of the various nutrients. Before we go on, however, let's look at Matthew 4:4:

> "It is written 'man shall not live by [emphasis on] bread alone,
> but by every word that proceeds from the mouth of God.'"

One weekend I attended a conference at which my husband, Keith, spoke. He was talking about how we might begin to recognize things in our lives that are more important to us than trying to live the way God wants us to. He asked, "What thoughts fill your mind when it's free, when it doesn't have to be busy thinking about something you're doing?"

At first, I couldn't think of anything, but then it hit me. I spent most of my free mental time thinking about food! This was true during all my previous attempts to lose weight, and even when I wasn't particularly trying to lose. I thought about what I could eat, what I wasn't going to eat, what I wished I could eat, what I didn't like to eat, what I had just eaten, what I was going to eat next.

After I focused on this startling discovery, my next thought was "What does that mean?"

Keith suggested to us that these things may be perfectly good things in themselves—like vocation, health, food, our mates, or our children. But they might also be what we worship instead of God, because after all, worship can be defined as freely giving our primary attention to something when we could choose to concentrate on anything. He also said that this can be compared to worshiping "idols."

I didn't like what I had discovered, but I felt he was right. For much of my life, I have thought a lot more about food than I have thought about God.

If we want to begin to change and to move closer to God, the next step, according to Keith, is to be honest with God by telling him, "God, I don't want you most in my life after all. What I want most is this thing I think about all the time. I'd *like* to want you most, but I can't seem to do it right now. So I ask you to come into my life and help me put that thing aside, and to want you most of all."

Boy, for some reason saying that prayer was hard for me! I didn't *want* to stop thinking about food. It was fun. It was a habit, and it didn't seem like such a bad thing to think about. And I thought I *needed* to think about it . . . to keep tabs on it so I could lose weight.

But then I realized something else. Even though I believed I *had* to think about food all the time so I could keep my weight down, I still didn't seem able to keep it down. Hmmmm. Maybe I *did* need to change my attitude.

So in the next few days I decided to give it a sincere try. I prayed, "Lord, I've just seen how much I worship food, and not you. I'm afraid to ask you this, but, just the same, would you come into my life and help me stop thinking about it all the time and to learn to think more about you?" After I prayed, I wondered what would happen next.

At first, the only difference I felt was that I was now *very aware* of how much I thought about food. I'd be sitting in the car at a traffic light and catch myself—"Oops, there I am again, imagining eating a big cheesy pizza!" just because I saw the pizza place across the street. I couldn't *believe* how many times I caught myself doing things like that!

But as the weeks went by I began to relax about food. I found I could go through a whole morning and be surprised that it was lunchtime and I hadn't even given a thought about what to eat.

There have been times during my study of nutrition when I have spent a lot of time planning menus, thinking about making healthy changes in the way I cook, and reading labels in the grocery store. But this doesn't feel like the old daydreams of forbidden foods that I used to have all the time.

I thought about the verse in Matthew: "Man shall not live by [emphasis on] bread alone . . ." And I realized that, for me, the best way to begin to take the emphasis of my thoughts off of food is to concentrate on something I need more—a relationship with Jesus Christ and a knowledge of his will for my life.

DEAR LORD, you know how much I like to think about food. Even though food is meant to be fuel for my body, I have

managed to turn it into a full-time entertainment enterprise for my own benefit. Help me to stop misusing food in
this way and to turn to you. Thank you that there are times
when I realize I haven't had these recurring thoughts. Let
me begin to learn how to love other people, to study your
Word, and to take care of my health in a way that is wholesome and good. In Jesus' name, AMEN.

## Which Foods Are the Good Foods?

During the whole eighteen years I've spent looking for a way to
lower my weight and to keep it down, I have wondered, "How much
and what kind of food would keep me healthy but not cause me to get
fat? Which food would give me energy and vitamins and will also
satisfy my hunger, so that I won't overeat and gain weight?"

In the last several years, writers have published in plain English
exactly what our bodies need. By making a few calculations, it's now
possible, without being a scientist or nutritionist, to figure out just
how much I should eat, and from which food groups, to maintain a
healthy weight.

One of my favorite writers on this subject is Jane Brody, personal
health columnist for *The New York Times.* In her book, *Jane Brody's
Nutrition Book,* she explains that there are four basic components
that make up the food we eat. And there are two other substances
which aren't exactly food, but are nevertheless important. These two
are water and fiber.

The names of these four food components are: simple carbohydrates, complex carbohydrates, fats, and protein. The nutrients
found in each of these are what our bodies need to grow properly,
fight off diseases, have energy, be emotionally stable, and repair
damages.

Let's take a brief look at the four components and at water and
fiber, to see what each contributes to our health and fitness. Chapters 19 through 25 give more detail about how these components are
"packaged" in real foods like meats, vegetables, fruits, and dairy
products, and how we can combine foods to get a healthy ratio of each
component.

## Simple Carbohydrates (Sugars)

Simple carbohydrates are basically sugars, and sugar is a source
of energy. Unfortunately, some sugars give us a huge overload of

energy that rushes like a tornado through our systems. It picks us up and we feel good and peppy. But when it's blown its way through us and is metabolized, it drops us in a crumpled heap and we come crashing down, feeling tired, depressed, and irritable. Examples of this kind of sugar are the ones called "refined" sugars—white sugar, brown sugar, honey, and corn syrup, to name a few.

Our bodies do need some sugar, however, since it is a source of energy. In fact, both the simple and the complex carbohydrates are eventually broken down into glucose and absorbed into the bloodstream. But the kind of sugars we need are the ones that enter the bloodstream gently and naturally, like a gently flowing creek, and that carry us along on a steady stream of energy for hours. These kinds of sugars are found in natural foods, not refined ones; they come from fruits, both fresh and dried, as well as from other foods like corn, wheat, and milk. You may be thinking that these foods aren't made of sugar. But there are ingredients in these foods from which our bodies *manufacture* the healthy kind of sugar we need.

## Complex Carbohydrates

Complex carbohydrates are also known as starches. Examples of the foods in which starches are found are vegetables, beans, and grain. In fact, beans and grain are very rich sources of nutrients because they are actually seeds for the next crop of plants. Since they are the sole source of nutrition for the little seedling, they are loaded with vitamins and energy.

## Fiber

Next, I'm going to discuss fiber, because it is from the complex carbohydrates that fiber comes. Fiber is the one form of plant carbohydrate that passes through our systems practically undigested. It provides two things: bulk, which helps satisfy our hunger, and roughage, which helps push waste materials through the intestines. Unfortunately, the majority of fruits and vegetables that we eat today are not in their natural form—raw. They are canned or frozen, and much of their fiber has been removed. There is much more fiber in fresh vegetables and fruits, especially if we eat them raw.

Whole grains provide a very high level of fiber, provided they are still in their natural form. Whole-wheat breads, other whole-grain breads, and breakfast cereals made from grains with little sugar or sodium added are very important sources of fiber. And miller's bran can be sprinkled on foods to add additional fiber. In fact, I like to put two tablespoons of bran on my breakfast cereal every morning. It blends right in and I hardly notice it.

Refined flours, like the white flour used in bread, have had almost all the fiber removed.

## Protein

Protein is in almost every food we eat! It is used for growing and for the repair of damaged tissue, and is important because if tissue damage could not be repaired, we'd probably fall apart very soon!

Protein comes from foods such as meat, milk, eggs, and cheese. It's also possible to get plenty of protein without the fat and calories of meats by combining plant foods like beans with grains or dairy products in the same meal. Examples are eating beans and rice, or beans and corn or wheat (as in Mexican tortillas!), or lentils and rice in a casserole seasoned with herbs, green pepper, and onion.

Since protein is so important to our health, we often believe we need much more of it than we actually do. But since adults are no longer growing, we need less protein than we did when we were teenagers.

## Fats

There are some dietary fats (by that I mean fats that you eat, not body fat) that are difficult for our bodies to digest and that tend to clog up our system—both the digestive system and the blood vessels. These are called "saturated fats," and you can recognize most of them pretty easily because they are solid at room temperature. Examples of foods which contain saturated fats are butter, lard, and the fat edges around meat.

But there are other fats which our bodies really like. They don't clog up anything, but rather seem to help break down deposits of cholesterol in the blood vessels and wash the cholesterol away. In addition, these fats are transportation for fat-soluble vitamins, which don't mix with water. These "good" fats are called "polyunsaturated fats," and are liquid at room temperature. Examples of foods which contain polyunsaturated fats are corn oil, sunflower oil, and safflower oil. (There are a few unhealthy fats that are also liquid at room temperature. Two of them are coconut oil and palm oil.)

Unfortunately, most of us eat too much of even the polyunsaturated fats. We can get all the fat we need for our bodies from one tablespoon of corn or safflower oil a day. Yet studies reported in *Jane Brody's Nutrition Book* indicate that Americans eat six to eight tablespoons of fat a day![1]

## Water

Water is a very important substance to our entire body. All the systems, including the digestive system and the circulatory system, need water to work right. And over 60% of our body *is* water. We'll talk about all the things water does for us in chapter 24. But for now I want to point out that it's recommended that we drink eight glasses of water a day.

Now that you have a little information about each of the four food components, plus fiber and water, we'll talk about how the components can be combined in a good, nutritious approach to eating (and losing weight). In the next chapter, we'll deal with the proper balance of these four components.

---

1. Brody, *Jane Brody's Nutrition Book*, 55.

# 17

## *How Much of Each Component Is Best?*

### Scripture and Devotion

As I mentioned earlier, it's important not only to eat the right number of calories, but to be aware of the proper combination of the four basic food components. Before we go into that, though, let's talk about Isaiah 40:31:

> "But they who wait for the Lord shall renew their strength,
> they shall mount up with wings like eagles, they shall run and not
> be weary, they shall walk and not faint."

There are days when it is all I can do to "walk and not faint." But when I try to understand the phrase, "they who wait for the Lord shall renew their strength," I think about how God intended for men and women to live. And that includes eating right and exercising, which are designed to renew our physical strength.

The basic trouble seems to be in my *desires.* When I really want something, I can argue my way right past all the reasons it's bad for me and just help myself. The result is that I never seem to reach my weight goal because I am basically unable to curb my desires.

So my prayers have two basic requests. One is for the Lord to change my desires so that it's not so important to me to have unhealthy foods. The other is for him to help me learn that I don't have to gratify every desire that passes through my mind. I can learn to live without every whim being satisfied.

"They who wait for the Lord shall renew their strength," I read. To "wait for" might mean to give up my own ideas about timing and to try to understand how and when things should happen from God's perspective. As I try to understand God's timing and how it is different from my own, I find that my desire for doing what God wants me to do is growing, and that my other desires are getting smaller. And I have hope that these desires can keep on shrinking until they do not control my life the way that they have before.

> DEAR LORD, help me learn to wait for you and understand your way of doing things. Renew my strength when I run out, and help me to walk and not faint. Turn my desires away from impatient thoughts, Lord, and keep me in your way. In Jesus' name, AMEN.

## How I Got Interested in Weight Loss

Four years ago, when I started studying about nutrition and exercise, I revisited my high school and asked for the medical chart from my student folder. This is a chart which was passed from teacher to teacher, and on which was written my height and weight each year.

When I looked at my chart, I saw that between the beginning of my fifth grade year, in September, and the end of that year, in May, I grew from 5'2" to 5'7" and my weight jumped up to 127 pounds. I was 11 years old that year, and I remember it quite well because the teacher read everybody's weight out loud to the class at the end of the year. One other girl, Peggy, and I were the only people (boy or girl) who were tall and who weighed over 100 pounds, and we both weighed more than 120! Needless to say, everyone in the class laughed out loud when our weights were read—except us. Peggy and I looked at each other, across all those short little people's heads, and cemented our friendship.

But weighing 127 at the height of 5'7" is not considered being overweight. The trouble was, I didn't stop gaining there. By the end of my sophomore year in college I weighed 160 pounds.

Something inside me snapped at that point, and I woke up as if from a bad dream. I got my weight back down to 140 and my dress size down to a 12 and I finished college at that weight and dress size.

Ever since that time, however, I have been haunted by a desire to weigh whatever the charts said was appropriate for my height. But whenever I dieted, I couldn't seem to lose, and I usually wound up sick with a cold or the flu. If I didn't get sick, I just felt tired and irritable and had almost no energy. I felt chubby, flabby, and miserable whenever I looked at myself in a mirror or shopped for new clothes.

## *A Physical Exam Is Worth a Lot*

Then in January of 1980, as I have mentioned, I took a complete physical examination at the Houstonian Preventive Medicine Center. Dr. Reg Cherry, the director of the Center then, said, "There's no reason you can't lose another ten pounds. In fact, after measuring you and considering your percentage of fat, I recommend that you get down to 129 pounds." I was amazed when later I saw that 129 was two pounds heavier than the weight on my chart from the sixth grade!

But I was fairly cynical by that time. Those ten pounds had been with me for 20 years. I thought I had tried dieting and couldn't lose because of some special medical problem. And I just *knew* Dr. Cherry wasn't paying enough attention to my "special problem."

I don't quite know how to tell you this delicately, but another problem I had, which I also mentioned earlier, was constant constipation, which had been a problem since high school days. I took a lot of laxatives, and they usually wouldn't work in "normal" doses. This same doctor simply said, "We can change that with diet, too." Since I'd had that problem for 15 years, I was really mad!

So, with a feeling of anger and frustration, I decided to try the nutritional advice he gave me *to the letter.* I thought I'd prove to him that I was a special case, and that *then* maybe he'd help me find out what my problem was. But to my relief and embarrassment, the constipation problem was gone in three days. And it hasn't come back, unless I forget to include enough fiber in my food or drink enough water.

I got really interested at this point and began a self-education experiment, the result of which, four years later, is this book. I found I can reduce the percentage of body fat I have and lose weight by following sensible exercise and eating habits. I guess that's nothing really new, only I've never known exactly what "sensible" eating habits and exercises were.

The two most important things I've learned are:

(1) Weight loss (for long-term weight control) doesn't happen quickly. It *shouldn't* happen quickly if it is to be a healthy, permanent weight loss. (This principle also applies to gaining weight, if that is what you need to do.)

(2) It is possible to lose weight that has been around for 15 or 20 years without crazy diets, food substitutes, or medication. But it takes time to get reeducated and to fit the new information into one's life.

While it may seem frustrating to you that it has taken us 14 chapters to get to this point, all of the things we've been talking about so far apply to the overall picture. You may be saying, "I'm in a hurry to start losing weight now!" And I'm glad you're feeling that much enthusiasm. But it's important, I think, to realize that successfully losing weight and *keeping it off* takes a gradual understanding of several different aspects of how our bodies and spirits work.

For a long time, I felt as if "anything goes" in the area of weight loss, because a "diet" is only a temporary way of eating until the weight is gone. But what has worked for me—what I believe to be the way I will live from now on—is a change of mental attitude which has come about gradually but which is the attitude I want to have for the rest of my life.

Health, as I now see it, comes from a combination of exercise and eating the right proportion of each food group, and from being at peace emotionally and psychologically. For me, this peace is possible only through a relationship with Jesus Christ.

So plunging into any old diet is not what we're after in this book. I want to share with you some of the insights I've gained as I've learned to let God into this area of my life. And I want to give you information about food, calories, and how our bodies use these foods, because by spending some time studying these facts, as well as by making regular exercise a part of my life, I've been able to more nearly regulate my health and fitness than ever before. I hope the same will be true for you.

## Balanced Eating Plans

From my studies, I've learned that unless the food we eat each day includes all four of the components we discussed in the previous chapter, it fails to give the basic nutrients our bodies need and therefore is bad for our health. (This is just as true for people with no "weight problem" as it is for those who need to lose or gain weight.) And the *ratio* of each component to the other is also important. It's as if we're trying to mix a certain color of paint from four different paint cans. Too much of one and not enough of another gives us the wrong color.

Below is a chart which shows the four food components. The figures on the left-hand side of the chart show the way we Americans on the average divide up our calories. The numbers in the right-hand column show the proper mix of components that is needed to paint the maximum picture of health possible. (This chart is from *Jane Brody's Nutrition Book* and uses slightly different terms than we've been using. In the chart, "Vegetables, Fruits, & Grains" refers to complex carbohydrates and "Sugars" refers to simple carbohy-drates.)[1]

| Present Division | FOOD GROUP | Recommended Division |
|---|---|---|
| 42% | Fats | 30% |
| 12% | Protein | 12% |
| 28% | Vegetables, Fruits, & Grains [complex carbohydrates] | 48% |
| 18% | Sugars [simple carbohydrates] | 10% |

To change what we eat so that we are eating a healthier diet would mean (1) *decrease* fats to 30% (an actual reduction of 29%); (2) *decrease* sugars to 10% (an actual reduction of 44%); and (3) *increase* complex carbohydrates to 48% (an actual increase of 71%). It is this 71% increase in the complex carbohydrate group that seems to me to be most important.

There is an important difference between simple carbohydrates—or refined sugar—and naturally occurring sugars. The component "simple carbohydrate" is made up of sugars such as white table sugar, brown sugar, honey, molasses, and corn syrup. The 10% figure recommended on the chart above represents the level to which we should try to *reduce* our intake of these sugars, and does *not* mean that we must have that many calories of sugar in order to be healthy.

The component "complex carbohydrate" includes many foods which also have naturally occurring sugars. Since the body can manufacture glucose from both naturally occurring sugars and starches, we would be perfectly healthy without any sugar from the component "simple carbohydrate" at all. Unfortunately, it is almost impossible to avoid simple carbohydrates. They are in baked goods that we make at home or buy at the grocery store. They are in breakfast cereals and other foods. So even though we may not eat refined sugar directly, we probably eat close to 10% of our daily calories from this food component.

Adjusting the ratio of foods we eat in the way we've been discussing does not reduce the amount of energy we have. It was once feared that cutting down on fats and sugar would also cut down on a person's energy level. But, as I mentioned, our bodies manufacture glucose (which is our energy source) from complex carbohydrates.

---

1. Brody, *Jane Brody's Nutrition Book*, 10. Her source: Dietary Goals for the U.S., 1977, prepared by the Senate Select Committee on Nutrition and Human Needs.

And researchers have discovered, to their astonishment, that complex carbohydrates provide the ingredients from which the body derives most of the energy we use during exercise.[2]

So what would all these percentages mean in terms of the number of calories needed from each food component? Let's divide 1,950 calories up according to the recommended percentages. (I'm using 1,950 calories because that's what I can usually eat to maintain my weight at a healthy level.)

| Food Group | Calories |
|---|---|
| Fats: 30% of 1,950 = | 585 |
| Protein: 12% of 1,950 = | 234 |
| Complex carbohydrates: 48% of 1,950 = | 936 |
| Simple carbohydrates: 10% of 1,950 = | 195 |
| TOTAL: | 1,950 |

If any one of these components is neglected, exaggerated, or left out completely (with the exception of simple carbohydrates—it's okay to leave these out if you can), our bodies can't get along as well as they are designed to. And so it seems to me that the healthiest approach to eating is one that ensures that our daily calorie intake contains the four basic food components in the right proportions.

I believe the easiest way to do this is to use an eating plan which already has the proportions of the four basic food components worked out. Such eating plans divide all our food into groups so that each group contains foods with similar calorie content as well as similar protein-carbohydrate-fat ratios. We already refer to most foods as being part of familiar categories or groups: fruits, vegetables, dairy products, and so on. But there are a few foods that, when classified according to the nutrients they contain, end up in a different food group than one might expect. For example, nuts have a high ratio of fat and are thus listed in the food group, "Fats."

In the next chapter we'll talk about how to plan your own balanced food-group eating plan, based on the number of calories you need for your particular weight and exercise level. These principles can be used to draw up eating plans for weight loss, weight gain, or weight maintenance. You can choose from your favorite healthy foods and put together your own menus.

If you prefer a diet that tells you exactly what foods to eat at each

---

2. Jim Fixx, *The Complete Book of Running* (New York: Random House, 1977), 258.

meal and how much of them, there are many good, balanced food-group diets available. I can recommend a few that I've tried and like. *The Southampton Diet*, a book by Dr. Stuart Berger, a psychiatrist who also lost 210 pounds and learned to keep them off, is well balanced. The Weight Watchers program is also very good. *Redbook* magazine regularly publishes new recipes in its "Wise Woman's Diet," which is a balanced food-group diet. And there are a number of other good ones with the menus spelled out.

It may seem like a lot of trouble to learn how to manage food components and food groups. And at first I didn't want to do it. But then I remembered that when I first learned to cook I spent a lot of time studying and experimenting. Eventually I developed cooking habits and favorite recipes that were quick, automatic, and easy. And as I've begun to exchange some of these unhealthy favorites for more healthy kinds of foods, I've found that this kind of cooking is also beginning to be automatic, quick, and easy. And I'm finding some new favorites.

The next chapter is about how to construct your own balanced food-group eating plan. This approach to food not only has helped me lose weight when I have needed to, but it represents the way I want to eat from now on, to give my body the best chance possible of functioning in a healthy, energetic way.

# Week Six
## (Three Days)

## *Aims and Activities*

(1) To continue with muscle-tone and aerobic workouts. (Can you see any improvement at this point?)

(2) If you have weight to lose or gain, to set a weight goal based on last week's calculations of ideal weight.

(3) To begin weighing yourself regularly and keeping a record of your weight. (Note: How often you do this is up to you. I like to weigh every day because I find that seeing the daily ups and downs helps me understand my body's fluctuations and keeps me from overreacting to minor gains or losses. Other people, especially people with more than ten pounds to gain or lose, find that weighing only once a week gives them a better picture of their overall progress. But either way, weighing yourself regularly will help "keep you honest" as well as help you keep in touch with how your body works.)

(4) Using the food lists and eating plans provided in this book, to draw up your own weight gain, loss, or maintenance plan—eating and exercise—and to determine approximately how much time it will take you to reach your goal. To set up a chart like the one on p. 293 to begin to keep track of your eating.

(5) To learn to be more aware of your body's signals and needs when it comes to food.

(6) To draw up some strategies for coping with difficult social situations while putting your new healthy eating plan into practice.

# 18

## *A Sensible and Effective Approach to Losing Weight*

### Scripture and Devotion

This chapter shows you how to calculate your own weight-loss, weight-gain, or weight-maintenance plan, keeping in mind all the things we've talked about up to now. (We've covered a lot of ground.) But first, let's spend a few minutes with a scripture and a prayer. The scripture is Hebrews 11:1:

> "Now faith is the assurance of things hoped for, the conviction of things not seen."

This passage is comforting to me when things are not going well. It can apply to so many areas of life that I see new hope almost every time I read it.

Sometimes when I begin to apply what I know about health and nutrition to my life, it seems as if nothing is changing. I don't lose any weight for a week. I feel sluggish when I run. I don't have the energy I had expected to have, and things just aren't working out like "the books" say they will.

At times like these I am "hoping for" results but not "seeing" any. Faith, I try to remember, is the assurance of things hoped for, and so I struggle to remember that over the long haul my health and fitness *will* get better. I try to keep on eating the right foods and doing the exercises even when I feel stuck.

Once during my first year of trying to get in shape I had to go on a five-day business trip. I had just reached my weight goal for the first time and I was fighting hard to keep my weight at that point. As I left town, I knew it was going to be difficult. I wanted to try to keep my new eating habits going, but the problem was that I had to start estimating the sizes of servings instead of being able to measure them. And I had to start thinking carefully about what I ordered in restaurants.

143

I remember that one evening at a restaurant I ordered baked fish. The dinner also included rice and some broccoli, and I remembered to ask the waiter not to put any kind of sauce on it. (I'd learned that restaurants love to garnish broccoli with hollandaise or cheese sauce and never mention the sauce on the menu!)

When the waiter put the steaming hot, fragrant plate of food in front of me, I couldn't wait to dig into that scruptuous dinner. But I made myself look at the sizes of the servings, and I could tell it was almost two dinners' worth of food.

So I cut the fish in two and scooted half to one side of the plate, along with half the rice. Then I tried to pretend it wasn't even there. I slowly ate the rest of the fish, half of the rice and—just to be safe—only part of the broccoli (about 2 stalks). I ate no bread, because I'd had plenty for the day, had iced water to drink, and drank decaffeinated coffee while the other people at the table had dessert. I tried to keep my mind on the people and the conversation instead of on "how sad it is that I can't eat dessert" (poor me).

All through the five days, I kept on doing things like this, but I had the sinking feeling that it wasn't really doing any good. I had always gained weight on trips! When we got back home, I dreaded weighing. But the next morning I gingerly stepped on the scales, and to my amazement I saw that my weight was still down at my weight goal. My new approach to eating had already worked in spite of not being able to carefully measure and weigh all my food! That was one time when hoping for good results and doing what I knew to do paid off, even though I couldn't see it happening.

> DEAR LORD, thank you that sometimes I can have enough faith to do what I know to do when it's difficult. Forgive me for the times when I lack the faith to stick to what I know is right. Help me to use the memories of those successful times to inspire me to trust the process and—more than that—to trust you. In Jesus' name, AMEN.

## An Approach to Weight Loss

After all my reading and experimenting, I have a lot of respect for approaching weight loss with a combination of diet and exercise. I haven't quoted many of the experiments I read about, but this one really impressed me. It was reported by Jim Fixx in his book, *The Complete Book of Running.*

Three groups of overweight women all attempted to lose weight by reducing their calories by 500 calories a day. The first group took their calories out of their diet, eating 500 calories a day less. The second group got rid of the calories by exercising enough to burn approximately 500 calories a day. The third group reduced their calories through a combination of diet and exercise.

The experiment went on for four months. At the end of that time the first group's average weight loss was 10.6 pounds, the second's was 11.7 pounds, and the third was 12 pounds. Now, you might say that there wasn't much difference in the three groups—and that's true. But the significant factor that the doctors found was that group three lost more *fat* and gained more *lean muscle tissue* than either of the other two groups. In other words, they wound up with a better percentage of body fat! The doctors concluded by saying, "We recommend that those interested in losing weight combine a lowered caloric intake with a physical fitness program."[1]

## How Much Should We Eat on a Weight-Loss Diet?

The goal of a good weight-loss program is to arrive at the new weight in a healthy, stable condition. Most of the sources I've read say that eating less than 1,000 calories a day does not promote this goal and is bad for one's health. Crash diets of 330 or 500 or 750 calories a day can be counterproductive and even harmful.

According to Dr. Ted Edwards, Jr., people need at least 1,000 calories a day to function normally. In fact, many people need even more than that. When we eat less than those 1,000 calories a day (or whatever our body's minimum need is), our metabolisms go into a shutdown/survival mode and slow way down in order to protect the body from death by starvation. Our bodies can't tell the difference between a famine and a reducing diet, so they quit burning up calories as fast as they were.

That's good if you're trying to survive in a concentration camp or lost in the desert. But it's not so good if all you're trying to do is lose weight. For one thing, a diet with fewer than 1,000 calories doesn't provide enough food to give you the vitamins and minerals you need. This situation can trigger a variety of possible problems, including low energy, depression, and susceptibility to colds and flu.

For another thing, because the body's metabolism slows down, weight loss also slows down after a few days on this kind of diet. While

---

1. Fixx, *The Complete Book of Running*, 76.

the body is in this mode, most of the food we *do* eat is stored as fat like the prehistoric cave men I mentioned earlier! This can happen within just a few days of not eating enough food. After a week, our systems become locked into this state.

Therefore, although we may lose a few pounds at first, what is lost is mostly water. Then, after the first two or three days, when the water is flushed out and it's time to burn fat, the rate of losing weight slows down to nothing. Meanwhile, our bodies frantically store up fat to use for energy in case the food supply should run out altogether. Furthermore, once we go back to eating over 1,000 calories, our bodies take up to six weeks to work back out of the fat-storing habit. So it's more than likely that we'll gain weight back even faster than we lost it—and many people do.[2]

If you are in the habit of fasting for spiritual reasons, it's a good idea to be aware of what is happening to your body's metabolism. Since it has slowed down, when you come off the fast, take care to keep your calories low and your exercise moderate to prevent gaining weight. When properly done, fasting can be a good spiritual discipline. However, in view of the effect that going without food has on one's metabolism, causing it to slow down and store fat more easily, fasting should probably *not* be done for the purpose of losing weight. Although a few pounds may be lost during the fast, they are likely to be quickly regained during the period of time the body is in its "low metabolism" period after the fast.

## How to Draw Up a Sensible Weight-Loss Plan

The solution to weight loss, it seems to me, is to learn how to lose weight on 1,000 calories or more. Dieting on fewer than 1,000 calories won't produce good, long-term *fat* loss, and it might hurt our health. But in order to lose any weight at all, it is necessary to reduce our daily caloric intake to a level below what we use up in energy. Since each person's metabolism is different, how do we figure how many calories we can eat and still lose the weight we want to lose? Jim Fixx's book shows one way to do this, and also shows how to get an estimate of how long it's likely to take.

Get a pencil and a blank piece of paper, and get ready to do a little arithmetic. There's a form at the end of the chapter and in the back of this book (pp. 151, 363) for you to use later on, but for now just use scratch paper while we go through the procedure. If you don't think

---

2. Ted Edwards, Jr., *Weight Loss to Super Wellness*, 17–18.

you're very good at mathematics, take this next section slowly. It may seem complicated at first, but if you take it one step at a time I think you'll find some worthwhile information at the end.

Using my own weight and goals, we can determine how fast I can safely and permanently lose ten pounds by combining a limited calorie intake with various amounts of exercise (in my case, running). Let's say I want to lose from 140 to 130. First, I would write at the top of the page the weight goal I have, which is 130 pounds, and label it "My Weight Goal."

Now, here is the weight-loss formula: Remember that we need 15 calories per pound of body weight to maintain our weight. So now figure the number of calories I need to eat for my *new* weight of 130 pounds. Multiply 130 by 15, and you get 1,950. Write that figure after the words, "No. cal. needed for new weight."

As I said earlier, aerobic exercise burns calories. The heavier you are, the more calories are burned. Look at the chart below. It shows approximately how many calories a runner burns in a mile at various weights:[3]

| Weight | Calories Burned | Weight | Calories Burned |
|--------|-----------------|--------|-----------------|
| 120 | 82 | 180 | 124 |
| 130 | 90 | 190 | 130 |
| 140 | 98 | 200 | 136 |
| 150 | 102 | 210 | 144 |
| 160 | 110 | 220 | 150 |
| 170 | 115 | | |

(I use running in this chart because that's what I do for aerobic exercise. But the reading I've done indicates that a person burns about the same number of calories when *walking* a mile, if the walking is done aerobically—with the pulse in the working heart rate range. However, if we were talking about *time* spent in aerobic activity, not *distance*, running does burn more calories. This is the way I understand it: A beginning 140-pound "walker" might be able to cover a mile in the 17½ minute minimum recommended for aerobic activity, and would burn about 98 calories. A beginning 140-pound "runner" might cover the same mile in 13 minutes and would also burn 98 calories. But if the "runner" continued running at the same rate for the rest of the 17½ minutes, he or she would cover approximately 1⅓ miles and burn about 130 calories. That is why many

---

3. From THE COMPLETE BOOK OF RUNNING, by James F. Fixx. Copyright © 1977 by James F. Fixx. Reprinted by permission of Random House, Inc.

people prefer running to walking; you can burn the calories *faster.* But if I run two miles in 26 minutes and you walk two miles in 35 minutes, we will have both burned the same number of calories—provided our weights are the same and our hearts are pumping in our working heart rate range.)

Next, multiply the number of calories I would burn if I ran two miles a day, weighing 140 pounds (assuming I'm in good enough shape to run that far). That would be 98 times two, or 196. Put that number underneath the 1,950 calories and add them together. The total is 2,146:

No. cal. for *new* weight: 130 x 15 =                1,950
Running bonus (2 miles x 98 cal.):                     196

                    TOTAL:                           2,146

Now, let's say I'm willing to diet on 1,200 calories a day. So put that number down in a new place on your paper. Call this "Number of Calories for Diet." Then add a little bonus because I'm willing to run. I think I'll add about 50 calories. (It has to be less than what I am really burning to make this work. I could add the full 196, but I don't want to because I want to lose weight a little faster.) So write the 50 underneath the number of calories for my diet, and add them together. That makes 1,250 calories in all:

No. cal. I choose for diet:                          1,200
Running bonus (less than above):                        50

                    TOTAL:                           1,250

Now figure up the difference in these two, or the deficit of calories I will have. When I subtract 1,250 from 2,146, I get 896 calories worth of deficit.

We know that 3,500 calories equals a pound of weight.[4] So divide the deficit above into 3,500 calories to see how many days it will take to lose one pound:

$$3,500 \div 896 = 3.9 \text{ or } 4 \text{ days}$$

To find out how fast I can expect to lose the weight I want to take off, I multiply the number of pounds I want to lose, which is ten, by the

---

4. Some sources say it takes a deficit of 4,500 calories to lose a pound, but we'll use 3,500 for the purposes of this study.

number of days it will take, which I rounded off to 4. That means I can expect to lose ten pounds in 40 days.

To lose 10 pounds will take 10 x 4 or 40 days.

With this information, my weight-loss plan would then be to:
(1)  Eat 1,250 calories per day;
(2)  Run 2 miles a day;
(3)  Stick to this for 40 days (five weeks and five days).

Any cheating on my part by either going over the calorie limit or skipping my run will mean that I won't lose all the weight in 40 days. (40 days? Hmmm. Maybe I could start this plan for Lent!)

Okay, now it's your turn. Take a few minutes to calculate your own eating and exercise plan. There is a form for this purpose at the end of this chapter. Choose the number of calories you are willing to eat, but make sure it does not go below 1,000. By doing this, you can get a realistic picture of how long it will take and what you will have to do to lose weight in a healthy way. Try calculating with several calorie levels, such as 1,200, 1,500, and 1,800 to see the difference.

## Is There Anything That Can Be Done to Speed Up the Process?

If I want to speed up my weight loss, there are three things I can do. One is to remove 250 calories a day from my diet, bringing it to the rock-bottom 1,000 calorie day minimum we discussed earlier. This will increase the calorie deficit to 1,146 calories and reduce the length of time to 3.1 days per pound, or 31 days for the weight loss to take place.

Another way to speed up the process would be to run three miles a day instead of two. I'd have to work up to that gradually, following the rule of thumb I mentioned earlier: increasing 10% a week over a period of three weeks. So this option isn't one I could put into practice for five weeks, and I'd nearly have all the weight lost by then, anyway. But if I were already in shape to run three miles, running that far each day would help me lose faster because, even without reducing any calories, the new deficit would be 994 and the new time period would be 3.5 days per pound or 35 days.

If I combine both methods—reducing the calories and running an extra mile—the deficit in calories becomes 1,244, the days required to lose a pound becomes 2.8, and the total length of time needed to lose ten pounds becomes 28 days.

With these facts before me I can decide how much to eat, how hard to exercise, and also how long my weight loss is likely to take.

## Knowing What to Expect Helps a Lot!

Before I found this formula, I used to get very impatient after about three weeks and think something had gone wrong if all ten pounds weren't gone. But when I know that the *fastest* healthy way I can approach this situation will take four weeks to bring off the ten pounds, and that a more comfortable way will make it five weeks and five days, my expectations are more realistic and I can usually be more patient and less frustrated.

To conclude our study of eating plans, the next chapter will give you a way to choose foods from the various food groups so that your menus are both balanced and within the calorie range you have chosen for yourself today. The plan is based on serving sizes, rather than counting calories, because I have found a "serving size" plan easier to put into practice.

## MY EATING AND EXERCISE PLAN[5]

MY WEIGHT GOAL: _____

No. cal. needed for *new* weight: _____ × 15 = _____
                                    *(new wt.)*

Exercise bonus (_____ miles x _____ cal.):     _____
                    *(use chart on p. 147)*

           (1) TOTAL:     _____

No. cal. I choose for diet: |     _____

Exercise bonus (less than above):     _____

           (2) TOTAL:     _____

Deficit in calories: (1) _____ − (2) _____ = _____

$$\frac{3{,}500}{(cal.\ per\ lb.)} \div \underset{(deficit)}{\rule{3cm}{0.4pt}} = \underline{\hspace{3cm}} \text{ days per pound}$$

To lose _____ pounds will take:
          *(desired no.)*

_____ × _____ or _____ days.
 [desired no.]     [days per lb.]

With this information, my weight loss plan would be to:
(1) Eat _____ calories per day;
(2) Run _____ miles per day or equivalent exercise;
(3) Stick to this for _____ days.

———————
5. From THE COMPLETE BOOK OF RUNNING, by James F. Fixx. Copyright © 1977 by James F. Fixx. Reprinted by permission of Random House, Inc.

# 19

## *Food-Serving Plans—
Weight Loss and Maintenance*

### Scripture and Devotion

The scripture for this chapter is from Paul as he writes in Romans 7:15, 24–25:

> "I do not understand my own actions. For I do not do what I want, but I do the very thing I hate. . . . Wretched man that I am! Who will deliver me from this body of death? Thanks be to God through Jesus Christ our Lord!"

When I read what Paul wrote in those verses, I liked him a lot! I can think of thousands of things I do which are the very things I hate. I will grab a handful of raisins or a spoonful of peanut butter when I pass by the kitchen. I get so mad at myself later, when I finally realize the effect these little "snitches" have on my health. (Even though they are more *healthy* "snitches" than I used to have, they still stand between me and my ideal weight.)

But what is most helpful to me about Paul's statement is that if *he* wrote it, then struggling with these feelings must be a normal part of being a Christian who is still a human being.

If I tried to analyze my progress during the last three years, the analysis would reveal the following kind of pattern: start, fail, start again, succeed, fail, give up, reconsider, start, succeed, get cocky, fail, get depressed, start again, succeed, keep on trying, fail, start again, etc.

When I read that Paul seems to have had the same kind of struggle, and realize that God seemed to love him and work through him just the same, I don't feel quite so inadequate about the start-fail-start-again way things have gone for me. In fact, instead of spending so much time being mad at myself and depressed about my failures, I try to pray, "Well, what do you know? Another failure. God, I did it again. Please forgive me and help me to get back on the track." When I remember to do this, I find I can get back to business sooner.

There's a song written by Bill and Gloria Gaither which came out in 1979. It's called "I Will Go On," and the words that have stuck in my mind all this time are these:

> I will go on.
> My past I leave behind me.
> I gladly take His mercy and His love.
> He is joy and He is peace.
> He is strength and sweet release
> I know He is and I am His.
> I will go on![1]

When I have failed, as apparently I will whether I like it or not, then I should try to recognize my failure quickly, tell God about it, and ask him to help me get back on the track. The time I spend feeling bad about it and telling myself how awful I am is really wasted time in the long run. It costs me enough to fail by cheating once. If I decide to keep on cheating "because I've already blown it," then I just make matters worse. But if I can catch the slip-up, confess it, accept God's grace, and go on again, things seem to go much better.

> DEAR LORD, deliver me from this body of death. Like Paul, I seem to do not what I want to do, but the very things I don't want to do. Help me to see that, if I'll just let you, you can help me get back to doing the good healthy things I want to do. I ask you to be with me now, to remove any sense of guilt from my past failures, and to help me along the way toward better health. In Jesus' name, AMEN.

## How to Spend the Calories: Choosing Menus

We discussed in chapter 15 the most healthful way to divide our daily calories among the four basic food components. Here's a brief review of the percentages—but this time I've added the calorie division for a weight loss plan of 1,250 calories.

---

1. "I Will Go On," by William J. and Gloria Gaither. © 1978 by William J. Gaither. Used by permission.

| 12% protein | 150 calories |
| 30% fats | 375 calories |
| 48% complex carbohydrates | 600 calories |
| 10% simple carbohydrates | 125 calories |
| 100% TOTAL | 1,250 calories |

By using one of the calorie counters that are readily available, I can plan my own menus. But this can be quite complex because some foods provide calories from more than one component. Meat, for instance, has protein calories *and* fat calories. And certain grain products have sugar in them, which counts in the 10% simple carbohydrate category.

I have found another helpful method, which is a guideline based on "food groups" already divided into servings very close to the percentages above. You'll find the plan on pages 289–290 in Part Three of this book under the heading "Food-Serving Plans for Weight Loss." There are food-serving plans which give you 1,000 calories, 1,200 calories, 1,500 calories, and 1,800 calories. The higher two would probably be used by men or very active teenagers. The lower two can be used by most women. I usually lose weight just fine on 1,200 calories.

In Part Three there is also a different set of food-serving plans for people who are not trying to lose weight, but who want to be sure they are getting the best balance of foods from all the food groups. It is found on page 290, is labeled "Maintenance Plans," and provides calorie levels of 1,600, 1,900, 2,200, and 2,600.

Plans like these spell out the number of food servings from different food categories which you can eat and still maintain the proper balance of the four basic components. The plans are based on the number of calories you have chosen on which to diet or to maintain your new weight goal once you reach it.

There are seven food categories or groups included in all the eating plans:

(1) Fish, poultry, meats, and meat substitutes;
(2) Fats (oils, salad dressings, nuts, etc.);
(3) Lowfat dairy products (milk, yogurt, cheese, etc.);
(4) Grains, breads, and cereals;
(5) Nonstarchy vegetables;
(6) Starchy vegetables and soups;
(7) Fruits.

In addition, the maintenance plans also allow a limited amount of "extras" such as desserts.

These seven food groups correspond in certain ways to the four basic food *components.* In fact, the four components are sometimes called "food groups," too. But in this book I'm using the term "components" to refer to the nutrients that make up all foods (proteins, fats, complex carbohydrates, simple carbohydrates) and the term "food groups" to refer to categories of foods in the forms they are actually eaten (fish and meats, oils and salad dressings, lowfat dairy products, and so on).

When I first started this plan, I chose to eat 1,200 calories and exercise in a swimming pool. So, if you look at the amount of food suggested under the heading, "1200 calories," you'll see that my food servings consisted of six ounces of fish, poultry, meat, or meat substitutes, three servings of fats, two of lowfat dairy products, four of grains, one of starchy vegetable, and three of fruits—and of course some nonstarchy vegetables eaten raw or lightly steamed. Keith decided to diet on 1,500 calories. That meant he was allowed more fats, grains, and fruits than I.

Now turn in Part Three to a chart called "Eating Plan Check Lists" (p. 293). If you're the only one dieting, just use the top part for one day and the bottom part for another. But if, like Keith and me, you diet with someone else, fill out each chart according to the calorie levels you each choose. I put my 1,200-calorie check list on the top, and Keith put his 1,500 on the bottom. That way, we could share the same sheet of paper each day. By filling in the number of servings from each group on the left, we could each keep track of what we ate. We just put a check mark to the right of the correct food groups after each meal.

For example, for breakfast I ate one-third cup of All-Bran with two tablespoons miller's bran in it, a bran muffin with a pat of margarine, half a banana sliced on the cereal, and a half-cup milk poured on it. I drank a 12-ounce glass of water and a cup of decaffeinated coffee. So, after breakfast, I checked off one serving of fats and oils (the pat of margarine), one-half serving of lowfat dairy (one cup milk is a serving, so my one-half cup is one-half serving), two servings grain (the cereal and the muffin), and one serving fruit (the half banana). You can make up your own breakfast using foods from any of the food groups. Just remember that, if you're following the 1,200 calorie plan, once you have put three check marks in the fruit category, you can't eat any more fruit that day.

This chart comes in handy in the afternoons when I want a snack and have to choose what to eat. By glancing at the check marks, I can see what foods are left. If I have saved a fruit, I eat fruit. If not, I have to choose from one of the other food groups or have something that has little or no caloric value—decaffeinated coffee, iced tea, herbal tea, or something from the nonstarchy vegetable group, like carrot sticks.

Keith worked out his food servings so that for a bedtime snack he could have a half-slice of wheat bread with a tablespoon of peanut butter and some banana slices on it, and a small glass of milk! (That's half a grain, one fruit, one fat, and one lowfat dairy.)

## Specific Information about Various Foods

In Part Three there are also some food lists. These answer many questions that come up when one starts to think about how to put an eating plan into practice—questions like: How big is a serving? Which foods fall in which categories? (For example, an avocado is listed in the fats category, not the vegetable one.) Are some foods in each group better for me than others? We'll also spend a chapter on each food group, talking about it in detail.

I want to stress again that this dietary guideline is not the only one that will produce safe weight loss. Many diets which offer a balance of all food groups are suitable, and I mentioned a few, such as the Weight Watchers plan, in a previous chapter. The American Dietetics Association has a food-exchange weight-loss plan similar to the one I've described in this chapter. You may know of others. Whichever balanced food-group plan you choose, I hope these formulas and guidelines will help you establish a goal and get a realistic look at how long it is likely to take you to achieve your goal.

## A "Quick Fix" Is Not a Permanent Solution

There are some aspects to this kind of approach which may be hard to accept but are extremely important if a healthy weight-loss process is to be achieved. Here's the hard news: If you have been overweight for five, ten, or twenty years, it seems only natural that it will take some time, perhaps even a year or more, to get back into shape. Developing the tolerance, patience, and discipline to begin to move our weight down instead of up seems to me to be the main goal. Diets which promise fast or instant results are, in my opinion, only playing on our human shortcomings of impatience and un-willingness to change our habits. They do not offer the kind of education and experience that will make it possible for us to live healthy lives. They offer only a "quick fix" that requires no thinking and that assumes human beings are too lazy or unintelligent to actually confront the roots of the problem.

There may be times when a person is so emotionally discouraged about a weight problem or about some crisis going on in her or his life that undertaking this kind of educational approach and beginning to change is extremely difficult. And perhaps a temporary "quick fix" is a good thing to get such a person out of the depths of despair and on the way toward health. But to rely on such a "fix" as a permanent solution when God has provided delicious, edible, healthy foods to nourish us seems sad to me. I hope these pages will help clarify some of the seeming complexity of basic nutrition.

## Wanting Something More

It has been said by philosophers that it is difficult to give up a bad habit until we want something else more. I can remember being so frustrated about my weight that I said, "I would do *anything* to get this weight off!" Well, now I know some of what that "anything" is, and the challenge is to begin to make the changes necessary to do it. When I get to the end of my rope and am sick of getting less and less healthy—then I try to turn to God with the prayer, "Teach me thy paths . . ." and begin to turn toward healthy living.

Developing the patience both to study about health and to wait for nature to give me results has been a large part of my life over the past three years. I've learned to trust God more and to face my own inadequacy to handle this myself. I've had to give up the idea that I'm a special case—unable to lose weight, exercise regularly, resist foods, or be disciplined because of whatever circumstances are in my life. I've picked up some ideas and risked trying some new things, and in the coming chapter I'd like to share some of these with you.

# 20

## *You Can't Rush Mother Nature—*
## *Father Time Knows Best!*

### *Scripture and Devotion*

In this chapter I'd like to discuss a little place in our brains which is supposed to control our appetite, and I'd also like to talk some more about why it's best to lose weight at a slow and easy rate, rather than rushing through a severe weight-loss program. But first, let's look at Philippians 4:8:

> "Finally, brethren, whatever is true, whatever is honorable, whatever is just, whatever is pure, whatever is lovely, whatever is gracious, if there is any excellence, if there is anything worthy of praise, think about these things."

I believe that if I'm going to get healthy I've got to improve not only my body, but also my mind and spirit. And I also believe that what I think about while I'm going through the physical motions of exercise can affect my overall health as much as whether I do the exercises correctly or incorrectly.

So while I'm exercising, I sometimes go through the parts of this passage and try to think of an example of each thing mentioned. For example, when I think, "whatever is true and honorable," a person I'm going to meet that day may come to mind. Will I be able to behave in an honorable way with her? If she shares a problem with me, will I find myself trying to straighten her out, to talk her into doing something my way, or will I be able to listen, try to understand it from her perspective, and be a friend who cares?

Am I being just? My mind takes quick review of my relationships. Is there a situation in which I'm not being fair? Do I need to forgive anyone? Have I done everything I promised to do?

Things that are pure and lovely are a joy—when I can find them! So often I get caught up in thinking thoughts about myself that I forget about anything else. But admiring a friend's beautiful hair and telling her so or noticing the way God put together a wildflower or a sunset and telling him so seem to have a good effect on me, too.

When I think about things that are gracious, I ask myself, "Can I look for God's grace in the good things which happen, the forgiveness and hope his love brings into my life, and the touches of concern and caring that come my way?" When I can do this, I *feel* gracious—I can see that my life is full of the signs of his grace.

And finally, "If there is any excellence, if there is anything worthy of praise, think on these things." A lot of the time when I start out running, my body seems to resist me. I feel out of breath, my legs are stiff, my calves ache. But as I go along, my system perks up and I feel better. Sometimes my mind tries to imagine what I could see if my skin were transparent—the intricate way my muscles are put together to hold the bones in place, the way the blood flows around my body taking oxygen to the muscles and going back to the lungs to get more, the way the kidneys and liver and intestines process waste materials. It's amazing to me! And I feel like praying "Thanks, God, for creating all this."

The more I can keep my mind on the things that are true and honorable, just, pure, lovely, excellent, and worthy of praise, the more I can live with the aches and pains, problems and failures, and not let them get me down quite so much.

> DEAR LORD, thank you that, in a world so full of problems and frightening things, there are still things worthy of praise. Your excellence alone amazes me, and I am grateful to you for all you've given me.
>
> I ask you to come into my mind and fill it with true and honorable thoughts, so that I can learn to love other people with your kind of love. In Jesus' name, AMEN.

## The Appetite Control Center

Now I want to talk a few minutes about the "hungries," about the appetite and what controls it. There's a little place in the brain which regulates appetite. Evidently it's very active in most animals, like cats and dogs and wild animals. Somehow they know to stop eating when they have eaten enough to satisfy their bodies' needs. This regulator exists in human beings, too, but in many of us it has become numbed and doesn't seem to work.

Have you noticed how some people can leave half of a delicious piece of pie on their plates, and sit there at the table carrying on a conversation without even seeming to notice it? Have you noticed how your pet dog or cat will sometimes leave part of its dinner in the dish? It is almost impossible for me to leave *anything* on *my* plate—especially something as delightful as a piece of pie!

The control center I'm talking about is an area of the brain called the hypothalamus. In it are various nerve centers which control several automatic body functions like hunger, thirst, sex drive, temperature, pleasure, and displeasure. One nerve center, nicknamed the "appestat," keeps watch over glucose in the bloodstream and signals when the body needs food. Then come the feelings we call "hunger"—slight stomach pains and growling and mild intestinal cramps.

## How It's Supposed to Work

When these signals happen, our thoughts turn toward food. We eat, and the glucose levels in the blood return to normal. At this point the appestat should signal the brain that we've eaten enough, and we should stop. But due to several overriding influences, many of us don't get the message from this part of the brain.

What's supposed to happen is this: When it's time to stop, the "appeal" of food should decrease. That means the aroma of food wouldn't be as enticing, the taste of it wouldn't be quite so delicious, and looking at it would not be interesting. But unfortunately I find that even after I have eaten a meal which I know in my head is enough, I still feel excited when I see a gorgeous dessert. Or I can look at the half-carved roast and be interested in eating another delicious slice.

I don't know exactly how my "appestat" got numbed. There are many theories about how this happens. For example, when we are children we are sometimes "rewarded" with food like ice-cream cones and cookies, or "punished" by having dessert withheld or being sent to our rooms without dinner. There is also social pressure to enjoy the company of other people over food—dates, celebrations of birthdays, anniversaries, business luncheons, dinners with friends, or church suppers.

But however it happens, I think it is important to recognize that a numbed appestat is like a handicap in the struggle to think of food as fuel for our bodies and not entertainment, reward, or punishment.

## The Time Delay in Receiving the Signal

I think God knew what he was doing when he put this signal in our brains. And the influence of the appestat on our approach to food is very important. I've read that it takes 15 to 20 minutes for the body to let the brain know that enough food has been eaten. So a person who is in the habit of eating fast might easily pass the point where he or she has had enough to maintain health and go far beyond that point before he or she feels any of the signals of being full. By paying attention to these body signals of fullness, and by eating slowly enough for the stomach to have time to signal the brain that enough has been eaten, we can, I believe, learn to resensitize the appestat.

When I first tried to become more aware of when I had eaten enough, I found that part of my problem was putting too much food on my plate to start with. When I saw how much was left when I noticed I was not "hungry" any more, I began to try to give myself smaller servings.

I found it interesting to realize how out-of-control I really have been for such a long time when it comes to knowing that I've eaten enough food. Ignoring my appestat for so many years seems like sleeping through the alarm clock and missing important appointments. God has some appointments for me to keep, and I can keep them better if I learn to get back in touch with the signals from my body.

## Impatience and Facing Reality: Two Tough Assignments

Now I'd like to look at the impatience that often comes with dieting. Some of the feelings that usually drive me to try to lose weight are being disgusted with myself for being a little fat, being ashamed of it, and thinking I'll have a lot more fun and like myself better if I can get my weight down. All of these feelings have made me want quick relief from the disgusted, embarrassed, or lonely feeling. So I'm usually tempted to try something *quick* that will *solve my problem.*

Along with wanting quick results goes the belief that I will be able to go back to the foods I ate before the diet—those foods I'm having to "do without" until I get my weight down. I refused to face reality for years, thinking that I just "had" to have my pizza, my chips and dips, my Mexican food, all the things I knew caused extra pounds, but without which I was convinced I could not live a normal, happy life.

The sooner I could "get the weight off" and get back to "normal" living, the better! So I would skip meals, try liquid protein formulas, eat grapefruit and eggs, all protein, no protein, whatever would "guarantee" me quick results. And as the first few pounds quickly fell away, I would be elated and convinced that "this time" I was going to solve the problem for good.

But when I started my study four years ago, I began to learn about how the body works, what kinds of foods are "easy" for it to digest and use for energy, and what kind of foods clog up the system. I learned that eating certain foods is like pouring grease down the sink drain, followed by cold water. By eating these foods I was clogging up my system and really asking for trouble, in terms not only of getting fat, but also of possible illness later on.

I began to see that God created my metabolism to need certain nutrients, and that he put in nature all the things I'd need for health and energy—protein, carbohydrates (simple and complex), fats, fibers, vitamins, minerals, all intricately combined and mixed in delicious edible foods so that I could have the fuel I needed to operate at my fullest physical potential.

As I read, my attitude slowly began to change. I realized that my desire for unhealthy foods was based on things I'd learned from the world around me, from the way I ate as a child, from the way television commercials played on my feelings of loneliness and inadequacy. But these desires had nothing to do with what my body was crying out for—good, solid nourishment for health and energy.

## Social Situations Expose Us to Tempting Trials

Even more than the foods themselves, the *things I did* while eating these foods were what I did not want to give up. And I couldn't figure out how to participate in social activities while avoiding the unhealthy food. I've been doing some serious thinking about that, and I've decided that I will always enjoy eating out or having friends over for dinner. But there are choices I can make which are still quite enjoyable, but more healthy. Here are some ways I have experimented with trying to order reasonable things from the menu, while *concentrating on the people* rather than feeling sorry for myself about not indulging in some of the unhealthy foods I used to order.

In Mexican restaurants, I have tried ordering à la carte once in a while. I'll have one taco and a salad instead of some huge Mexican dinner. Tacos al carbon are also a good lowfat Mexican selection. In regular dinner restaurants I often eat just the salad bar, and sometimes add either a baked potato or a cup of soup (not the creamy kind, though!). Sometimes Keith orders one meal for both of us. Then I order the salad bar, and we split one meat and baked potato (about one-third for me and two-thirds for him). Both of us come out feeling better. Chinese restaurants offer many good low-calorie choices. Two people can each order soup, then split one meat/vegetable entree. These changes are hard at first, but I find that the more I practice them, telling myself it's the *people* I want to enjoy, as much as or more than the food, the easier the changes are getting to be.

## Healthy, Permanent Weight Loss Takes Time

One of the most important things of which I keep reminding myself over and over *is that real, healthy, permanent weight loss takes time.* My body has spent years storing up all this fat, and it's going to take some time and effort to "burn it up" and wash it out of my system.

But even though I realize weight loss takes time, a pound or two a week seems so slow when there are many pounds to lose. My impatience often gets the better of me when I start a new diet.

It helps to know that the way the body must get rid of excess fat is to burn it off, and that it takes time to metabolize fat properly. If I am losing weight faster than one or two pounds a week, that means I am either (1) losing water, not fat, or (2) losing valuable muscle—protein.

When I remind myself of these facts, I seem to have more patience with the process. Since I'm planning to make many of these changes permanent anyway, I'm not in such a rush to lose weight and to get it over with so I can "go back" to my old ways of eating.

When I started on the eating plan given to me by the doctor at the Houstonian, I faced the fact that for me to cut my calorie intake in half—from 2,000 to 1,000 a day—would be quite an adjustment for both my mind and my stomach. I felt that such a drastic change would be hard to stay with for the long period of time I now knew losing weight safely was going to take. It was then I realized that the greater my impatience, the greater the likelihood that I will start out on a program too tough to stick with for a long time. Eventually I decided to try 1,200 calories. Even that adjustment was hard at first, but not so overwhelming as dieting on 1,000 calories would have been.

Now I am trying to face reality, which is the fact that I need to be more aware of what I eat. I consider this to be a lifelong project. But even at the slow rate of a pound a week, a person could lose 52 pounds in a year. That is quite a lot!

In light of all this, I've become very reluctant to use the word *diet* at all. I prefer to refer to this approach to food as an "Eating Plan," which means I am developing healthy eating habits and learning to use food to nourish and improve my health, rather than just sliding by, using old unhealthy habits, or eating just to gratify certain emotional needs. I have not totally changed my ways, but when I look back over the past four years I can see that I have made some significant changes and that I'm working on others.

Now we've seen an overall approach to food, along with a food-serving eating plan and a brief definition of the components in various foods. Next, we'll look at each specific food group more closely, beginning with the fruit and vegetable groups.

# Week Seven
## (Three Days)

## *Aims and Activities*

(1)  To continue with muscle-tone and aerobic workouts.

(2)  To begin putting a food-group eating plan into practice.

(3)  To become familiar with the first five food lists in Part Three: fruits; vegetables (2 lists); grains, breads, and cereals; and animal sources of protein.

(4)  To go to the grocery store to evaluate what's in the produce section, the bread and cereal section, the meat counter, and the dairy case. Read labels and try to decide on the best choices for good nutrition.

(5)  To try at least one new recipe from Part Four, and to adapt at least one of your old recipes, substituting healthful ingredients and cooking techniques for those that are not so healthful.

# 21

## *Fruits and Vegetables*

### *Scripture and Devotion*

This chapter begins a series of chapters about the various food categories on your eating plan—what the best kinds of foods are in each category, and how much of those foods makes up a serving. I'll also mention some foods in these groups to cut down on or eliminate. But first, here is a thought from Genesis 1:30:

> "And to every beast of the earth, and to every bird of the air, and to everything that creeps on the earth, everything that has the breath of life, I have given every green plant for food."

I once knew a man with extremely limited food tastes. He was a beef, potatoes, salad, and green beans man. Period. No squash, no rice, no broccoli, no Brussels sprouts, no carrots, no coleslaw. Fried chicken or fish was okay with him, but not baked or broiled. He often said about broccoli, "If I wanted to eat a bush I'd go out and chew on the hedge!"

This may be okay for people who don't care about eating. But to those of us who love food, a life of "meat and potatoes" would be boring indeed. I've often found that variety is the very thing that keeps me interested in wholesome foods.

If this scripture is true, then many green plants (and some white, brown, and yellow ones, too) are wholesome food for people. For instance, raw spinach makes a good leafy base for a delicious salad. And the vitamin content of spinach is very rich. I heard a man who is a fitness instructor at a health club say "When I think of the nutritional value of a leaf of spinach, I don't ever want to waste time eating lettuce again!"

Keith and I enjoy experimenting with fresh vegetables we've never eaten. We look through the grocery store for interesting things. A few months ago I was shopping with Keith, and we saw an interesting white vegetable labeled "J-i-c-a-m-a." I first tried to pronounce it "Jamaica," but when I looked at the word more closely, I didn't know what to call it. We decided to try it, so I put some in a bag and took it to the cash register. The cashier knew what it was! She told me it was pronounced "hick'-uh-ma," and it could be eaten raw in salads or lightly steamed. It's a member of the turnip family. We enjoyed it both ways, and it was as if we'd found an exciting new food treat like a great new dessert—only this one wasn't fattening.

> DEAR LORD, thank you for the varieties of healthful foods you've provided. I'm so glad to be learning about more of them and about how to enjoy them. Let my interest in and curiosity about food be channeled into good directions. In Jesus' name, AMEN.

## Food Lists

In chapter 19, I suggested a food-serving eating plan based on foods from various food groups including meats, dairy products, vegetables, fats, and fruits. Now, I'd like to take each one of those food groups in turn and talk about which foods in these categories are good for us, and which ones aren't so good. There are lists in Part Three on pages 297–305 which summarize what I'll be discussing. If you decide to use the food-serving eating plan described in chapter 19, you can refer to these lists to find out which foods are recommended and how much of each is a serving.

For the first month that I was trying to learn how to manage food groups, I kept these lists in the kitchen and looked up serving sizes. I also served the foods first into a measuring cup and then poured them out of the cup onto the plate. That way, I began to see how a half-cup of something looks on the plate, so that later, I could better estimate the servings. At first, when I had tried to estimate and then measure, I had found I would estimate almost half again too much.

There are also two main parts in each food list; one is called "recommended" foods and the other is "not recommended." By reading through each part, you can see which foods are the better choices in terms of good nutrition and weight control.

When I talked about the four basic food components earlier, I mentioned that there are two kinds of carbohydrates, complex and simple. In this chapter I want to begin to talk about food groups that consist mostly of complex carbohydrates, the component that should make up 48% of our calories. This chapter will be concerned in particular with two food groups: vegetables and fruits.

## Vegetables

Most vegetables are very low in calories and are rich sources of many vitamins and minerals, especially vitamins A and C. They also give us dietary fiber, which as I mentioned before is important in helping the body get rid of waste materials.

There are two food lists for vegetables, found on pages 298–299. "List One" consists of nonstarchy vegetables which are very low in calories. Although your food-serving list says you can have all of these you want, I've found that when I eat very, very large servings of them I don't lose as fast. Some eating plans I've seen do limit these vegetables to a serving of a half cup, because they do have a few calories. I regard them as the foods I can have seconds of if I'm still hungry, or the ones to snack on in the afternoon or evening.

But almost all of the plans I've read say that the leafy green vegetables like lettuce, kale, and endive are virtually "free." So enjoy them in salads all you like, and use your own discretion about the others.

The vegetables listed in "List Two" are considered "starchy" vegetables and are somewhat higher in calories. These should definitely be limited to one half-cup serving per day. Certain soups are also included in this group, and as you can see at the top of the list, a serving is one cup. Popcorn is also in this group, and a serving is two cups. If you decide to have two starchy vegetables, like soup for lunch and a baked potato for dinner, skip a grain serving.

Since all vegetables are healthy choices, the "not recommended" division points out less healthy ways vegetables can be prepared— using batters and oils for frying, for example.

## How to Serve Vegetables

*The best way to serve vegetables is raw*, as in salads or party appetizers. Raw vegetables retain the most vitamins, minerals, and fiber. For serving at meals, they can be lightly steamed and seasoned with herbs and spices. (I usually don't season mine much; they all have good natural flavors.) Another way to serve them is to add them to casseroles and soups.

Even the skins of such vegetables as carrots and potatoes are nutritious. In fact, many of the vitamins found in these vegetables are just below the surface of the skin. So I scrub carrots and potatoes well, then simply cook and eat them, skin and all. Eating the skin provides more fiber, too.

Part Four of this book contains a few "fancy" vegetable recipes, in case you want to make them a little more entertaining. Also, the minestrone soup recipe is a great way to serve vegetables in a thick, hearty soup.

Although canned vegetables are convenient because they last a long time in the pantry, many of their vitamins have been destroyed by the heat necessary to can them, and the cooking process used in canning usually destroys the fiber. Also, some canned vegetables have preservatives and salt added to help keep them from spoiling. Too much salt has been linked to certain health problems for some people; we'll discuss these problems in a later chapter.

Frozen vegetables are a little better than canned because they haven't been subjected to high heat. The main problem here is buying vegetables frozen in butter or sauces. These sauces add to the fat intake and are hard to digest because of the kind of fats (saturated) used in them. There are preservatives and artificial colors in them, too, which we can avoid by buying fresh vegetables. But buying plain frozen vegetables (with no sauce, butter, or breading) is the best alternative if you can't get good-quality fresh ones.

## Fruits

Fruits are higher in calories than most vegetables, but raw fruits have lots of dietary fiber in them, as well as vitamin C and other vitamins. You'll find them listed on page 297.

The most nutritious way to serve fruit is raw and whole. They're great for snacks, in salads, or as desserts. Sliced oranges in a sherbert bowl make a delicious dessert after a nutritious dinner. And eating fruits like apples and pears with the skin on provides a lot of fiber as well as vitamins and energy. There are recipes for a fruit salad and several fruit desserts in Part Four of this book.

The same comments I made about canned and frozen vegetables can be applied to fruits, too. If you buy frozen fruit, watch out for added sugar or syrup. I've seen frozen fruit with no sugar added in several grocery stores.

## The Rest of the Complex Carbohydrate Food Group

In addition to fruits and vegetables, there is another large category of foods that fall under the general heading, "complex carbohydrates." The next chapter will be devoted to this category, which consists of breads, grains, and cereals.

# 22

## Grains, Breads, and Cereals

### Scripture and Devotion

This chapter deals with another food group which provides the component complex carbohydrates—breads, grains and cereals. But before we discuss this group, let's look at Psalm 119:11:

> "I have laid up thy word in my heart, that I might not sin against thee."

When I was a little girl growing up in Tennessee, I belonged to a Baptist church. I was a member of just about everything there was to join in that congregation. And in the process of attending Sunday school, Girls' Auxiliary meetings, and choir, I learned a lot of Scripture. In choir, we sang anthems that were scriptures set to music. I remember with joy an energetic setting of "If God be for us, who can be against us? Who can separate us from the love of God?" I still am tempted to say it in the musical rhythm of that anthem!

When I was young, however, I thought having to memorize so many Bible verses was rather pointless. I didn't understand the meanings of half of what I learned, and the other half didn't apply to me because I wasn't old enough to know how selfish, lazy, and weak I really am! But now, when I'm really interested in knowing God's will for my life and in trying to put into practice everything I can learn about what his will might be, I find myself repeating fragments of Bible verses I learned as a child. And these fragments are inspiring, comforting, confronting, educating, and motivating.

I realize that memorizing parts of God's Word has helped me so much today because I can carry promises of God's care and guidance with me wherever I go. These verses sometimes guide me through difficulties or help me celebrate joyful times.

A woman I know told me she uses the time she spends jogging or doing exercises to memorize scriptures. She puts a verse or two on an index card and carries it in her hand while she's running. Or she puts the card on the mat beside her and studies it while she works out. Then at some other time, when she doesn't have her card with her, the verse is there to inspire her because it's memorized. Since one of the big problems for some people in exercising regularly is boredom, it seems to me this is a great way to use the time!

> DEAR LORD, thank you that you can communicate with us through the Bible. Help me to want to learn your Word and keep it in my heart so I can know how to be your person all through the day. Guide me to the places in your Word which will speak to me in areas I need to hear. And thank you for my friend, whose example of studying the Bible during exercise has shown me that there is time to do both, if I am willing. In Jesus' name, AMEN.

## Grains, Breads, and Cereals

In the last chapter we talked about two kinds of foods which give us complex carbohydrates: vegetables and fruits. Now let's discuss another group of foods with this component: grains, breads, and cereals.

I mentioned that fruits and vegetables eaten raw are a good source of dietary fiber. But grains, breads, and cereals are an even better source of it. While the exact human requirement of fiber is not known, the current recommendation is that we try to eat 7–10 grams of crude fiber per day. The list for this food group divides grains, breads, and cereals into three sections according to the amount of fiber they contain (pp. 300–303).

The first section contains the highest known sources of fiber. These items have about 2 grams per serving, which goes a long way toward the recommended 7–10 grams. The foods in the second section are also good sources of fiber, and they have from .4–2 grams per serving. As you read down this list, you'll probably recognize some favorites. A serving is approximately 1 slice of bread, ½ a bun, and ¾ cup of cereal.

There is a third group of grains, breads, and cereals which don't have much fiber, but which are still recommended bread choices because they are lower in fat and higher in vitamins than some other bread choices you could make.

It is suggested that we stay away from baked goods that are made with saturated fats like butter and coconut oil. You'll find these listed in section three under the column headed "Not Recommended." You'll see under this "Not Recommended" heading that commercially baked cakes, pies, cookies and so on are not so good for us because of the high saturated fat content. But there are many delicious recipes for whole-wheat spice cakes, muffins, and quick breads that you can make yourself using polyunsaturated fats such as corn oil or margarine. In fact, three muffin recipes are included in Part Four—two for breakfast (BRAN-Bran and Zucchini) and one for other meals (Three-Grain Muffins).

## Cereals

A good thing to have for breakfast is cereal. I've already mentioned some cereals which are nutritious and have a lot of fiber in them. In fact, I get most of my daily fiber from a bowl of shredded wheat or All-Bran with miller's bran sprinkled on it. The sodium content of cereals varies, so I try to choose a cereal which has a low sodium rating. I've discovered that there are even different sodium contents for Raisin Bran made by different companies!.

Cereals can be incorporated into other recipes to make delicious variations with increased fiber and vitamins. Companies like Nabisco will send you pamphlets with interesting nutritious recipes. (I got some addresses from the cereal boxes themselves, but they are included in Part Five under the heading, "Materials Which Can Be Ordered at No Cost." Some companies ask you to send a small amount of money, like 25¢, for handling.) And there are often recipes printed right on the box which are worth trying. Just watch out for less healthy ingredients like butter (a saturated fat), lots of sugar and so on.

## Rice

I've always thought brown rice had more fiber than white rice because most high-fiber breads are brown. Actually, brown rice has only slightly more fiber than white rice—not quite enough to move it to the list of foods with higher fiber. But I still prefer to serve brown rice because it has so many of the B vitamins in it.

In fact, one book I read explained that *all* rice is brown when it is grown. But because people like the fluffy white look of white rice, manufacturers go to all the trouble to scrape off the outer brown hull, leaving only the low-vitamin white insides. Then they sell the hulls they scraped off to pharmacists, who use them to make vitamin-B tablets, which some people buy to make up for the fact that they didn't get any vitamin B from white rice! When I learned that, I was delighted to switch to brown rice. White rice has very little flavor, while brown rice has a subtle nutty flavor which I think is very good.

## Wheat

A similar thing happens to a wheat kernel when it is ground up into white flour. The inside part of the kernel is called the endosperm (see illustration). Wrapped around the endosperm is an outer layer called bran, which is nothing but dietary fiber. And at the base of the kernel is a section called the germ. The germ contains valuable vitamins such as the B vitamins and vitamin E.

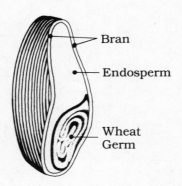

Bran

Endosperm

Wheat Germ

WHEAT KERNEL
(Enlarged Longitudinal Section)

White flour was developed for looks and taste—people liked the pure-white softness of it. But it is made by scraping off the bran and germ, which are brown. When these are lost, it means that 80% of the vitamins and all of the fiber are removed. When it is bleached, even more of the vitamins are lost. Some white flours have been "enriched," which means that some (but not all) of the vitamins, and none of the fiber, have been put back.

Whole-wheat flour is the kind of flour that offers the most vitamins and fiber. The best kind of whole-wheat flour to look for is "stone-ground." This method causes the fewest nutrients to be lost.

Other methods of grinding (for example, with metal blades) generate more heat and cause more vitamins to be lost. There isn't much difference in calorie content between white and whole-wheat flour. The wheat flour is better because it has fiber and more vitamins. And *whole* wheat flour is better than flours labeled "cracked wheat," or simply "wheat."

When I buy whole-wheat breads, I've noticed that some of them do not list whole-wheat flour as the first ingredient on the label. The manufacturers are legally allowed to call it whole-wheat bread because they've added a little whole-wheat flour, but you'll find that it's listed as the fifth or sixth ingredient on the label, with enriched white flour as the first, and main, ingredient. So I try to choose breads listing whole-wheat flour, preferably stone ground, as the very first ingredient.

As I learned about the higher vitamin and fiber content of breads, I decided to try to spend my "grain and bread" calories on these whole-grain foods. But an occasional roll or slice of bread made with white flour is not bad for you. To me it just seems like wasting an opportunity to get more vitamins and fiber into my system.

# 23

## *Protein—Fish, Poultry, and Meat*

### Scripture and Devotion

In this chapter we'll begin looking at the food component protein, which should make up 12% of our daily calories. We'll talk about animal protein in this chapter, then go on with vegetable sources and dairy products in later chapters. Before we go on however, let's take a look at 1 Corinthians 10:13:

> "No temptation has overtaken you that is not common to man. God is faithful, and he will not let you be tempted beyond your strength, but with the temptation will also provide the way of escape, that you may be able to endure it."

I woke up this morning and weighed myself. I had gained a pound! In my head I know that gaining a pound even when I've stuck to my diet is a common thing, possibly due to water retention or extra muscle weight. But my heart sank anyway. I could hear the taunting voice of this beast in my head, a fat woman with scraggly hair and puffy cheeks. She tries to convince me I will never reach my goal.

"See, you're wasting your time with all this health business," she taunts me. "You're never going to make it!" And this morning I believed her. I was so tempted to throw the whole plan out the window and treat myself to a day off, a week off—maybe even the rest of my life off! Wild thoughts crashed around inside me as I headed for my quiet time.

Then I read this scripture. The promise God has made to us leaped off the page: ". . . but with the temptation will also provide the way of escape . . ." I asked him, "Really, Lord? You promise? Then why do I feel so discouraged because of one itty-bitty pound?!"

I thought of many other times when I've felt helpless in the face of the pressures of my world . . . the times when special friends were coming over for dinner and I felt obliged to serve "standard" foods such as desserts and creamy casseroles, that I knew were not healthy . . . the times when I was out of town in a strange city and didn't have the courage to put on shorts and jog around the streets for fear of what might happen to me.

But with God's promise that there would always be a way of escape, I pushed my thinking further and asked myself, "What could I do in those cases?" With this new attitude, the answers seemed to pop up like the numbers on an old-fashioned cash register. "When those guests come you could search harder for delicious ways of fixing standard foods without the unhealthy ingredients. If dessert is a must, you could not eat yours, or serve yourself dessert and only take a bite or two, throwing the rest in the garbage."

When that last thought came, the voice of the beast laughed at me and insisted, "But that's too hard for you." I wondered, "Could I really find the discipline to serve myself a dessert and then not eat much of it?" Well, reluctantly I admitted, "Yes. It *is* an escape, and God has promised to help me. Maybe I could try it."

Then the beast spoke up: "But what about the danger of jogging in a strange town?" With my newfound confidence in God's promise, I responded, "I could stay in my hotel room and jog in place. I could take a small tape recorder and do an aerobic tape in my room. I could jog with someone else at a safe time of day. If the hotel has a swimming pool, I could go swim some laps." Wow! I couldn't believe how these answers came to me when I kept God's promise in front of me, and I was shocked when I realized that no answers had come before when I was really faced with those situations.

I got the message. As long as I am convinced there is no solution to the situation, the answers eluded me. I resolved to remember that, when that helpless feeling comes up, I am *not* helpless. I'm going to try to make an extra effort to look at the situation with God's promise in mind, and to pray for his answers to my "impossible" situations.

DEAR LORD, your promises for help are so good, and I have seen that without your help I am really helpless. Thank you for showing this promise to me again today, and help me to remember it whenever I feel helpless. Arranging my schedule, disciplining my will, and adjusting to changes are all things I struggle with. Keep me in your care and remind me often that you will not let me be tempted beyond my strength, and that you will provide the way of escape. In Jesus' name, AMEN.

## The Many Faces of Protein

I used to think of protein as a big, juicy 12-ounce steak. But during my studies I've found out two important things about protein that changed my image of it. One is that I don't have to eat as much as I once thought to get the protein I need. The other is that there is plenty of protein in foods besides meat, and protein from other foods comes with a lot fewer calories. Furthermore, protein from plants is much easier to digest than protein from meats, especially red meats like beef. In this chapter we'll talk about animal protein—found in chicken, fish, and red meats. The next chapter is about how we can get a lot of our protein from vegetable sources.

Protein is very important to the body. All cells contain protein, and it is used in building new tissues to replace ones that die and are sluffed off. Hair and nails are made up of protein, and so are muscles and bones. Also, protein is needed to make antibodies, which help us fight off sickness. And it is needed in forming scar tissue and clotting blood (part of the repair work), as well as in carrying oxygen and nutrients in the blood.

Protein is made up of 31 amino acids which travel through the bloodstream to the various parts of the body, where they are used in many ways. The living tissue in our bodies contains 22 of these amino acids, and can manufacture these 22 from carbohydrates and nitrogen. But there are nine others that the body cannot make and must get from food. Therefore, these nine are called the *essential amino acids.*[1]

Meat, chicken, fish, eggs, milk, and other dairy products contain all nine of these essential amino acids, along with small amounts of other nonessential amino acids. These foods are called "complete" proteins.

## How Much Protein Is Enough for Health?

Protein is measured in grams, and there are charts available giving how many grams of protein women, men, and children need per pound. Jane Brody has come up with a formula by which we can calculate how many grams of protein we need according to our age, weight, and whether or not we are pregnant.

The formula is as follows: Adults, both men and women, over the

---

1. Brody, *Jane Brody's Nutrition Book*, 35–36.

age of 18 need .36 grams of protein per pound of body weight.[2] If you weigh too much, figure your protein requirement according to what you *should* weigh. Our need for protein is determined by the amount of lean tissue in our bodies, not by how much fat we've got.

According to the formula, if my weight is 130, then I need 46.8 grams of protein a day. A single three-ounce slice of lean roast beef will give me 24 grams, over half my daily requirement. And since there is protein in other foods such as peanut butter (two tablespoons has 8 grams), milk (a cup of skim milk has 8.8), and beans (a half-cup of cooked navy beans has 7.4), it's possible for me to get plenty of protein without that 12-ounce juicy steak . . . and all the fat that goes with it.

The Houstonian Preventive Medicine Center dietary guideline recommends that adults eat no more than eight ounces of cooked protein per day. This would be the same as a ladies' filet steak for dinner and no protein at all for breakfast and lunch. (One thing that I want to point out here is that meat loses about 25% of its weight when it is cooked. So a ten-and-a-half ounce raw steak would become an eight-ounce cooked one, and it's the cooked weight that counts.)

But that's for a man-sized maintenance-type eating plan (see Weight Maintenance Plan, 1,900 or 2,200 calories). For a person like me who weighs 130 pounds, only six ounces is recommended (but that's still more than enough to keep me quite healthy). As we discussed earlier, our healthy goal is to eat 12% of our daily calorie requirements in the form of protein. That would mean that if I were eating 2,000 calories per day (which is about 15 calories times 130 pounds), only 240 of those calories should be protein. That is the equivalent of five ounces of roasted chicken without the skin or five ounces of lean roast beef. (While this much meat does not give me the full 48 grams per day of protein I need, I can easily make up the remaining 8 to 10 grams with other foods in the other categories— like milk, cheese, beans, peanuts, and so on.)

Please note that none of the figures I have mentioned even comes close to that juicy 12-ounce steak! A steak that size would be 50% more than a person who was eating a man-sized maintenance-type plan would need in an entire day—and double what I need in my 2,000 calorie plan. I'm saying this in all these different ways to point

---

2. A pregnant woman needs .62 grams per pound, and one who is nursing needs .53 grams per pound. Children need higher amounts per pound, but since they weigh less the actual total is the same or less than an average adult woman. The exact figures for different children's ages can be found on p. 48 of *Jane Brody's Nutrition Book.*

out that what we usually think we need in the way of protein is a lot more than we *really* need.

## The Source of the Protein Is Important, Too

Another problem with that 12-ounce steak is that animal protein, especially red meat, is loaded with saturated fat, the kind that clogs the veins and arteries and can lead to heart disease. (Even *lean* red meat is higher in fat than poultry, fish, or vegetable sources.)

Also, eating too much protein, and too much red meat in particular, has been linked to increased risk of colon cancer. Our bodies have to work so hard to digest meats that the waste products sift through the bowels slowly. And uneliminated waste remaining in the colon might create conditions that could encourage cancer to grow.

For all these reasons, it is recommended that no more than four ounces per day of protein should come from red meat, with the rest coming from fish, chicken, dairy products, and vegetables. (In the next chapter we will discuss how to combine certain vegetables to meet our protein needs.) Eating fish and chicken four or five times a week, having "meatless" meals once a week, and eating red meat only once a week is an even healthier plan.

## One Way to Be Sure You're Serving the Right Amount

I highly recommend getting a small scale for your kitchen with which to weigh foods. You can find one for ten dollars or less at most large grocery stores or hardware stores. I started out by weighing everything, so I'd know how big a four-ounce piece of steak looked. I even bought a larger roast, cut it up into 16-ounce sections (this is raw weight; when cooked, these pieces become two six-ounce servings) and froze them. That way I could pull out only the amount I needed to cook for the two of us without having to cook a whole roast and then eat beef the rest of the week.

### Fish

Fish is low in saturated fat and therefore low in calories. I live on the Gulf Coast, so it's not hard to buy freshly caught fish. But I've also tried the frozen fish fillets from the grocery store. They can be delicious, also!

Many people don't like fish because it becomes tough when cooked, but that's because it's usually cooked too long. A general rule of thumb I now go by is one my friend, Betsy, told me about. When I bake or broil fish I cook it at 500° for about five minutes per inch of thickness. The fish looks white and is flaky when done. If it is cooked longer it gets tough and dry, and that's not good. Some thin little fillets should be cooked only two or three minutes.

Some fish has a strong "fishy" taste that is distasteful to many people. Other kinds of fish are mild, even sweet and tender—very unlike the typical "fish" taste. Flounder and red snapper are two of these. Also, the fresher the fish is when it is cooked, the milder the flavor.

I like to squeeze a little lemon juice on fish and sprinkle on some seasoning salt or a few sprigs of dried basil. Craig Claiborne has a charcoal-broiled fish recipe in which he uses a little melted unsalted margarine and some finely chopped garlic as the seasonings. Other delicious seasonings for baked fish are parsley, dill, chopped and sauteed vegetables like green pepper and celery, and lime juice.

Try to stay away from commercially breaded and fried fish. The fish is okay, but the breading and fat used in frying is very unhealthy. Even when you fry it yourself the added calories and fat are undesirable.

## Poultry

Poultry is also much lower in saturated fat than red meats, and there are many ways to serve it. It's important to remember to skin the chicken before eating it, since this cuts the calorie content in half. You can skin it before you cook it in some recipes, or after it's done in others. If you're out for lunch at a fried-chicken place, order the chicken, remove the skin and that delicious crust, and eat the meat underneath. You'll be doing your digestive system an enormous favor *and* cutting your calories by more than half (the skin calories plus the breading and frying fat calories). With a few prayers and some determination, it can (sometimes) be done!

Buying frozen turkey parts such as breast or thighs and roasting them can give a delicious variety to meals. The recipe for Turkey Breast Singapore is a good way to serve turkey either at Thanksgiving or during the rest of the year.

My friend, Betsy Manis, a nutritionist, gave me a recipe she wrote for marinated chicken which I'm including in Part Four of this book. You marinate the chicken in low-calorie Italian dressing, tomato juice, and chili powder overnight, then bake it. Wonderful! Keith and I also enjoy making crockpot chicken dishes with low-calorie sauces.

## Red Meats

For those occasions when you are serving red meat, here are a few tips that will help cut down on fat. Choose the leanest cuts of meat you can find. (The meat food list on pp. 304–308 points out some cuts of beef that are lower in fat than others.) Then, trim away any fat that's visible on the meat before you broil or roast it. Taking a small amount of meat, say two ounces, slicing it thinly, and stir-frying it with a lot of Chinese vegetables (or regular vegetables like carrots, green peppers, celery, onion, mushrooms, and cabbage) is a way to enjoy red meat in small amounts. Charcoal grilling is another delicious way to serve beef. And in Part Four there's a great recipe for Veal Chops with Lemon Sauce to add a little variety to your cooking.

## Luncheon Meats

There are some luncheon meats which are good choices, and are listed on your food lists. Another good sandwich filling is tuna salad made with a minimum of salad dressing and lots of chopped celery, green pepper, and hard-cooked egg. Sandwich fillings made with chopped vegetables can also be good. Some of them provide excellent protein, and we'll talk about them in the next chapter.

## Other Sources of Protein

There are lots of foods besides fish, poultry, and meat that contain protein. For example, as I have mentioned, dairy products such as milk and cheese are good sources of protein. But these foods also contain a lot of fat. (The beauty of the food-serving eating plan is that it allows for foods such as meats and dairy products that provide more than one food component. When you eat the specified number of servings in each group, you will be assured of getting the components in the right proportion.)

We'll be looking at dairy products in some detail in a later chapter. But first I want to look at another source of protein in the diet that is frequently overlooked—protein from vegetable sources.

# Week Eight
## (Three Days)

## *Aims and Activities*

(1)  To continue with muscle-tone and aerobic workouts.

(2)  To continue finding realistic ways to work into your life the eating plan at the calorie level you've chosen.

(3)  To become familiar with the next three food lists in Part Three: vegetable sources of protein, dairy products, and fats.

(4)  To study the charts on complementary vegetable proteins, and to try at least one of the "meatless" main dishes from Part Four.

(5)  To concentrate on drinking at least eight eight-ounce glasses of water (not including coffee, iced tea, or carbonated beverages) daily.

# 24

## *Protein from Vegetable Sources*

### *Scripture and Devotion*

This chapter is also about foods with protein in them. But before we get into it, let's take a minute for a word from the Bible.

The scripture for this chapter is longer than usual, because it tells a story. This story really "rang a bell" for me as I thought about trying to treat my body with healthful respect according to God's wishes even though I live in a society that seems to "push" unhealthy foods. It is about Daniel, and the reference is Daniel 1:8—16. Here it is:

> "But Daniel resolved that he would not defile himself with the king's rich food, or with the wine which he drank; therefore he asked the chief of the eunuchs to allow him not to defile himself. . . . And the chief . . . said to Daniel, 'I fear lest my lord the king, who appointed your food and your drink, should see that you were in poorer condition than the youths who are of your own age. So you would endanger my head with the king.'
>
> "Then Daniel said to the steward . . . 'Test your servants for ten days; let us be given vegetables to eat and water to drink. Then let our appearance and the appearance of the youths who eat the king's rich food be observed by you, and according to what you see deal with your servants.' So he hearkened to them in this matter, and tested them for ten days. At the end of ten days it was seen that they were better in appearance and fatter in flesh than all the youths who ate the king's rich food. So the steward took away their rich food and the wine they were to drink, and gave them vegetables."

When I read this scripture, I realized that the truth it illustrates fits what nutritionists today are telling us—that meats and rich foods are hard on our systems, and vegetables and water are healthy. A ten-day test like this on ourselves would tell us a lot about what kind of foods are friendly to our bodies and what kind are harmful. (Before you get worried about the fact that Daniel and his friends wound up "fatter in flesh" than the other young men, let me say that I checked on that. I found out that the original Old Testament word for "fatter" conveyed our idea of "healthier" or "fitter.")

When I first began my own experiment, I had some big decisions to make. I was willing to change the way I ate and to add some exercise to my life. But I wondered if doing this would make me any "fitter in flesh," as it had Daniel and his friends. After just a couple of months, I did notice some differences, not just in terms of weight loss and stronger muscles, but in some basic areas I thought could never change.

For instance, I have never been a "morning person." Some people wake up smiling and chatting and singing in the shower, but not me! When I first got up, I used to feel stiff all over and sluggish. I couldn't speak in complete sentences. When Keith would talk to me, all I could manage in response was a sleepy nod or a quiet "Um-hmm."

But out of a desire to find a better quality of life and to be more available physically to do God's will, I reluctantly agreed that we would start getting up at 6:30 A.M. so that we could be through with exercise, breakfast, and showers, and ready to work by 9:00. (Without children to send off to school, this was a workable schedule for us.)

By the end of a month or two, we had established this pattern of getting up at 6:30. And along with this we had begun making some difficult food choices, too, such as choosing to sweeten our breakfast cereal with bananas and raisins *instead of* sugar. I began to notice a difference in the way I felt in the mornings. I was a different person. I became more talkative, started walking with a bounce, and was more creative at my work for the rest of the day. I would not have thought that such a change could take place in a confirmed "night owl" like me. And as I see the good results in the *overall* way my body functions, I am even more motivated to keep on changing. I still enjoy sleeping in when I get the chance. Saturday mornings are my favorite time of the week now because I don't get up until 9:00!

But back to Daniel. Using the idea of a "trial run" or experiment might not be a bad thing to do. Try a diet that seems to be healthy to you for a few weeks, or try a new daily schedule that allows time for exercise, and see how you feel. I predict that, like Daniel, you will look and feel better than you did before. Let that feeling be a positive memory on which to build in the future as you begin to turn your approach to eating in a more healthy direction.

DEAR LORD, thanks for the way you built in the marvelous potential for health and energy that we all have. Help us to have the courage not only to learn what foods are best for our digestive systems, our muscle tissue, and our blood flow, but to put what we learn into practice.

Lord, it seems like everything in our society points against this way of eating and living. My schedule is pushed to the maximum with deadlines, commitments, obligations, and chores. It's so tempting to stop and grab a fried-chicken dinner or a hamburger when I'm on the run. It's so easy to open a few cans and mix them together and serve a hot casserole to my family after coming home late from all the things I have to do. But I am *so glad* you are helping me to make healthy eating a priority and are giving me the insights and courage to put these new ideas into my life.

Thanks for Daniel's example of asking for vegetables to eat and water to drink when he could have had rich foods and wine, or in my case pizza and Pepsi. In Jesus' name, AMEN.

## *Meat Substitutes: Protein from Plants*

In the previous lesson, we talked about the fact that protein is made up of 31 amino acids. Our bodies can make 22 of them for themselves, but it has to rely on foods for the nine "essential" amino acids. The foods we discussed in the last lesson contain all nine, and are called *complete* proteins.

But it is possible to provide good quality protein for our bodies by eating foods which have only part of the nine essential amino acids. These foods are called "incomplete" protein. If two or more of these "incomplete" proteins are eaten at the same meal, they provide "complete" protein to the body. This is because each supplies different essential amino acids, and the combination results in all nine being present. Since the body can't use the protein from a food if even one of the nine is missing, combinations of all nine must be eaten in the same meal—but not necessarily in the same food.

For example, rice has almost all of the nine amino acids, but it is low in an amino acid called lysine. But beans have plenty of lysine. So when beans and rice are eaten together, all nine amino acids arrive in the stomach at the same time and the body uses them all together as protein. Also, beans combined with other grains such as corn or wheat provide all nine essential acids.

Dairy products are also sources of protein. So beans or grains eaten with a small amount of a dairy product (like cheese) provide complete protein. Another way to enhance the protein value of a vegetable food is to eat it along with a small amount of animal protein, like meat. Just an ounce or so will be enough to complete the protein content of beans or grains.

Jane Brody gives in her book a diagram which shows how vegetable sources (grains, legumes, seeds) can be combined to give complete proteins. You'll find it and a list showing how to combine vegetable sources with dairy products on p. 310.

There are some very good vegetarian cookbooks which give recipes for casseroles which have all the ingredients to give complete proteins. One of my favorites is a recipe my friend, Betsy Manis, gave me. It's a rice and lentil casserole topped with a little melted cheese, and with her permission, I've included it in Part Four.

## Sandwich Fillings and Other Lunch Ideas

I mentioned in the last chapter there are some good vegetable sandwich fillings which make nice, light lunches. One good one is peanut butter and banana slices on whole-wheat bread. Peanut butter and whole-wheat bread combine to make a complete protein.

Combining chopped fresh vegetables like zucchini, spinach or shredded carrots with a dressing made from yogurt (a dairy product) gives a very healthy salad or sandwich filling. The dairy product, yogurt, helps complete the protein available in the bread.

Another lunch favorite of mine is to make a miniature pizza from half a whole-wheat hamburger bun, a little tomato sauce seasoned with Italian herbs, some sliced fresh vegetables like zucchini, green pepper, and tomato, and some grated cheese. I toast it all under the broiler until the cheese is bubbly. Great! And the cheese enhances the protein value of the bread.

## More Plant Sources of Protein

Seeds constitute another incomplete protein that combines well with grains or beans. Sesame seeds and sunflower seeds are two good examples.

Bean sprouts are like beans in terms of their protein content. Sprinkling them on salads and in sandwiches can increase the protein value of them.

There is another food which is made from soybeans. It's a little unusual and, while I don't usually go for strange "health-food" type concoctions, I kind of like this one. It's called tofu (pronounced toe-foo), and you find it in the fresh vegetable section of the grocery store in small plastic containers, packed in water. It's also sometimes referred to as soybean curd, and it looks like white cakes of some kind of cheese. It has almost no flavor of its own. But, like soybeans, it's loaded with protein. Combined with a grain, like rice, it can make a very nutritious meal. There is one recipe I learned while taking a natural foods cooking course that makes tofu very delicious. I've heard of many other recipes that weren't so delicious, and you may have, too. But if you want to be adventuresome, I recommend giving this one a try. It's marinated tofu broiled with a whole lot of fresh vegetables and served over brown rice. And it's become a favorite at our house. You'll find it in Part Four.

I hope I've given you some new ideas to try. In the next chapter I'll talk about two more food groups: dairy products and fats.

# 25

## *Dairy Products and Fats*

### *Scripture and Devotion*

Today we'll talk about both dairy products and fats. As I mentioned earlier, dairy products are good sources of protein but are also pretty high in fat. So I've decided to discuss them along with the food group, fats. But first the scripture for this chapter is John 8:31–32:

> ". . . If you continue in my word, you are truly my disciples,
> and you will know the truth, and the truth will make you free."

Of course, this scripture has a general application to more than just getting in shape, but when I think of it in relation to health, my thinking goes something like this. This scripture says to me that when I know the truth it can set me free. But this is apparently hard for me to accept, because I'd rather *not* know the truth—so that I can keep enjoying my favorite, though unhealthy, foods.

The truth about health and fitness seems to include what I've been saying in this book—that there are certain foods and ways of living which nurture and improve our health, and others which do not. And I must admit that most of the time I've been studying about this I've wished that what I was learning weren't true.

I've wished it weren't true that peanuts are so loaded with fat that they make a poor snack choice. I wish it weren't true that to lose weight I've got to limit the *amount* of food I eat—yes, even healthy food!—and get some exercise.

The scripture says that "the truth will make me free." If I believe that, then I have the chance to put what I know to be true into my life and to be free from these extra pounds, free from being so tired and catching so many colds, free from certain kinds of back pain.

I sit at my desk, writing this, knowing that after four years of work I have gained back three pounds. I've had to face some more truth once again as I am writing to you: I will not take these pounds off until I decide that weighing the correct amount is more important than my favorite foods.

This past weekend I met with a group of five women for a weekend retreat. Two of them were having a birthday in the coming week, so there was a delicious and healthy whole-wheat carrot cake with a no-sugar cream cheese icing. I ate a slice on Friday night and another one on Saturday. Today I'm facing the truth again—the truth that having a piece of Debbie's and Heidi's birthday cake, even if it's a healthy kind of cake, is more important to me than losing weight.

I believe that when I really know the truth, the next step is to be able to allow it to make me free to lose the weight. In the meantime, as I behave in ways that are the opposite of the truth I'm learning, I will not be free of this weight.

So this passage as I've related it to my health is a message of hope, and yet of responsibility. I have the means with which to become healthy, but I have the responsibility to learn the truth, believe it, and act upon it. And it is only through a relationship with Jesus Christ that I can begin to do this. That seems to be the *only* way it works for me.

DEAR LORD, thank you for your willingness to let me choose how I will live my life. I know that you make truth available to me, if only I will look at it, believe it, and act upon it. Forgive me when I behave as if I don't believe what is true, or as if I don't respect the truth enough to do the things I know I should do. Help me want to begin to try harder to learn about my body and about the foods you provided for its care.

I want to be free, Lord, free to do your will and to live as long as you want me to. I shall try hard to learn the truth, with your help, and to believe that eventually it will really make me free. In Jesus' name, AMEN.

## *DAIRY PRODUCTS: MILK, CHEESE*

The food group dairy products includes milk, cheese, yogurt, and cottage cheese. These foods give us protein, calcium, and riboflavin, a B vitamin.

## Calcium

Milk is a valuable source of calcium, which is important for having strong bones and teeth. According to *The Houstonian Preventive Medicine Center's Nutritional Advice* booklet, adults need about 800 milligrams of calcium daily, and this can be obtained from only two cups of milk. Teenagers and pregnant women, or women who are nursing babies, need more like 1200 milligrams of calcium, or three cups of milk.[1] But calcium is also available in other foods such as soybeans, sardines, salmon, peanuts, sunflower seeds, dried beans, and many green vegetables. So it's not necessary to drink two cups of milk every day to ensure that you get enough calcium.

## Fat Content

Because dairy products have so much fat in them, it is recommended that all people, whether overweight or not, eat only lowfat dairy products. Our systems just don't need to put up with all that fat.

Whole milk is 3.5% to 4% milkfat. Milk that has been reduced to 2% is not that much better in terms of fat content. So when I refer to lowfat milk, I mean milk which has had the milkfat reduced to 1% or less. Other kinds of milk that are good choices are skim milk, buttermilk made from skim milk, nonfat dry milk, evaporated skim milk, and lowfat *plain* yogurt made with skim milk. (Incidentally, plain yogurt can be flavored with vanilla extract, almond extract, or spices like cinnamon and nutmeg and is very tasty.)

Cheeses are very high in fat, with some being as high as 50%.[2] These regular, high-fat cheeses should be limited to one or two ounces a week. There are some new lowfat cheeses on the market now which are quite good. Some I like are Danalette (by Otto Roth), Laughing Cow reduced-calories variety (Green Label), and Nutrend (by Vantage Foods/Merrywood Farms). Sometimes I can find these in rare-foods stores and health-food stores by asking for them by name.

If you look at the food list on page 311 of this book, you'll notice that some dairy products are very high in fat. Learning to do without these is really the best approach. When people read sour cream on that list, I often hear moans of protest. If you love sour cream on your baked potato, you might be interested in the recipe for a sour cream substitute given in Part Four. We've tried it on baked potatoes and

---

1. Elizabeth Manis, R. D., compiler and Mary Pat O'Malley, editor, *The Houstonian Preventive Medicine Center's Nutritional Advice* (Houston, TX: The Houstonian Preventive Medicine Center, 1979), 13.
2. Ibid., 47.

think it's quite tasty. In fact, I've served it at two dinner parties at which my guests were people with very sensitive "diet food" detectors. And they never realized it wasn't real sour cream until after dinner, when I told them!

## Nondairy Products

When we first started working to lower Keith's cholesterol, I looked around at the nondairy substitutes, especially the coffee creamers. Using a nondairy creamer instead of real cream in coffee seemed like a good idea. But then I learned that many nondairy products are made with coconut oil, palm kernel oil, or some kind of saturated fats, which are all high-cholesterol, high-fat items. When these fats are listed on the labels, they're called "hydrogenated" fat. A few nondairy coffee cream substitutes are made from soybean oil, however, which is a polyunsaturated fat. So I began to look for "soybean oil" as the main ingredient on the labels of these products.

## FATS

A misconception I've always had is that if I avoid eating fats, I can keep from *getting* fat. But I've learned that I don't have to eat fats to acquire body fat. *Any* food I eat that isn't used for energy or repair work is stored by the body as two things: glycogen and fat. Glycogen is my energy reserve, because it can be quickly converted to glucose, which is what "burns" and gives me energy. I have about a pound or less of that around for emergencies. The rest of the excess is stored in fat cells as fat. It can be converted to glycogen, which then becomes glucose and is used for fuel, provided I get through burning up that one pound of glycogen that's already in reserve.

The point is, avoiding dietary fats completely won't keep me from getting fat, because my body can make fat from carbohydrates and protein just fine. I can be assured of having some body fat around even though I cut out fats completely. In other words, I can create body fat from any excess food, not just fatty foods. Nonfat foods like carbohydrates and proteins don't just pass through my digestive system and out again if I eat too much of them. They get stored up as fat! Only the nonessential, non-digestible part of foods and the residue from burned fat get flushed out of my system.

With all this emphasis on getting rid of body fat, one would think that the more body fat we can eliminate, the better. But a certain amount of fat on our bodies is necessary for health and has good uses. It is a good insulation against cold; it supports the internal organs and cushions them against possible injury; and fat deposits in our muscles provide the muscle with a readily available source of energy. And the presence of body fat in women's bodies helps regulate the sex-hormone balance and menstrual cycle.

The trick is to get to the right *ratio* of body fat to muscle tissue, not to eliminate all body fat. Even the leanest female Olympic athlete still has about 7% body fat! And as I said earlier in this book, a healthy percentage of body fat for women is 22% and for men is 19%.

Of course, cutting out fats completely is next to impossible. And to be healthy, we need to eat a tiny amount. The formula I mentioned for a healthy distribution of fats says that 30% of our calories should be fats. That sounds like a big percentage—more than one fourth! But remember that small packages of fat contain high amounts of calories. I can get all the calories I need in one day from a little less than two tablespoons of corn oil. Thirty percent of 1,950 calories is 585. A tablespoon of corn oil has 360 calories, so my total fat intake could consist of about 1⅔ tablespoons (5 teaspoons) of corn oil—hardly enough to decently cover one salad! (That's why good low-oil or no-oil salad dressing recipes mean so much to me.)

But now that we've talked about the importance of having the right amount of body fat, and about where body fat comes from, let's switch now to talking about the group of foods listed as "fats" in Part Three. Some of these are better for our health than others, and since the amount of fat foods we can eat is so small, it's important to know the difference.

## Cholesterol Levels in the Blood

One of the most common contributors to heart disease, heart attack, and the need for bypass surgery is the clogging up of our arteries by a fatty substance known as cholesterol. Actually, there are two kinds of cholesterol. One contributes to heart problems, as I've mentioned. The other, called HDL cholesterol, is a "good" kind of cholesterol. It helps to wash away the other kind and to keep the blood flowing smoothly through the arteries and heart.

One type of fat, called saturated fat, is believed to *raise* the unhealthy cholesterol level, while another kind, polyunsaturated fat, can help the body make HDL cholesterol, which *lowers* the level of bad cholesterol. Therefore, if one's cholesterol levels are above the safety levels recommended by preventive medicine doctors, one should eat what little fat is allowed from the foods which contain polyunsaturated fats.

Preventive medicine doctors have studied research data showing at what cholesterol levels heart attacks and strokes occur. Their recommendations for healthy cholesterol levels are much lower than what most other doctors recommend. A person can have a cholesterol level of 250 and be told by some doctors that it's in the moderate range, "so keep an eye on it." But the preventive medicine doctors like to see cholesterol levels at or below 200.

When Keith had his first preventive medicine physical three years ago, his cholesterol level was 249. The doctors recommended that he lower it. After one year of changing the way we ate and doing aerobic exercises, his level was down to 221, and after the second year it was 209. He had lowered it by 40 points in two years by following the advice of these doctors—exercising and changing his diet.

Women seem to be protected by nature from getting higher cholesterol levels during childbearing years. But after menopause, many women find that their cholesterol levels shoot up to equal or pass those of men unless they take the same precautions. Therefore, changing your eating and exercising habits as early as possible might help you avoid this sudden rise.

## Which Fats Come in Which Foods?

Part of the problem is to learn to tell which foods have which kind of fat in them. As I studied and talked to nutritionists, I learned a basic way to tell the difference between the "good" and the "bad" fats. I mentioned in an earlier chapter that saturated fats are solid at room temperature—for instance shortening, butter, the fat on roasts, and so on. Polyunsaturated fats are liquid at room temperature and include corn oil and safflower oil (but not palm oil or coconut oil).

Even the liquid oils vary in the amount of polyunsaturated fats they contain—called their P.S. ratio. The best oils have a P.S. ratio of 5 or higher, and there's a list of them on the food list in Part Three with the best oils being first on the list.

There are other fats which have a lower P.S. ratio—1 to 5. These are still recommended over foods containing saturated fats, and there's a list of them in Part Three, too (p. 314).

## Choosing Margarine

The best kind of margarine to buy is tub margarine, either regular or diet, which lists liquid safflower, sunflower, corn, or soybean oil as the first ingredient. The important word to look for is "liquid." Some tub margarines and diet margarines list other things, like "partially hydrogenated" oil, as the first ingredient. The word "hydrogenated" means the oil is solid at room temperature; these solid oils are the same ones used in stick margarine to make it stay in stick form. But there are some brands which list a liquid oil first. Reading the label will tell you which brands to buy.

The serving sizes for all these foods are very small. One teaspoon is a serving of most oils. The servings for other foods are accordingly tiny—one-eighth of an avocado, ten peanuts, seven almonds, or six pecan halves.

## Hidden Fats in Cooking

But just counting up your servings of fats like these isn't close enough. We've got to watch out for other fats that are hidden in our foods. When we use cooking oils, it's good to remember that the amount of fat used must be subtracted from our daily allowance. A way to allow for this is given in the food list.

Basically, the thing to remember is that only 30% of our daily calories should come from fat, and that lots of fat calories come in small packages. Baking or broiling meats will cut a lot of fat out of our diets. And trying to completely eliminate saturated fats, the ones that are solid at room temperature, can keep our blood more clear of "bad" cholesterol.

That completes a look in some detail at each of the food groups. But there are other substances which affect our health, and one of them is water. I was surprised to learn that it can affect my health dramatically. And I'll tell you more about it in the next chapter.

# 26

## *Cleansing the Body from the Inside*

### *Scripture and Devotion*

In this chapter we're going to talk about the value of water to our health. But first, our scripture is Proverbs 3:5–8:

> "Trust in the Lord with all your heart, and do not rely on your own insight. In all your ways acknowledge him, and he will make straight your paths. Be not wise in your own eyes: fear the Lord, and turn away from evil. It will be healing to your flesh and refreshment to your bones."

I've mentioned how many times I've tried to rely on my own insight and strength and how I have to keep running back to God over and over with my frustration and failure. But I'd never known anybody to write about why this might happen until I read *The Southampton Diet,* by Dr. Stuart Berger.

Dr. Berger gave a warning in one of his chapters about an emotional danger that comes with dieting. He said that after we've been on a diet for a week or so and we've lost some weight, we'll probably start feeling pretty cocky. We'll feel like we're really in control of getting good results and success. These feelings can lead us to start thinking things like, "I'm doing so well, I can afford to eat this one extra little piece of cheese," or "I think I'll add another slice of bread to my diet today. Surely it won't hurt." That's when it all starts to fall apart. And you know what? That's exactly what's happened to me many times, and it's usually the point at which I stop losing weight, even though I "think" I'm still dieting.

As a matter of fact, it seems that the closer I get to my goal, the more likely it is to happen. I start to think the momentum I've begun by losing weight will carry me on to my new weight goal without my having to stick to the diet. It's like pushing a grocery cart around the store, then assuming the momentum it built up from being pushed all over the grocery store will carry it through the checkout line! Most of the grocery carts I've ever seen have to be pushed constantly or they stop dead on their flat little wheels. And that's the way my weight-loss momentum seems to work.

Richard Foster, in his book, *Celebration of Discipline*, also talks about this cocky feeling. Foster points out that "the moment we feel we can succeed and attain victory over our sin by the strength of our own will alone is the moment we are worshipping the will."[1] Heini Arnold, in a book called *Freedom from Sinful Thoughts: Christ Alone Breaks the Curse*, also looks at this problem of attitude. He says, "As long as we think we can save ourselves by our own will power, we will only make the evil in us stronger than ever."[2]

So, after reading these things in the Bible and in these three books, and after thinking things over, I'm recommitting myself today as I write this to try to drop my cocky attitude and get back to work. I'm going to trust in the Lord more than I ever have and try to stop thinking I can handle this myself.

I keep thinking I can find a shortcut around what it takes to shape up my body. But now I know that one of the problems I have is in my head. And I believe the cure for the problem in my head is to let God change my attitude toward who is God around here.

DEAR LORD, I want the refreshment to my flesh and healing to my bones that is promised in this scripture. Help me to trust in you and to stop pretending that "I can handle it now, so you don't have to bother, God." *Please bother!* I need you.

Thank you that you can make my paths straight—straight past the refrigerator and out of the kitchen. In Jesus' name, AMEN.

## A Fountain of Youth—Any Old Fountain Will Do

One of the most amazing things to me about my health is what a difference I feel when I drink enough water. Sixty percent of each person's body is water. Water is needed for every kind of bodily function.

---

1. Richard J. Foster, *Celebration of Discipline: The Path to Spiritual Growth* (New York: Harper & Row, 1978), 4.
2. Heini Arnold, *Freedom from Sinful Thoughts: Christ Alone Breaks the Curse* (Rifton, NY: Plough Publishing House of the Hutterian Society of Brothers, 1973), 94.

One of the most important things water does is flush out waste materials, like the leftover wastes from burned calories and also the parts of foods that remain after digestion. The "poisons" (such as artificial preservatives, colors, and flavors, nicotine, and caffeine) that get into our systems from things we eat, drink or inhale are also flushed out with water. This happens not only through elimination, but also through sweating.

When I first started doing aerobic exercise, I noticed a strange thing. I couldn't sweat. I belonged to a health club at that time, and after exercise I would get in a hot whirlpool, then a dry sauna, then back in the hot whirlpool. Yet I still didn't sweat. My skin got wet from the whirlpool, but when I dried off, it stayed dry! I know that sweating is a vital, necessary function that cleanses the body and also cools it during exercise. I noticed that the other women around me could sweat just fine, and that my husband seemed to perspire for a long time after heavy exercise. I was surprised, and also worried, about my lack of perspiration.

Along with not sweating, I would feel an uncomfortable itching sensation on my skin, particularly on my upper legs. The muscles and fat were flabby and they jiggled a lot when I ran, and before I'd been running five minutes the itching was very irritating. It was so bad I considered giving up exercising. But instead I decided to change from running to swimming laps for a while.

One of the things the preventive medicine doctor told me was that it is important to drink at least eight cups of water (eight eight-ounce glasses) every day. I don't think I had ever drunk even two a day for most of my life.

So I decided to try it. A few days after I started keeping track of how much water I drank, I noticed that I could break into a light sweat when I exercised. And as the years have gone by, I have found that I can really get up a good sweat during a workout or a run. It's great!

I've also noticed that, thanks to water and fiber, I can throw the laxative bottle in the trash. And another thing I've found is that my skin doesn't itch when I run, and the skin on my face isn't quite so dry. Since I have oily skin, the dryness in the midst of the oily patches was hard to understand. But I know now that it was partly due to not drinking enough water.

Drinking water helps to improve other things, too, like fingernails, toenails, hair, and skin all over the body. I've always had brittle splitting nails, but now they can grow out better than they ever have.

At first, I kept forgetting to drink water until late in the evening. Then I would either have to drink four or five glasses right before bed (and we all know what that leads to!) or go to bed without having drunk enough water. So I started leaving an eight-ounce glass out beside the sink during the day. Every time I'd go by the sink in the kitchen and see that glass, I would be reminded to fill it up and drink. That helped a lot.

It's good to drink the water evenly spaced throughout the day. Some doctors recommend drinking most of it before 4:00 P.M. to avoid the multiple-trips-in-the-night problem. And besides, drinking it all at once can flood the system and cause vitamins and minerals to be rinsed out before they can be absorbed into the body.

One concern I had when I started drinking all this water was that it would add to a problem I already had now and then—water retention. But when I asked about it, I learned something interesting. Water is so vital for our survival that, if we *don't* drink enough of it each day, our bodies will "hold on to" the water they already have so it can do the most vital life-maintaining jobs in the blood, cells, and internal organs. Things like perspiration, elimination, and skin moisture have to take second place. In other words, not drinking enough water can *increase* the problem of water retention!

Later, I learned that when I feel those puffy knuckles and swollen ankles due to water retention, the best thing to do is to drink *more* water! I would have thought the opposite is true. But now I try to drink a steady amount of fresh water, and doing that helps alleviate the problem.

I also heard that drinking a mild tea brewed from fresh parsley and water can help relieve water retention. So I made the tea by boiling two or three sprigs of parsley in four or five cups of water, and I kept it in a pitcher in the refrigerator. I'd drink a little bit, like four to six ounces, once or twice during the day. The taste isn't so good, but it's mild, and you don't have to drink much to have a good effect. I noticed the effect by evening when I drank the tea in the morning after breakfast. And to me, a small drink with a slightly unpleasant taste was worth it!

Many women I've talked to avoid drinking water because they don't like having to make a lot of trips to the bathroom. But since going to the bathroom is the natural way of cleaning out our system, not going often enough seems to me almost like not sweeping out our house or dusting the furniture. Even though it is inconvenient, it's worth so much to my health that it's worth it to me!

## How Much Water Do We Need?

Drinking two to two-and-a-half quarts of water a day is very healthy. Don't count other liquids as part of the two quarts. Milk, coffee, tea, and soft drinks all contain other ingredients which affect the body's ability to utilize the fluid as water. Only water, herbal teas, and fruit juices fit the bill. And fruit juices contain calories—so watch out!

On the other hand, it's not good to drink too much water. Anything over two-and-a-half quarts might be too much, unless you're really dehydrated from being out working in the sun. I found that, if I wanted to, I could probably get a whole gallon of water down in one day by drinking a large glass every hour or so. But I later learned that after two-and-a-half quarts the water only washes out important nutrients before the body has a chance to absorb them. This can leave us with vitamin or mineral deficiencies.

So I started the habit of drinking water during the day, and was careful not to wash out the vitamins and minerals I was getting from food. But this raised a question in my mind: How many vitamins do I need, and am I getting enough?

# Week Nine
## (Three Days)

## *Aims and Activities*

(1) To continue with muscle-tone and aerobic workouts.

(2) To continue with your chosen food-group eating plan.

(3) To consider how you store and cook foods, looking for ways you can better preserve the vitamins and minerals in them.

(4) To read the labels of boxes and cans in your pantry, paying special attention to how often sugar and salt appear in the lists of ingredients.

(5) To begin experimenting with ways you can cut down on sugar and sodium. For a week or two, to try removing the sugar bowl and salt shaker from the table.

# 27

## *Vitamins and Minerals*

### Scripture and Devotion

In this chapter, we'll talk a little about vitamins and minerals and whether or not we should take vitamin supplements. But first, here is 1 Corinthians 6:13:

> "'Food is meant for the stomach and the stomach for food'—and God will destroy both one and the other. The body is not meant for immorality, but for the Lord, and the Lord for the body."

As I have set out to find out what foods will help me be healthy and which ones will not, I've realized an interesting thing about myself. My rational attitude towards food says that if I only eat what will make me healthy I'll conquer this weight problem. But I quickly lose my calm, rational approach when I realize that some of my favorite foods are not healthy!

My birthday was only a week away, and Keith asked me what I'd like to do to celebrate. I answered immediately, "Go out to eat someplace really fancy." My mental image of having a good time is to sit in a semidark restaurant enjoying plates of fragrant, steaming food soaked in rich sauces.

A friend in my exercise group said last week, "When I get to where I can do this whole tape without dropping out, I'm going to go get a candy bar!" And as I've said before, that's the way I am: I think of foods when I believe I deserve a reward for something.

Also, when I'm reading or working on a writing project, things seem to go better when I have a bowl of peanuts or a couple of slices of cheese to munch on. It's food for thought, I guess. And when I am depressed, I think that a peanut butter sandwich or a bowl of ice cream would cheer me up.

How many times have I told myself, "Go ahead and eat that cake. You *deserve* it." Now that I know what I know about the unhealthy effect of sugars and unrefined white flour on my health, how can I say I deserve to eat cake? When I think of it this way, it seems that I don't really like myself or that I want to *punish* myself for doing something bad. So I try to imagine saying to myself, "Go ahead and eat that rotten, moldy piece of meat. You deserve it!" And I have to laugh. The meat would not only taste bad; it could make me very ill. Yet I ignore the fact that the ingredients in a piece of cake can lead to poor health, too.

The scripture for today seems to be saying, "Food is for the stomach"—not for entertainment, reward, or comfort. It also says that my body isn't for immorality, but for the Lord. Although the kind of immorality Paul was talking about probably involved sexual promiscuity, I believe it could also include other kinds of carnal abuse such as consuming unhealthy foods, or eating too much food. Once again, I remember that the reason I should be in good health is so I can do what God wants me to do during my life.

My turning to food as comfort and reward is not, I believe, what God had in mind when he created food. My appetite was given to me so that I would eat what I needed to stay alive and healthy—but that's all. So, if I stop turning to food for reward or comfort, then to what can I turn? I think God wants me to turn to him for these things. By learning how to put God first in my priorities, I can begin to put food in its proper perspective.

There are times, though, when I feel I need something concrete to comfort me, reward me, or entertain me. Here are a few alternatives I have decided to try.

When I am disappointed, lonely, or depressed, I'm going to try a hot bubble bath and a good book. If it's early enough in the day, I might drive to a park where I can go for a walk. Or if I've just *got* to have something to eat or drink, I'll fix a tall glass of mineral water with ice and lime.

The next time I've done something really great that deserves a reward, I'm going to make an appointment for a manicure and/or a pedicure. Or I might make a long-distance telephone call to a friend I haven't talked to in a while. Or, instead of spending money on an expensive dinner, I might shop for something new to wear.

When it's time to be entertained, I'll try going to a good movie. Or maybe, just to be different, I'll take a trip to a museum or a zoo. Another thing I might do is go to a concert or play, and invite friends over for fresh strawberries and coffee (decaffeinated, of course!) afterward.

DEAR LORD, help me to learn how to manage food. Thank you that there are other healthy things to which I can turn for comfort, reward, and entertainment. And help me to turn to you for a reminder of this when I feel my old desires for food creeping up on me. I want you—not food—to be what I worship with my desires. Help me to change as time goes by, until I am free of these unhealthy habitual attitudes toward food. In Jesus' name, AMEN.

## Vitamins and Minerals in Our Food

Now let's talk about vitamins and minerals. If we lived on a farm and could control the kinds of soil, fertilizer, and insect repellant that were used on our foods, and if we could eat the foods the same day they were harvested, then we wouldn't have to worry about any kind of vitamin or mineral supplements.

In fact, most preventive medicine doctors say that we should try to get our vitamins from foods and not worry about vitamin tablets. That's the best way to give ourselves vitamins. Our bodies were designed to digest food and to sort out all the nutrients and send them to the right places.

But not all of us are in a position to get our food directly from the farm on a regular basis. So let's talk about some things we can do to make sure the food we get from the grocery store is as rich in vitamins and minerals as possible.

In the first place, choosing fresh fruits and vegetables instead of canned or frozen ones, and whole-wheat products and brown rice instead of the white, processed varieties, is a step toward getting more vitamins from food. And once we get these foods home from the market, we can store them in ways that help preserve their nutritional value.

The three main enemies of vitamins are heat, light, and air. After a vegetable or piece of fruit is picked, all three begin to rob it of its vitamins, so I try to be careful about how I store these foods. Since heat and light are bad for fresh vegetables and fruits, I keep them in the refrigerator where it is cool and dark. But air is also bad for them, so I try to keep them sealed somehow, either in a plastic bag tightly sealed or in a plastic dish with a snap-on lid.

Flours and cereals should be kept away from heat, light, and air too, but they don't need to be in the refrigerator. Keeping them on a low shelf in the kitchen, however, exposes them to less heat than they would get on a higher shelf, since heat rises. I like to keep mine at the counter level away from the stove. I've also bought some large jars with rubber rings around the lids for flour and other dry goods. I think this kind of jar seals out air and moisture better than just letting the flour sit on the shelf in its paper bag.

Certain cooking methods are better than others for retaining the vitamins and minerals in foods. Vegetables benefit from being lightly steamed (or eaten raw!) instead of boiled. (Steaming a vegetable means to cook it *above* boiling water. I use a little metal steamer basket inside my saucepan to keep the vegetable from soaking in the hot water while it's cooking. By "lightly steaming" I mean leaving the food slightly crunchy; some cooks call it "tender crisp.") Another good way to cook vegetables and protect the vitamins is to stir-fry them a very few minutes in a wok or skillet.

## Vitamin and Mineral Supplements?

All these things can be helpful when it comes to preserving vitamins and minerals in foods after we get them home from the grocery store. But since we can't control what happens to the food *before* it gets to the store, there is bound to be a certain loss of vitamins. For this reason, many people take some kind of vitamin supplement in tablet or capsule form.

To determine whether such a supplement is a good idea, I decided to take a look at the vitamin requirements of the human body. I bought three different vitamin books and started doing a comparative study. I made a list of every vitamin and mineral I could find and noted the quantities recommended by each particular author. I was shocked at the wide range of recommendations I found in these three books. So I made note of the *range* of amounts of vitamins recommended by my three sources and tried to come to my own conclusions.

I think each person will have to come to some kind of decision based on what she or he feels is the right amount. I certainly don't think people who are conscious of what kind of foods they eat and how the foods are cooked need to take megadoses of vitamins. But at the same time, it might be a good idea to take a well-balanced vitamin supplement.

But before you choose a vitamin, be aware that it is possible to take too much of a few vitamins. Most vitamins are water soluble, which means that they dissolve in water. These vitamins pass through our digestive system and the body absorbs what it needs. Then any extra amount passes right on out and causes no harm.

But a few vitamins are not water soluble, but rather fat soluble, so they are like a coating of grease on the side of a pan. You know how hard it is to rinse that grease off the pan with just plain water. In the same way, the extra amounts of fat-soluble vitamins which the body does not absorb and use are not washed out of our systems. So if we take too much, the fat-soluble vitamins not absorbed by the body build up. The intake of the four fat-soluble vitamins, vitamins A, D, E, and K, should be monitored carefully.

Again, eating a sound, nutritious diet will provide you with vitamins and minerals in a form our bodies can absorb much more easily than they can vitamins in tablet form. In fact, there is some question as to whether vitamins taken in tablet form can be absorbed at all before they are destroyed by the stomach's acid digestive juices. I prefer to take smaller doses of vitamin supplements and to eat balanced foods, rather than taking huge megadoses of vitamins.

There's one more fact about vitamins that you may want to consider if you're trying to lose some weight by cutting down on the number of calories you eat. As I mentioned in chapter 18, nutritionists stress that it is almost impossible to get the vitamins and minerals we need from food if we eat fewer than 1,000 calories. Since that's the most natural way for bodies to absorb vitamins, this is another good reason—besides the other reasons I mentioned before—to choose a sensible weight loss plan of 1,000 calories or more. If you have questions concerning whether vitamin supplements are right for you, check with your doctor.

As I studied about foods that can improve our health, I also became aware of some other substances that are often in foods and that can affect our health. Sugar, salt, and caffeine are three of them. I learned that a few things I struggled with, such as feeling too tired at times or too keyed up at other times, were related to them.

# 28

## *The Sweet Tooth Bites Back*

### Scripture and Devotion

I hope you're not too overwhelmed by all we've talked about so far. At the end of the book there's an entire chapter devoted in some detail to how I began to work all of this into my life. I think we are unrealistic when we think we can begin to change everything all around us in a week—or even in ten weeks! To begin with one area, to work on that area until the changes we make become routine, then to take a second area and work on it seems to me to be much more realistic. So hang in here with me until we finish up a few loose ends, then we'll tackle the problem of working this information into our lives.

The scripture for this chapter is Isaiah 55:2:

"Why do you spend your money for that which is not bread, and your labor for that which does not satisfy? Hearken diligently to me, and eat what is good, and delight yourself in fatness."

When I first read this I thought, "Oh boy, it says to 'delight yourself in fatness'! What could this mean?" But then I remembered from the story about Daniel that the word *fatness* has been used in this instance to mean "health." Then I chuckled at myself for the way I keep hoping for biblical approval for having a little extra fat. That shows just how irrational I can be when it comes to thinking about this problem.

One of my wishes when I was suffering through a semi-starvation diet years ago was, "I wish there were foods I could eat that would reduce weight, just like there are plenty of foods that increase weight." Since I love eating, I thought I'd do fine with a food like that. Then one day I was in the grocery-store checkout line and I saw one of those little mini-books on a rack by the counter. The title was *Foods That Melt Body Fat*. Needless to say, I grabbed it up and took it home.

It turns out that the foods these writers claim will "melt" body fat are foods that have very few calories, but that do provide valuable vitamins and protein. The book listed 30 of them, including asparagus, green beans, broccoli, cabbage, cucumbers, lettuce, mushrooms, radishes, and turnips. This little booklet turned out to be a nutshell version of the most basic philosophy of healthy eating I have read.

Now, I know, doctors know, and you know there are no foods that melt body fat. But the interesting thing is that what sold me that book in the first place was the hope that there really were foods like that. The claim on the back of the book was, "Yes, you will be able to eat, eat, and eat and remain slim and trim forever." But the little book seemed to be saying, like the author of Isaiah, "Eat what is good, and delight yourself in health!"

I saw a television program, part of the *Nova* series, called "Fat Chance in a Thin World." One mind-blowing fact which came out is that if we eat just one little pat of butter over our body's calorie limit every day, we could gain ten pounds a year! So my tiny little snacks of one tablespoon of peanut butter before bed could easily stop me from losing weight, or maybe even add some weight, even if I'm following a diet in every other way!

But God seems to be saying to me, "Listen . . . eat what is *good*. And be happy with the good health you'll get." And I'm beginning to find out how right he is. When I do what I know is right for me, I feel great.

> DEAR LORD, thank you that there are foods that don't create extra fat. Help me to learn how to enjoy these foods, and thank you that, at long last, I am really enjoying the things which are good for me. In Jesus' name, AMEN.

## Refined Sugar in Our Food

There are three common food additives that are creating numerous health problems in America. They are sugar, salt, and caffeine. Of these, sugar is by far the most popular one, and I'd like to talk about it in this chapter. In later chapters I'll talk about the other two.

Jane Brody says that we eat ten times more sugar than the other 2,600 or so food additives, except for salt, which is a distant second. The average American eats about 128 pounds of sugar a year, which is about a third of a pound every day. This means about 24% of our daily calories come from this food component, when the recommended percentage is only 10%.[1]

Also, more than two-thirds of the sugar we eat is added to our food by the food manufacturers; we only add about a third of it at home. There is sugar even in foods that aren't sweet—like ketchup, crackers, peanut butter, breading mixes, and salad dressings.

Sugar in foods goes by many names, such as fructose, dextrose, corn syrup, sweeteners, and honey. So a manufacturer can break down the sugar content into two or three groups and list them on the label in several places. But if you could actually add up all the sugar, it would be clear that sugar was a primary ingredient. So it's good to start paying attention to *all* the ingredients on the label and not just look for the word "sugar." There will be more detail about reading and interpreting what is on labels in chapter 31.

## Health Problems Linked to Sugar

The main medical problems caused by sugar are tooth decay and obesity. There is even some evidence that relates sugar consumption to hypoglycemia and heart disease, although the main culprits in the latter are cholesterol and dietary fats, as we discussed in the previous chapter.

But even if you don't have any of these problems you can still be affected by sugar. When we eat something sweet like a candy bar or a soft drink, all that sugar rushes into our bloodstream and we feel a lift of energy or even a slight high feeling. But then a few hours later, when all the sugar has been metabolized, our energy level drops and we feel tired, depressed, and irritable.

The cause for this seems to be that, as sugar doses send our blood-sugar levels shooting upward, our pancreas responds by sending out large supplies of insulin. This lowers the blood-sugar level again, sometimes to a lower level than it was before. If a person is genetically inclined toward diabetes, these sudden rises and drops in blood sugar can contribute to its onset, although I want to add that being overweight or consistently eating a high-calorie diet seems to bring diabetes on more often than occasionally eating a candy bar.

## What Good Is Sugar?

The main concern about sugar, I understand, is that it has *no* nutritional value, yet it has *a lot* of calories. The only effects it has on

---

1. Brody, *Jane Brody's Nutrition Book*, 119.

our bodies seem to be negative—tooth decay, obesity, and energy letdowns.

Many people believe that sugar is a quick source of energy. Well, that's true, but the only problem is that whatever energy we get also runs out quickly. And another important factor is that our bodies can make all the sugar they need for energy from other sources—complex carbohydrates—without the rapid burst of energy followed by the huge letdown.

The problem is that many of us are so accustomed to the sweet taste of sugar that we think we can't do without it. It's like an unnecessary habit, almost an addiction, from which it's hard to back off.

The healthiest approach to this problem, it seems, would be to cut out sugar altogether. The only thing it contains is calories, so we wouldn't be missing any vitamins or minerals.

## Are Other Sweets More Healthy?

Some people have turned to other sweet substances such as honey, raw sugar, brown sugar, fructose, and molasses to replace white sugar. Except for molasses, none of these has nutritional value. And they all react the same way in our bloodstream. Brown sugar is only white sugar colored with a little molasses. Fructose can help because it is almost two-and-a-half times sweeter than sugar, so you can get the same amount of sweetness for a third fewer calories.

Molasses is the liquid left over after the white crystals have been taken out of sugar cane or sugar beets. It has some minerals and B vitamins in it and is somewhat more nutritional than sugar. The darker the molasses, the more nutritious it is, and blackstrap molasses is the best.

I can already hear the question in your mind about artificial sweeteners. These have no nutritional value either, and they have few calories. For heavy sugar users, these might provide relief while learning to decrease the amount of sweets in the diet. But I want to tell you an interesting thing I learned from a book I've mentioned before, *The Dieter's Dilemma*, by William Bennett and Joel Gurin. I wrote earlier about the setpoint, and how there are three things which lower it. But there are also a couple of things which tend to raise our setpoint. One of these is the presence of sweet tastes in the diet. That includes artificial sweet tastes!

The experiments we have just described suggest that artificial sweeteners could make people still fatter, by driving up the setpoint. The more convincingly sweet and less artificial they taste (as is claimed for the new sweetener, aspartame), the more effectively they should stimulate users to fatten. . . . Enormous quantities of artificial sweeteners—the safety of which is at least doubtful—are consumed in this country, yet they have never been shown to accomplish what they are supposed to.[2]

So again, without meaning to be harsh, I would say the best approach to sugars is to cut them out completely. (Incidentally, another factor which influences a higher setpoint is a sedentary lifestyle.[3])

But there is still that old "sweet tooth" to satisfy, and there are some healthy alternatives to the unhealthy sweet things like candy, cakes, and pie. One thing to do is to get in the habit of serving fruit for dessert, preferably fresh fruit. If you do resort to canned or frozen fruit, be sure there is no sugar added to it. Another thing to do is learn to bake your own cakes, pies, or cookies using recipes in which the sugar is cut down to about a third of what you used to use. Using spices like cinnamon and extracts like vanilla can also help.

When we had taken the sugar bowl off our table for several weeks, we were fascinated to discover how we began tasting the natural sugar in fruits and cereals. Whereas before we had thought we "needed" extra sugar, now bananas and raisins on cereal tasted very sweet.

While we're talking about sweets, there are actually some desserts that are a more healthy choice than others, and I've included lists of them in the food-list section of Part Three (pp. 316–317). The main thing to remember is that, if you're trying to lose weight, there isn't room in a daily eating plan for the empty calories of sweets. But if your weight is down and you're using a maintenance plan, a dessert a day is acceptable. The foods we should try to avoid are the sweet foods with high-fat content such as ice cream, commercially baked pies, cookies and cakes, and deep-fried pies. But many things, including angel food cake, ice milk, and jams, jellies, and marmalades are acceptable on a maintenance plan.

## Helping Children Avoid Bad Habits

An important thing to think about if you're raising children is to try to avoid rewarding them with sweets. One afternoon a young mother in her early twenties came to visit us with her two-year-old.

---

2. Bennett and Gurin, *The Dieter's Dilemma*, 100.
3. Ibid, 248.

After half an hour the little girl got upset because her mother had to take a glass knickknack away from her, and she continued to cry and reach for it. Her mother pulled out a bottle of apple juice, which quieted her down. I thought that was a very healthful solution. But when the bottle was gone, the little girl got upset again, and the mother pulled out a cookie.

I could see the pattern that was likely to develop. The little girl was learning that if she wanted food—specifically cookies—she might be able to get them by crying. The cookies helped her mother keep her quiet while she visited with the other adults. But they probably didn't help the little girl's health very much, nor her tendency to see food as a reward for being good.

I have another friend who's discovered that her eight-year-old son becomes very energetic and agitated after eating sweets or drinks with red food coloring in them. So when he's at home he doesn't eat those. But every two weeks or so he goes to stay with his grandmother, who brings him back home complaining about how hard he is to discipline. My friend had asked her mother not to give him cookies or red drinks, but her mother had laughed off this request and ignored it.

Finally my friend said to her mother, "Don't complain to me about his behavior anymore. If you want him to behave, stop giving him those cookies and red drinks!" Her mother finally decided to try it on his next visit. And now my friend's son gets along a lot better with his grandmother.

# 29

## Saltaholism—A Newly Discovered Health Risk

### Scripture and Devotion

A second food additive (in addition to sugar) we've gotten carried away with is salt. But before we discuss how excess salt may affect our health, let's look at Philippians 3:13–16:

> "Brethren, I do not consider that I have made it my own; but one thing I do, forgetting what lies behind and straining forward to what lies ahead, I press on toward the goal for the prize of the upward call of God in Christ Jesus. Let those of us who are mature be thus minded; and if in anything you are otherwise minded, God will reveal that also to you. Only let us hold true to what we have attained."

As I sit here writing these last few chapters, I can't help but think back over the months I've spent compiling this book . . . and the months before that when I was beginning to learn about the kinds of eating and exercise that bring health and energy instead of illness and tiredness.

I remember my first talk with Dr. Cherry at the Houstonian and my feelings that I could not succeed with this kind of plan because of all my past failures. But when I read Paul's words in Philippians about "forgetting what lies behind and straining forward to what lies ahead," I realize my doubts were so large because I kept remembering how I had failed in the past. So now I try to keep my mind focused on what lies ahead.

This passage reminds me, when my weight is at or near my goal, to "press on toward the goal of the prize of the upward call of God in Christ Jesus," as Paul encourages us to do. The prize is a close relationship with Jesus Christ, and through this relationship we can continue to improve our health by using all we have learned as a way of living from now on.

Paul says he does not "consider that [he has] made it [his] own." And I realize, too, that I haven't done all the learning, habit changing, and improving I can do. In reality, I haven't quite made this way of living my own, although I have committed myself to it in my soul and mind. But through Jesus Christ I believe I can continue to find the strength, desire, and grace to continue to improve. Following Paul's example, I hope to press on.

From time to time there may creep into my way of thinking thoughts that lead me away from healthy living. These most often come to me in the form of influence from other people, who may wrinkle their noses and refer to my healthy meals as "rabbit food" without even knowing how delicious and appealing they are. Or these thoughts may come from an unusually hectic time in my schedule, like having the whole family home for Christmas, when my exercise time is filled by added responsibilities and I skip it. But my wish now is for God to reveal to me those thoughts leading away from health. Paul wrote to the Philippians, "If in anything you are otherwise minded . . . God will reveal that also to you." And when I ask him to, and he does . . . then I can get back on the track a lot faster.

> DEAR LORD, thank you that you are with me as I try to live for you. Help me to forget the failures which lie behind me and to strain forward to what lies ahead. Help me to hold true to what I've attained so far, and show me whenever my mind strays away from what you can teach me and help me to do. Be with me, and guide me in my life as I go forward. In Jesus' name, AMEN.

## Saltaholism—A Newly Discovered Health Risk

A food additive that has been under a lot of study lately is salt. Salt even made the front cover of *Time* magazine in March of 1982. *Time*'s article said that Americans eat, on the average, two to two-and-a-half teaspoons of salt a day.[1] That didn't seem so bad to me until I read that our bodies only need less than an eighth of a teaspoon each day. Our bodies need only 220 milligrams of salt a day, and there are 12,500 milligrams of salt in two-and-a-half teaspoons. Jane Brody reports that Americans eat from two to four teaspoons a day—a figure even higher than the *Time* magazine report.

---

1. Claudia Wallis, "Salt: A New Villain," reported by Patricia Delaney and Jeanne Saddler, *Time*, 15 March 1982, 64.

It is virtually impossible to eliminate enough salt from our diets to bring us down to the small amount our bodies need, 220 milligrams, but doctors suggest that even a daily intake of 3,000 to 5,000 milligrams, or three to five grams a day, is a much better level than most of us currently take in.

The main health problems to which salt contributes are water retention and high blood pressure (hypertension), which is a stealthy silent killer today.

## Salt Assaults the Taste Buds

What happens when we eat salt is that it creates a salty background taste in our saliva, which dulls our taste buds. With dull taste buds, we don't notice ordinary amounts of salt in our food, and so we add more. This tendency can keep building up until our natural ability to recognize salt is almost completely gone, and it takes more and more salt to satisfy our taste for it.

As you may have noticed, when you cut out salt, at first food tastes very dull. But gradually, over the months, our palates can become more sensitive again, and our taste buds can enjoy food with smaller amounts of salt or no salt at all.

From the figures I gave you at the beginning of this discussion, you've probably figured out that most of us run no risk of eating too little salt. Three to five grams a day is still a great deal more than our bodies need, and yet it's one-fourth to two-fifths less than what *Time* magazine reports we eat on the average.

There are some basic steps we can take to help reduce the amount of salt we eat. Removing the salt shaker from the table and experimenting with other seasonings is one step—the one most recommended by doctors and nutritionists. And avoiding high-sodium foods such as potato chips, salted peanuts, and pretzels is another.

## Beyond the Salt Shaker

The chemical name for salt is sodium chloride, and it's the sodium part of this formula that gives us all the problems. Just like sugar, salt is hidden in many foods today. In fact, according to the article I read in *Time* a lot of foods that taste *sweet* have salt in them. A single serving of instant chocolate pudding can have more sodium than a small bag of potato chips. And a scoop of cottage cheese has three times the sodium of a handful of salted peanuts. Soft drinks contain lots of sodium.

But our number-one source of salt is baked goods and cereals. So

to minimize the amount of sodium we get from this source, I've started trying to read the labels and to note the sodium content of these
foods. For example, when I buy cereal I try to buy varieties that have a
sodium level of less than 200 milligrams per one-half cup serving. I've
found only three or four which meet this standard. One cereal we've
come to love is shredded wheat, which has *nothing* in it but wheat—
no salt or sugar. As for other baked goods, whole-wheat breads are
about the only ones I buy any more.

A very helpful book I read about how to season foods with very
little salt was written by Craig Claiborne, the *New York Times* food
editor. He was ordered off salt by his doctor after he developed extremely high blood pressure. He's found that by experimenting with
herbs, condiments, and spices he can cook foods which taste delicious—without salt. His book is called *Craig Claiborne's Gourmet
Diet Book,* and is loaded with good ideas about saltless cooking. He
uses onions, garlic, peppers, dry mustard, lemon juice, and even
fruits. If you substitute like this, just be sure not to use garlic salt,
onion salt, celery salt, seasoned salt, soy sauce, MSG (monosodium
glutamate), Worchestershire sauce, hydrolyzed vegetable protein, or
bouillon cubes, since they're all loaded with sodium.

One little booklet I ordered is full of recipes using angostura aro-
matic bitters as a salt substitute. There was no charge for this booklet, and the address is given in Part Five of this book (p. 357).
Angostura bitters is a blend of spices and herbs first compounded in
1824 by Dr. Johann Siegert, Surgeon-General in the Army of Simon
Bolivar. He spent four years finding the exact combination of flavors
to improve the appetites of troops. Although it is often used to flavor
alcoholic drinks, there is no alcohol in the mixture at all, and only
small traces of sodium. It is named after the city of Angostura, Vene-
zuela, where the doctor had his headquarters.

The booklet shows how angostura bitters can be used in meat
loaf, gravy, white sauce, soup, fresh vegetables, salad dressings,
fresh fruit compotes, and even on grapefruit.

# Week Ten
**(Three Days)**

## Aims and Activities

(1)   To continue with your exercise program and eating plan.

(2)   If you drink a lot of coffee or tea, to try experimenting with decaffeinated varieties and herbal teas.

(3)   To go on a label-reading trip to the grocery store, looking for healthy substitutes for unhealthy favorites.

(4)   To use the time map given in Part Five to help you draw up a schedule that helps you work your exercise program and eating plan into your life.

# 30

## *Caffeine—Approach with Caution*

### *Scripture and Devotion*

One thing that has helped me stick to my fitness program has been having someone to share it with me. Not only is it good company, but it makes me accountable to someone else for what I do. This passage in Hebrews illustrates this idea. It's Hebrews 12:1—2:

> "Therefore, since we are surrounded by so great a cloud of witnesses, let us also lay aside every weight, and sin which clings so closely, and let us run with perseverance the race that is set before us."

Sigmund Freud said that we have "people" in our subconscious minds who reach up and try to control our behavior. These people in our minds can often be the grownups we remember from our childhood—like our parents, schoolteachers or grandparents. They tell us things like, "You'll always be fat. You can't lose weight. Look at the rest of us. We're fat, too," or other, similar things.

But the late Carlisle Marney used a different image to describe what we Christians can be for each other while learning to live the Christian life. Take a minute to imagine that the room you are in as you read this is your mind. Along the wall to the right there is a balcony filled with people, living or dead, who love you and/or inspire you to do your best. Dr. Marney called these people in our minds "balcony people," and whenever we're out somewhere by ourselves and are struggling to do what we know is right we can imagine those people cheering us on, saying "Go on, you can do it! You can do those sit-ups and walk those miles. I know you can!"

Among my balcony people are my husband, Keith, my friend Heidi, my junior-high-school gym teacher, that doctor at the Preventive Medicine Center, Bobbie and Judy, Cathy, Thomas à Kempis,

Richard Foster, Debi, and some other people who are members of the prayer support group to which I belong. There may be people in your exercise class or in your family who can be balcony people for you.

When I read this passage from Hebrews, "since we are surrounded by so great a cloud of witnesses," I realize that my balcony people are like the cloud of witnesses to which Paul refers and can help inspire me to do my best. When I'm in a restaurant about to order dinner, thinking of these people being proud of me for ordering the best thing helps me do so. When I don't feel like running, I imagine having a slow run and a good talk with one of my balcony people, and I find the strength to get out and exercise.

Paul's suggestion that we "lay aside every weight, and sin which clings so closely" brings to mind an obvious image of extra pounds. But another thought I've had is that when I'm overweight I usually feel too embarrassed to put on a leotard or running shorts. This feeling keeps me from exercise. So in one sense, I am "laying aside weights and sins" when I refuse to let my embarrassment keep me from doing the things that will bring me health.

> DEAR LORD, I want to begin to lay aside every weight and sin and to live my life for you. Thank you that there is a great cloud of witnesses available to inspire and support me. Help me learn to be a good support for my friends as well. Teach me to do what is best for me, and to learn to love others and support them, too. In Jesus' name, AMEN.

## The Caffeine Kick

The last thing on my list of problem substances is caffeine. The coffee habit has become almost a national pastime. Coffee is a wonderful drink because it's warm and has no calories. But caffeine is actually a drug. In small, ordinary amounts, such as two cups a day, caffeine can have beneficial effects. It often increases mental and physical efficiency and makes our attention spans longer.[1]

But the danger of caffeine is that of any drug. People can become dependent on it, and caffeine in large doses has some unhealthy side effects such as jittery hands, heart palpitations, and irregular heartbeats.

There has been a lot of controversy over the dangers of caffeine,

---

1. Brody, *Jane Brody's Nutrition Book*, 240.

and the most current reports I've read indicate that it's not as bad as was once thought. But people who are heavy coffee drinkers find that when they try to stop they experience painful withdrawal symptoms such as headache, drowsiness, lack of energy, yawning, nervousness, and mental depression. So if you want to break your caffeine habit without going through all this, it's recommended by some doctors that you cut back one cup a day until you are totally off caffeine.

One thing that is interesting to me is that caffeine is suspected to aggravate a benign condition of the breast called fibrocystic disease. Two years ago I was diagnosed as having this condition when I discovered a lump which had to be removed. The lump turned out to be an ordinary cyst wrapped in some fibrous tissue. Two doctors recommended that I stay away from caffeine, which I did. When I had my final checkup six months after the surgery, the surgeon said, "That's the most normal breast check you've had so far!" And even now, a year and a half later, my new doctor in my new town finds few fibrous growths. Jane Brody reports a study which showed similar results in other women.[2] While the medical evidence is not conclusive, the testimonies of many women seem to indicate that there may be a link between caffeine consumption and fibrocystic disease.

Caffeine is found in other foods besides coffee. Chocolate and tea have caffeine in them. And soft drinks that are dark in color, like Pepsi, Coke, and Dr. Pepper, include caffeine. Some root beers use caffeine and others do not. Reading the label provides the right information. And now there are caffeine-free versions of many of these dark-colored soft drinks on the market.

## Decaffeinated Coffee and Coffee Substitutes

There has been some concern over the safety of decaffeinated coffees because of the chemicals used in removing caffeine. But most companies have switched from harmful chemicals to others which leave no harmful residue in the coffee. There are some more expensive decaffeinated coffee beans and ground coffees that have the caffeine removed by a steam process developed in Switzerland.[3]

Other substitutes for coffee are two grain-based drinks: Postum, made from bran, wheat, and molasses; and Pero, made from barley, rye, chicory, and beets. Both of these have only a few calories per cup, and come in a powdered form similar to instant coffee.

---

2. Ibid., 242.
3. Ibid., 244.

## What about Herbal Teas?

In trying to avoid caffeine, many Americans are enjoying herbal teas. And while herbal teas are now becoming popular, some doctors and pharmacologists are concerned. Over half our prescription drugs come from plants and can have unpleasant and even fatal side effects. So don't automatically assume that because herbal teas are made from plants (herbs), they are all safe and harmless. And some concoctions sold under the name of "herbal teas" may not be made solely from plants, but may contain chemicals with potentially harmful side effects. Most herb teas, however, when drunk in moderation, cause no harmful effects in otherwise healthy people. Still, they should not be considered a food, but a drug. And they should not be drunk like water. Enjoying a weak cup or two in a day is not harmful. But it's best to be careful about choosing herbal teas, and read labels.

I've learned that it is relatively safe to buy herbal teas made by major companies like Lipton, Celestial Seasonings, Morning Sun, Bigelow, and others. The ones to watch out for are the loose-pack teas in unmarked jars from which you serve yourself.

When I began to understand how all these things might work together to create conditions of health, I wanted to learn what to eat to replace some of my unhealthy snack foods. Also, I needed to learn a little bit about what's on the labels of foods in the grocery store and how to choose better foods based on the information given on those labels. So we'll go on with our study by talking about those two subjects next.

# 31

## *Better Food Choices*

### *Scripture and Devotion*

Today we're going to talk about some healthy alternatives to popular but unhealthy foods, and also about reading labels in the grocery stores. But first, here is the scripture for this chapter, Luke 11:24–26:

> " 'When the unclean spirit has gone out of a man, he passes through waterless places seeking rest; and finding none he says, "I will return to my house from which I came." And when he comes he finds it swept and put in order. Then he goes and brings seven other spirits more evil than himself, and they enter and dwell there; and the last state of that man becomes worse than the first.' "

When thinking about this passage, I compare my former unhealthy habits to an unclean spirit. My attempts to change some of them are like throwing the unclean spirit out of my mind, heart, and body. I find that if I don't replace that habit with a good habit or fill up the place left by its absence, then several other habits, just as bad or worse, may develop.

For example, I want to stop thinking about food so much. But it's hard to turn off my mind after all these years of planning, denying, wishing, giving in, and dreaming. I need to replace those thoughts with new things to think about.

One way I approach this is to stay so busy that I don't have any free time to think *at all.* But that usually ends up exhausting me and seems to be only running away from the problem instead of facing it. Besides, I've learned that getting too busy can quickly lead me back into compulsive behaviors.

Another way of looking at the situation is to realize that, before I can cut out bad food choices, desserts, fried foods, and junk food, and really be able to do without them, I need to have substitutes to turn to for the times when I usually enjoy these unhealthy foods. Instead of cakes or ice cream for dessert, I try to have fresh fruit. Instead of corn chips and dips, I'll have fresh vegetables and lowfat dip. Instead of frying chicken, I've learned some new recipes for cooking it in my crockpot, or for marinating the chicken and then baking it.

By planning and trying out other choices that are healthy and also taste good, I can fill the gap left by not doing old recipes. When I have these new recipes handy, and I've tried them so I know they're good, I stand a much better chance of making a change.

Apparently it's a normal human problem to need to put something in place of things we've cut out of our daily lives, because this parable seems to be saying that throwing out something bad and not replacing it with something good leaves us vulnerable to being filled with the original bad thing—plus more!

> DEAR LORD, I admit it. I don't want to give up some of my favorite things, even though I know they can lead me to bad health. I ask you to come into my mind and soul and fill me with your love and assurance that you will be there for me. Help me know what healthful alternatives I can have to replace my unhealthy habits. And help me not to let my grief and anger over giving up these things get in the way of being able to let the love of them go and learning to love healthy foods.
>
> Be with people who read this book as they begin to discover their own healthful alternatives and to replace the unhealthy foods with good, wholesome ones. Help them as they guide their families in these changes. And thank you again that you are there to support us. In Jesus' name, AMEN.

## Cracking the Code on the Labels

By the time I became aware of the potential for damaging my health by eating sugar, too much salt, and caffeine, I had already become very fond of certain "bad" foods. Coffee, Christmas candy, carbonated drinks, and chips and dips were a few of the things on my list that I realized had some pretty unhealthy consequences.

Also, having decided to try to improve my choices at the grocery store, buying whole-wheat bread, margarine made with polyunsaturates, and high fiber cereals, I wanted to make sure I was getting the best kinds. So I began trying to read labels.

The federal government requires that manufacturers list certain ingredients on the labels. These are listed in descending order of prominence. That means that the first ingredient on the label has the largest percentage of the total, the second has the next largest and so on.

## A General Way to Look at Healthy Food Choices

In the grocery store, foods can be put into two categories: whole foods and processed foods. Here's what I mean by each of those words:

(1) *Whole foods* are free of chemical additives, artificial flavors, or artificial colors. They are usually left in a whole, raw, unrefined state or processed as little as possible to make them edible. Some whole foods are apples, raw spinach, potatoes, and bananas.

(2) *Processed foods* have been treated in some way—refined, cooked, and/or blended with other foods. Chemicals are usually added to processed foods, although in some cases they aren't necessary. And the preparation and handling usually destroys many of the nutrients which were in the foods before processing. Frozen and canned foods are processed foods, as well as mixes, quick dinners, boxed and packaged foods.[1]

As you have probably guessed, whole foods are the most nutritious, having the most vitamins, minerals and fiber. I try to buy whole foods like fresh fruits and vegetables, dried beans, whole-grain brown rice, etc. In fact, a friend who has studied healthy eating for a long time once gave me what I think is some great advice: "Shop around the edges of the store and stay away from the middle." The edges are usually where the produce, dairy and meat products, or whole foods are. The middle is usually where the processed foods are.

## Healthy Alternatives to Popular Snacks

*The Supermarket Handbook*, by Nikki and David Goldbeck, gave me some good information about how to make wiser choices in the grocery store. The book was first published in the seventies, and

---

1. Nikki and David Goldbeck, *The Supermarket Handbook*, rev. ed. (New York: Signet Books, 1976), 148.

contains a lot of warnings about additives that were used then but have now been banned. And the Food and Drug Administration has been doing a lot in the last 15 to 20 years to eliminate additives and chemicals as they were discovered to be harmful. But the rest of the book is helpful because it also gives healthy alternatives to popular unhealthy foods like candy, soft drinks, and chips.

## Candy

For example, the authors reminded me that dried fruits were the sweets of the day in biblical times—before Milky Way and Snickers came along. Dates, raisins, figs, and other dried fruits which have been sun-dried *without* being dipped in sulphur dioxide, and which have no added preservatives and sweeteners, make delicious and healthy snacks and can satisfy our craving for sweets. (Check the package label to find out if sulphur dioxide, preservatives, or sweeteners have been used.)

## Soft Drinks

Instead of soft drinks, I try to have natural fruit juices, especially ones with no added sugar or preservatives. Apple juice (unfiltered or filtered); freshly squeezed or frozen orange juice; grape juice; pineapple, prune, and tomato juices are all good suggestions. Drinking them diluted with water reduces the number of calories without taking away the refreshing, sweet taste. The frozen concentrates have higher vitamin contents than canned juices because, according to the Goldbecks, the heat required for canning kills off many vitamins.

Fruit juices have calories, however. So if you're trying to keep your calories down, I recommend plain iced water, mineral water, or herb tea—iced or hot. I've had a lot of fun experimenting with herb teas. I buy the boxes of loose-pack tea leaves (not tea bags) and brew the tea right in my drip coffee maker. As I said in the previous chapter, be sure to choose herb teas carefully and not drink large amounts. In moderation they are very good.

## Chips

Now let's talk about alternatives to chips. The process by which corn chips, potato chips, and tortilla chips are made includes adding saturated fats. So instead of these, when I want a crunchy salty snack, I use popcorn, popped in a little oil or melted margarine. (Hot-air poppers or microwave poppers, both of which work without fat, are also available.) Roasted nuts and seeds are healthy. While nuts and seeds have fat in them, it is the polyunsaturated kind, which is better for our health. All fats have calories, though. So if you're watching your weight, fresh raw vegetables and occasionally a little fruit really make a better snack.

## Soups

Canned soups are a quick and easy lunch treat, but precooked food from a can has lost most of its nutrients. There are many ways to make homemade soups that are healthy and nutritious. Some are elaborate and time consuming, but others are quick and simple. Making up a big batch and freezing it or using it over several days can be as efficient as—and much more healthy than—opening a can of soup.

I have a friend who saves leftover steamed vegetables from each dinner. Then, when there is enough, she runs them through the blender and heats the liquid in her microwave: delicious creamed vegetable soup! Another thing to do is to take all the little scraps on the counter after you make a tossed salad—the little bits of tomato, onion, lettuce, and so on—and put them in a plastic bag kept in the refrigerator. These can be dumped into chicken broth with a little rice to make a great rice/vegetable soup. Just be sure to use them every three or four days, before they get soggy and rotten.

## My Choices Can Make a Difference in the Food Market

I have noticed that it isn't as easy to find wholesome foods in the supermarket as it was just to grab the quick and easy boxed mixes and canned vegetables that I used to combine to make tasty casseroles. So I sometimes imagine what it will be like when more and more people become convinced that life will be better if we stop eating "fast foods," "junk foods," and rich sauces served to us by the food industry, both restaurants and supermarkets. If more and more people refuse to buy these unhealthy foods and turn toward whole, natural foods, then in a free enterprise system like ours the food industry will have to change to meet that demand and to survive.

Already in the last three years I've seen improvements. I have bought whole-wheat flour and bran flakes on the shelves of some supermarkets—not just in health-food stores. There are fairly good brands of whole-wheat breads and frozen orange juices *with the pulp left in*, as well as lowfat milk, cottage cheese, yogurt, and margarine. Soft drink companies are making caffeine-free and sugar-free versions of their original best sellers. I've seen syrup for pancakes with one-third less calories. Fresh fruit and vegetables are becoming more available than ever before. And the Kiplinger editors, who report on trends in the business world, commented recently that the "lite" version of prepared frozen ("TV") dinners has helped improve the sagging market for frozen prepared dinners.

Of course, it's obvious that right now some of these healthy things cost more than the unhealthy counterparts. But I think that's probably due to at least two things. One is that foods in their natural state don't have the additives and preservatives, so they have a shorter shelf life; more of the food spoils before it can be sold. The reason those additives were put in foods in the first place was so food wouldn't spoil when it was shipped long distances or stocked on supermarket shelves or in our own pantries for long periods of time. When a store stocks whole, unprocessed foods, we can't expect these foods to have the same long period of storage time. So I buy only enough fresh vegetables and fruits to last three or four days. That way I can have fresh foods on the table instead of buying too much and having some of it lose its crispness—which means I have to figure out how to disguise old, limp cabbage in some kind of mystery casserole.

The second reason I think fresh foods and wholesome things like whole-wheat hamburger buns, good lowfat cheese, and decaffeinated coffees cost more right now is that the demand for these products is not yet large enough to allow the manufacturers to move a big enough volume, which would keep prices lower. Both of these factors, and probably some others, make these items cost more. But I'm convinced that as we continue to vote "yes" to the manufacturers and distributors of wholesome foods—by buying their brands—and "no" to the makers of unhealthy junk foods and foods loaded with artificial nonfood items—by not buying them—the costs of the more healthful foods will drop.

In the meantime, as far as my food budget goes, I've found that as I've cut down on expensive red meats and tried meatless meals for one or two days a week, I've saved money. Also, prepared foods (like macaroni and cheese in a box to which you just add milk or water and serve!) are more expensive than ones I make from scratch (buying a bag of macaroni and a package of cheese).

So making the switch has sometimes cost us a little more, but hasn't run our food budget up as high as I was afraid it would. A meal of brown rice, pinto beans, steamed squash, tossed salad, and a whole wheat roll is really quite inexpensive.

Well, needless to say, there are many, many approaches to beginning to make the changes necessary to move toward good health. Both exercise and nutrition are important to weight control, lowering the risk of heart disease and cancer, and improving health in general. And I didn't manage to get all these areas of my life changed in a month or even six months. It's been a four-year study so far, and I'm still finding areas in which I can improve. So the next chapter is about how to fit these new things into one's schedule. I think it's important to take these changes one at a time until they are gradually worked into one's life.

# 32

## *Making Time for It All*

### *Scripture and Devotion*

As we close this study of exercise and nutrition, let's look at one last scripture, which is 2 Corinthians 4:7–9:

> "But we have this treasure in earthen vessels, to show that the transcendent power belongs to God and not to us. We are afflicted in every way, but not crushed; perplexed, but not driven to despair; persecuted, but not forsaken; struck down, but not destroyed."

This scripture seems to speak to me about the overwhelming task of fitting into my life everything that I know is good for me. A quiet time with God, time to exercise, time to plan healthy meals, and time to do all the other things involved with living—the chores, church meetings, work, cleaning, time with my family and friends.

With this reminder that the power to overcome the battle with the clock belongs to God and not to us, I have hope. There have been many days when I felt perplexed, and even driven close to despair. But when I remember to trust God with the outcome and to take each thing one step at a time, things usually work out.

One way I seem to make my life more complex than it has to be is by expecting myself to be able to work all of this out in a few days or weeks. When I can't manage to do that, it seems like it's all too complicated. "Good grief!" I think. "Nobody could do all this." Well, that may be true. But I can do a little, and when that becomes easier I can add a little more.

To me it seems just like the way my muscles have improved with exercise. At first, I couldn't do all of the sit-ups or leg lifts on my exercise tape. But as I kept on working, I found that I could do a few more each time, until finally I could make it through the entire workout. As I kept on working out, before long the tape was easy, and my muscles needed a harder workout if I was going to improve them.

By the same token, I realize, at first I won't be able to make every single bite of food the most healthful that it could be. And I live with other people whose eating preferences must be considered. If the other people in my life want to change, too, then we can work together. Keith and I both wanted to change, so we agreed to eat the kinds of foods I was learning about. And he asked me to explain why one food is better than another.

Having another person on the same "experiment" helped me stay motivated. But I also resolved that, even if the other people in my life don't want to change, I must find a way to make my changes in the midst of living with these other people.

And then there were the weeks when I got tired of it all and went back to some old unhealthy habits, just because they were easier. This is when I felt I had "struck down" the whole plan. But this passage says that although we are "struck down" we are "not destroyed." And I found it true. Even though I had not been on my plan 100%, all was not lost. I could turn to God, confess, and be forgiven. And then I could get up and start where I had left off.

Sometimes circumstances made it impossible to do the things I had been doing to improve. I might need to go on a business or vacation trip, or I might have company for the weekend or for dinner. These times seemed to be the hardest to handle, because I didn't always have time to test out healthy "company" recipes so I could serve them with confidence to guests. But over the months and years, even these areas have become easier.

So I take great comfort in the fact that with God in our lives we are not forsaken, not crushed, and not destroyed.

> DEAR LORD, thank you for the hope that I can change, and for the amazing fact that I already have changed! A lot. Thank you for being there when I cry out, "This is too much! I'll never be able to do it." Thank you for the strength to keep on trying to learn to care for this body you have given me so that I don't lead it toward disease and death but toward health and life. Your example of facing death for us gives me the courage to believe that with your help I can overcome my resistance to doing all I can to be healthy.
>
> Now go with me into the rest of my life and help me to continue trying to be who you made me to be—physically, mentally, and spiritually. In Jesus' name, AMEN.

## Putting Twenty Pounds of Flour in a Five-Pound Bag

When I first took that life-changing physical in January of 1980, my life was already full. The decision to take the advice of the doctors at the Preventive Medicine Center and begin to exercise and learn about more healthy eating was difficult to make. But I tried to approach the obstacles with an attitude of prayer and a willingness to experiment and be flexible. I tried various time schedules and talked with my husband about ways we could both fit the time for exercise into our busy lives.

## Setting Priorities

One of the things I recognized was that I couldn't make all the changes I wanted to make at once. I had some studying and learning to do. So I decided to make the changes one at a time.

In the food category, I started by picking out one or two books from a reading list (like the ones listed on pp. 343–356 of this book) and reading them from cover to cover. I noted the page numbers of recipes inside the front covers, and I underlined key passages in the books. Keith said he wanted to learn what I was learning, so at dinner I would tell him what I had read. I realized as I was talking to him that doing so helped me to remember more of what I was reading.

As soon as I had learned some basic things, I went through the kitchen and pulled out everything I knew to be unhealthy or poor quality and threw it away. I realized I really didn't need most of it, anyway. And when I went grocery shopping, I began to buy more fresh foods, chicken, and frozen fish. I planned simpler menus that I knew I could handle.

If I were asked to make a list of things to do to make such changes and to put them in some kind of order of how to begin, this is what I would list now. I don't know exactly what I did first or second, but this might give you some ideas as to how you might begin to handle all this new information. I'd probably spend anywhere from a week to a month on *each* of these steps:

FOOD AND COOKING

(1) Read and learn.
(2) Clean out kitchen.
(3) Change shopping habits.
(4) Change cooking habits (steam vegetables and bake meats).
(5) Review favorite recipes. Cut out unhealthy ingredients and substitute more healthy ones (e.g. evaporated skim milk for heavy

cream, etc.). If they can't be altered, throw them away. If they can, keep using them in their new form. Try some experiments with them.

(6) Search out new recipes.

(7) Try one new recipe.

(8) Plan an entire meal of new recipes.

(9) Continue step by step to find ways to adjust or replace your old food favorites.

EXERCISE

(1) Go to exercise class or work out at home three times a week.

(2) Begin an aerobic program. Early in the day is a time which probably has fewer interruptions, and for me this is the best time to do aerobic exercise. But lunchtime is popular with some people. Another time is after work or dinner (at least one-and-a-half hours after dinner), or maybe in the morning right after the kids and husband leave for work.

(3) Evaluate daily schedule (see time chart in Part Five).

(4) Try out new proposed schedule for two weeks. The first week will be full of disasters. I don't know why, but it always is. The second week shows what really will work and what is unrealistic.

## Time Map

In Part Five of this book is a "Weekly Time Map" with the days of the week across the top and half-hour time slots, from 6:00 A.M. to 11:00 P.M., down the side. I have used a chart like this to help me map out where my time is going (p. 358).

Sometimes I have the overwhelming feeling that there isn't enough time in the day to do everything I need and want to do. But by filling out the chart, I can find out whether or not that is really true. Most of the time it isn't true; the feeling of being overwhelmed comes mostly from not having a plan and from being afraid I'll forget something.

The way I use the time map is to begin by writing in the known obligations I have—meetings, working hours, car pools, lunchtime, breakfast time, dinner time (and cooking time), and so on. Each little box represents a half hour of time. So, if you want to take one hour for lunch from 12:00 to 1:00, write "lunch" in the box by 12:00 and draw a short arrow down through the next little box, which is marked 12:30, stopping right before the little box that is labeled 1:00. When everything I must do during the day is filled in, then the blank places on the chart are the times I have available to exercise, take my "time out" for myself, and study nutrition.

PART ONE: THE BODYCARE ADVENTURE

## Keeping Control of the Time Map

A helpful thing I always do is fill in this chart with a pencil, not a pen. One of my fears is that I'll dream up a schedule I can't possibly live by and then feel guilty when I don't keep it. But when I write in pencil, I know that if something I wrote down just plain won't work, it's okay because I have the eraser! I control the chart—it doesn't control me.

When you fill out your chart, if there are no blank spaces, perhaps it's time to do some creative thinking about your priorities. Maybe there are things on your list that other family members could do for you, or things you can eliminate. Try to clear them out. When I first made my chart, I could put only two or three hours a week to study nutrition, but it was a start.

I've found that this kind of schedule map has helped me get a handle on my time when I felt overwhelmed with things to do. I made several blank copies of the master chart, because I find I have to redo my chart every so often when the responsibilities in my life change. But it really helps me to have a picture like this when I am frantic.

## After Four Years, Is Anything Better?

You may have begun seriously looking at sound nutrition and sensible exercise ten weeks ago, when you began reading this book. And as you finish, I hope you feel that your goal has been to get a good idea about what it might take to put healthy practices into your life and to begin putting a few to work right away. But the goal was certainly not to get it all done in ten weeks! I've been moving in better directions for *four years,* and I still have more to accomplish.

But what has happened to me is that I now have a sense of making choices within the framework of a specific kind of lifestyle. It's like choosing what to major in at college—once you've decided on computer science, you don't have to struggle with a decision about taking advanced German or not. There's not room for it in the framework of your chosen major. And I feel there's not much room in my life now for things that lead me away from health. I either avoid such things or find a way to change them so that they are healthy choices (like going out to eat at restaurants even though there are unhealthy food choices on the menu).

There are a few concrete improvements I can see, too. I never thought I'd be able to go out and start running and not stop for three miles! (I've even run four on a couple of occasions, which just about blows my mind!) And I have increased my flexibility so that when I

238

bend over I can reach well beyond my knees and almost to the floor. I hope to keep improving in that area.

Another thing I've done is buy a size-8 skirt. When all is going well and my weight is at the low end of my range for a while, I really enjoy putting on that skirt. And seeing it in the closet when my weight has gotten to the upper end of that range helps me remember that I have lowered my weight before and I will be able to do it again—sooner this time.

Now that my muscles are stronger I can carry two fully loaded bags of groceries into the house together without dropping one, and I can handle my luggage at airports much more easily. Carrying the dirty clothes basket to the washing machine is a breeze now. And I don't get out of breath going up a flight of stairs—or even two or three flights. And, of course, that mad dash for the plane we made last January is another sign of better health.

## Where to Begin?

I've told you about health from my perspective, and I'm really excited about what it's doing in my life. I feel I could write volumes more about it because there's so much to learn. But the sad thing to me is that I can't *do* all the things in this book for anyone else. If I could, I would, because I'm that convinced about them. But each person must come to a place where she wants to improve her own health and must make a decision to begin. Not only that, but we can most influence others around us, like our husbands and children, by our example—by what we enjoy and what we complain about. The adventure of finding health through exercise and good nutrition can be interesting, delicious, and enjoyable. It doesn't have to be a grim, tasteless task.

I closed this book by talking about scheduling because I think it's a good place to begin. After absorbing this overall approach to health, including exercise (three kinds) and good, basic, balanced food-group nutrition, some prayer time and thinking time might be in order. While it is a big picture, it's not too big, especially if broken down into smaller steps. With God's help, Keith and I have been able to put much of it into our lives. The rest is yet to come.

So as you continue to develop your health plan, you'll probably begin to notice more and more changes and improvements in the quality of life you're living. And I believe they'll make you more and more the person God had in mind when he first thought of you.

# Part Two

# THE
# BODYCARE
# WORKOUT

*Exercises for Flexibility and Strength*

# Introduction

Here is a muscle-tone exercise routine you can do at home alone or with a friend.

There are three levels of workouts given: I, II, and III. The exercises are the same, but the higher levels require more repetitions, which you'll be able to do as you develop muscle strength. Remember, however, if you start at level I of this routine and find your muscles are not ready to do the number of repetitions suggested for this level . . . STOP. Do not force your muscles to do the recommended repetitions until you are ready. You risk two things: (1) suffering from sore muscles, which takes away from the fun of exercising; and (2) injuring yourself by trying to increase your repetitions too fast or to do more than your muscles are ready to handle. If you haven't read chapter 6 about how to pace yourself, please do so before beginning these exercises. Also, please review chapters 2 and 3 regarding muscle tone.

We'll progress through this workout by body groups. First a warm-up, then exercises for arms, waist and torso, stomach, legs, hips, and finally buttocks. To end the workout, there will be some stretches, since warmed-up muscles can flex better. These will also help ease your muscles out of the tension of the heavy work they've done. Depending on the number of repetitions you do, you'll need about 30 to 45 minutes to do the exercises. When you first start, you may be able to finish sooner, because you'll be doing fewer repetitions.

## Warm-Up and Cool-Down

Many people tell me they are tempted to skip the warm-up and cool-down sections of exercises, especially when they are short of time. If you find yourself with less time than you'd like and are considering cutting out one or both of these, let me urge you to reconsider. It would be better to cut out one exercise from each body group than to fail to protect your body from injury. Even though the warm-up and cool-down don't feel strenuous, they are very crucial to preparing your body for the hard work of exercise.

## How This Part of the Book Is Structured

First is a section describing the movements involved in the exercises, illustrated with photographs. After that, there is a chart listing the exercises by name and suggesting a number of repetitions to do at each level. I suggest spending two to four weeks on each of the levels, working out three times a week. (Begin at the lowest level, even if you feel you can already do the higher levels.) If, after two weeks on a level, your body feels ready to do more, move to the next level. But if you still feel pushed to complete the repetitions given on a particular level, stay with that level until you feel ready to move on.

## Some Tips for a Better Workout

Disconnect your phone and allow plenty of time to get ready, go through the routine, and relax a few minutes at the end. Time to shower and get dressed again should also be included. Remember, this is your time to spend on bringing yourself to a better level of fitness. Interruptions will reduce the effectiveness of your workout.

It's fun to put some music on while you're doing your workout. In fact, the number of repetitions suggested are multiples of four so that they will fit the rhythm of most music. But please remember, if the tempo of the music is too fast or too slow for the exercise, to disregard the beat of the song and do the exercise at the best speed for you to keep control of the movement. Gradually you'll get a feel for which songs are good for leg lifts, abdominal exercises, and so on.

## Control Is Important

Be sure to do all the exercises with a controlled motion. If you do them too fast, the momentum resulting from swinging around a body part (such as an arm or a leg) will "help" you with the motions. Your muscles won't have to do as much work, and therefore won't get stronger. You don't have to look like a slow-motion movie, but do the exercises at a reasonable speed at which you can control the movements.

Remember to *put* your arm, leg, or body deliberately into the position, then to *put* it back in the starting position just as deliberately. Try to work the muscles going both ways in a movement. With a leg lift, for instance, raise your leg, then try not to just relax the muscles and drop it with a thud to the floor. Instead, bring the leg consciously down until it is about three inches above the floor, then raise it back up again. Don't relax or touch down with the leg until you have done all the repetitions. That way your muscles will get a better workout.

As I mentioned in chapter 3, the proper form for an exercise is very important. It is far better for you to do fewer repetitions using the proper form than to do more repetitions with the incorrect form. When you work at using the proper form, your muscles will gradually strengthen, and you'll be able to increase your repetitions naturally.

# Overall Body Warm-Up

### 1. WARM-UP WALK

Walk briskly around the room or from room to room. If there is not space for this, walk briskly in place. Take steps rapidly, raising feet off floor about a foot, and swing arms widely. Do not run in place or break contact with the floor at this stage of the warm-up. Each time right foot touches floor is one repetition.

### 2. WALK WITH PUNCHES

A. Continue walking and punch your fists alternately into the air in front of you. Punch forward with your right arm when you step on the left foot, and with your left arm when you step on your right foot. Each time right foot touches floor counts as one repetition.

B. Switch to punching fists up toward ceiling (not pictured).

# The Exercises

### 3. STEP-KICKS

Return to your exercise place (if you've been walking around) and place your hands on your hips. Step on your right foot, then raise your left foot out in front of you in a kick. Bring that left foot down and step on it, then kick the right foot out in front. (Count, "Step, kick, step, kick.") Each time you step on your right foot counts one.

*By now you should be feeling your pulse rate go up as your blood begins to move around a little. You should be breathing harder, so that oxygen is getting to your muscles.*

### 4. GENTLE JOG

Jog gently in place. Count one each time your right foot touches the floor.

*Shake out your arms, breathe deeply, and get ready for your workout.*

# *Arms*

### 1. ARM CIRCLES
A. Stand with feet hip distance apart. Bring straight arms out to sides. With palms up, circle forward in small circles, fairly rapidly. Circle backward in small circles.

B. Repeat with palms facing down, circling arms forward and backward.

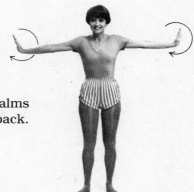

C. Bend hands at wrist so that palms face side walls. Circle forward and back.

D. Repeat with hands bent down.

## 2. BACK-CROSS SHOULDER TOUCH

A. Bring arms down to sides. Raise right arm straight up overhead, with elbow close to ear.

B. Bend arm at elbow and touch left shoulder. Keep elbow pointed at ceiling, head straight up. Straighten arm.

C. Repeat with left arm touching right shoulder (not pictured).

## 3. ALTERNATING
## SHOULDER TOUCH

A. Bring straight arms up and out to sides. Bend right arm and touch shoulder, keeping elbow on the same level as shoulders.

B. Now switch, bringing left arm to shoulder and straightening right arm.

C. Keeping elbows high, continue alternating. Each time you touch your right shoulder is one count.

251

## 4. *THREE-WAY*
## *SHOULDER TOUCH*

A. Touch both shoulders with both hands, keeping elbows out to the sides and on the same level as shoulders (top). Then straighten arms out to sides, keeping elbows high (bottom). Repeat this three times, for a total of four.

B. (Pictured above.) Then touch shoulders, moving elbows out in front of you, and straighten arms in front. Remember to keep elbows high. Do four times.

C. (Pictured below.) Last, touch shoulders with elbows in front of you (as in B), then straighten arms up overhead. Repeat three times for a total of four.

Each complete pattern is one count.

### 5. STRAIGHT-ARM OVERHEAD TOUCH

A. Bring arms down to sides. Turn palms in so that they face your legs.

B. Then, keeping elbows straight, raise arms out to side and up overhead until the backs of your hands touch.

C. Lower arms, keeping elbows straight.

## 6. BUTTERFLY

A. Bring arms straight out in front of you with palms touching.

B. Keeping elbows straight, open arms to side and slightly back—as wide as you can.

C. Close arms. Throughout this exercise, keep arms parallel to the floor, knees slightly bent. Make your arm muscles, not your back, do the work.

## 7. LAWN-MOWER START

A. With knees slightly bent, bend forward. Place your right hand on your right knee. Bring your left hand to your right toe.

B. Bend your elbow as you lift it up high toward the ceiling, as if you were starting a lawn mower.

C. Return hand to toe. Bend forward and keep both knees slightly bent throughout entire movement, twisting slightly at the waist as you raise the elbow. Do required number of repetitions with left arm. Then repeat with left hand on left knee, moving right arm.

## 8. WINDMILLS

A. Keeping body in same position, knees slightly bent, touch right hand to left toe, bringing left arm up high in back with elbow straight.

B. Now reverse, touching left hand to right toe and swinging right arm up high in back.

C. Continue to alternate touching left and right. Each time right hand touches left toe counts as one repetition.

### 9. SLOW ROLL-UP
Bring feet together. Then, with both knees bent, slowly roll up, one vertebra at a time, to a standing position.

*Shake out arms, and we'll move on to exercises for the waist and torso.*

# Waist

### 1. SIDE BENDS—ARMS FOLDED
A. Stand with feet hip distance apart. Fold arms over chest.

B. Bend torso to right, keeping shoulders back and seat tucked under. At the same time, straighten right arm and pull down with it diagonally while moving left elbow up toward ceiling.

C. As you return to a standing position, return arms to folded position. Do the required number of repetitions bending right. Then do the same number of repetitions bending to the left, reversing arm movements.

## 2. THREE-WAY SIDE BENDS

A. Raise left arm up, curving it slightly over your head. Curve right arm in front of you. Bend to right side, keeping left shoulder back and seat tucked under, and "pulse" down gently (no big bounces).

B. Interlace fingers behind your head, keeping elbows spread and shoulders back. Continue pulsing gently to the right.

C. Grasp your left wrist with your right hand and pull it gently over your head to the right. Continue pulsing to the right.

D. Return to standing position. Lower arms. Repeat all three movements to the left, reversing arm positions.

### 3. TORSO BENDS

A. Stand with feet only a few inches apart (less than hip distance). Bend knees slightly and keep them bent throughout this movement.

B. Bend from side to side, letting your fingertips slide down the outside of your thighs toward your knees. *Don't bend forward*, and *do* keep your seat tucked under. Don't let your hips sway from side to side. Try to let your fingertips work their way down to your knees. Each time you bend to the right is one count.

## 4. WAIST TWISTS— FOUR EACH WAY

A. Stand with feet hip distance apart. Bend knees. Bring arms up to sides and flex your hands up.

B. Twist four times to the right, then four times to the left. Each time you complete this pattern is one count.

## 5. WAIST TWISTS—SINGLES

Continue twisting in same position as above, twisting once to each side. Each time you twist right is one count.

*For the rest of the waist exercises, which will be done on the floor, you will need an exercise mat or large towel to sit on. During these exercises, try to keep your head up and your spine straight.*

### 6. SITTING STRETCH

A. Sit with your legs open, leaning forward out of your hips. Straighten both legs and open them as wide as you can, toes pointed.

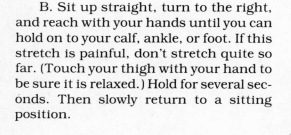

B. Sit up straight, turn to the right, and reach with your hands until you can hold on to your calf, ankle, or foot. If this stretch is painful, don't stretch quite so far. (Touch your thigh with your hand to be sure it is relaxed.) Hold for several seconds. Then slowly return to a sitting position.

C. Twist to the left and repeat. Hold. Slowly return to a sitting position.

D. Facing straight ahead, reach forward with both arms and lean out (not pictured). Hold. Return to starting position. Each set of right, left, and center stretches counts as one repetition. (Note: I'm not flexible enough to reach beyond my calf in this exercise. But if you can reach your ankle or toe, by all means do it! Don't settle for your calf just because that's what I'm doing in this picture!)

## 7. SITTING TWISTS

A. Remain seated with your legs open and your back as straight as possible. Flex your feet. Reach your right arm toward your left foot, twisting your body out of your hips.

B. Then twist the other way and reach your left arm toward your right foot. Each time you twist to the right is one count.

## 8. BENT-LEG STRETCH AND TWIST

A. Bend your right leg so that the sole of your foot is facing the inside of your left thigh. Twist and reach toward your left foot twice. (Concentrate on two separate reaches, rather than a bounce.)

B. Then sit up straight and twist toward the right, snapping your fingers twice. Each time you complete these four counts is one repetition.

### 9. SOLES OF FEET TOGETHER

A. Bring the soles of your feet together, hold on to your ankles or feet, and use your elbows to press your thighs gently toward the floor. Keep your back straight and your chin up. Rest your hands on your ankles as you take a deep breath.

B. Exhale as you lean forward over your feet (not pictured). Hold, then return to a sitting position.

C. Now, let go of your feet, close your knees, and wrap your arms around your legs. Round your back and place your forehead on your knees. Hold.

D. Repeat both steps above.

*Good job. Now we'll move on to the abdominal muscles.*

# Abdominal Muscles

*REMINDER: Never do sit-ups with straight legs. This causes excess strain on the lower back. Keep knees bent whenever you are doing curls or sit-ups.*

*REMINDER: Never raise both straight legs at the same time while you are lying on your back. Bend one leg when you raise the other one straight, or tuck both knees up to raise legs. This protects your back from excess strain.*

## 1. CURLS WITH ARMS FOLDED

A. Lie on your back. Bend your knees and place the soles of your feet on the floor, hip distance apart. Fold your arms across your chest.

B. Curl your head and shoulders up until they are off the floor, pulling your stomach muscles *in* at the same time. (Do not let the tummy muscles push out as you do this.)

C. Roll back down partway toward the floor. (Each curl is done from a partially lifted position.)

D. As you develop more muscle tone, you can place your hands behind your head (not your neck) and interlace your fingers. Be sure to keep your elbows out to the sides and not folded up alongside your head. (See photo for exercise 5.)

## 2. CURLS TOUCHING KNEES

Now, unfold your arms and reach them out to touch your knees as you curl up, keeping your stomach pulled in tight. Roll partway down and continue curling up from a partially lifted position.

### 3. KNEES TO CHEST

Hug your knees into your chest and take a deep breath. Relax your stomach muscles. Exhale. Hold this position for the time listed on the chart, breathing deeply.

### 4. KNEE TUCKS

A. Place your hands under your hips (for support) and your feet flat on the floor, knees bent and together.

B. Tuck your knees up toward your chest as far as you can.

C. Lower your legs, knees still bent, until your pointed toes barely touch the floor. Then tuck again.

D. As you develop better muscle tone you can actually roll your hips up off your hands as you tuck.

## 5. KNEE TO ELBOW

A. Place the soles of your feet on the floor. Place your hands behind your head (not your neck), with fingers interlaced and elbows open wide.

B. Curl up and raise your right knee. Touch your left elbow to this knee over your waist. Return to a flat position.

C. Next, curl up and raise your left knee. Touch your right elbow to this knee over your waist. Roll back down. Each time you touch your left elbow to your right knee is one repetition.

## 6. KNEES TO CHEST

Hug your knees into your chest, take a deep breath, and relax your stomach. After a few seconds, release the breath. Hold the position for the time listed on the chart, breathing deeply.

## 7. CURLS WITH LEGS UP

A. Tucking your knees, raise both legs and straighten them into a perpendicular position.

B. Curl up, bringing your hands alongside your legs on the outside. Roll partway down and continue curling up from a partially lifted position.

## 8. ABDOMINAL RELEASE

A. Tuck your knees up to your chest and swing them over toward the right while moving both arms to the left. This twist will help release your tense abdominal muscles. Take a deep breath and let it out.

B. Then reverse your position, swinging your bent knees over to the left and your arms to the right. Breathe in and exhale. Knees swinging right, then left, counts as one repetition.

# Legs

## 1. SIDE LEG LIFTS

A. Lie on your right side, propped up on your elbow. Bend right leg at the knee to protect your back. Keep left leg straight, with toe pointed and knee facing the wall in front of you.

B. Raise left leg and lower it, being sure to control your movements. Do not let the knee rotate toward the ceiling, and do not touch the floor when you lower the leg.

C. After completing the repetitions listed in the chart, repeat with foot flexed.

## 2. KNEE TUCK—STRAIGHT LEG BACK

A. From the same position, bend your left knee and bring your left leg forward in a tuck position.

B. Now straighten the leg as you swing it out in back of you. Move your left arm in opposition to the leg to help with balance (see photographs). Remember to keep your right leg (on the bottom) bent.

## 3. KNEE TO SHOULDER

A. From the same starting position, bend the knee, bringing it up toward your shoulder. Straighten the leg to the beginning position. Right leg (on the bottom) is still bent.

## 4. PERPENDICULAR LEG LIFTS

A. Remaining on your right side with lower leg (right leg) bent, bring your left leg forward until it is perpendicular to your body, your foot even with your waist.

B. Keeping your leg straight and foot flexed, raise it and lower it in a slow, controlled movement.

C. Now lift it at double time, keeping movement smooth and controlled.

## 5. HIP RELEASE—
## CROSS-LEGGED SIT

Sit up and cross your legs with your left leg in front. Lean forward to stretch out the leg and hip.

## 6. INNER-THIGH LIFTS

A. Lie back down on your right side. Bend your left knee and place your left foot on the floor in front of your right knee (holding your foot at the ankle).

B. Lift your straight right leg (which is on the bottom) up, making sure that your knee is facing the wall opposite you—not the ceiling. Then lower the leg *almost* to the floor.

C. Do the required number of repetitions with toes pointed, then repeat with foot flexed.

## 7. INNER-THIGH CIRCLES

Keep your left leg in front of your right, holding on to your ankle. Make big circles forward with your right leg, foot flexed, then circle backward.

272

*Shake out your legs and relax. Then lie on your left side and repeat all leg exercises listed above, using the opposite leg. This time, do the Cross-Legged Sit (exercise 5) with your right leg in front, to release the leg muscle. The next body part we'll work on is the hips.*

# Hips

### 1. SIDE BENT-KNEE LIFTS

A. Move up onto your hands and knees, weight evenly distributed. Keep your head up, stomach muscles tight, and back flat.

B. Raise your right bent leg out to the side as high as you can without twisting your hips or back. Then lower the leg back to the starting position.

## 2. BACK LEG LIFTS

A. Keeping your head up, stomach muscles tight, and back flat, extend your right leg straight out behind you, pointed toe touching the floor.

B. Now raise the leg until it forms a straight line with your back, then lower it.

## 3. DONKEY KICKS

A. Raise your right leg out behind you until your knee is even with your hip (or higher), and flex your foot.

B. Bend your knee and try to kick yourself in the seat. Then straighten leg, keeping knee high and foot flexed.

274

## 4. SIDE STRAIGHT-LEG LIFTS

A. Bring straight leg out to the side with foot flexed.

B. Raise and lower leg, trying to keep your foot even with your waist.

## 5. HIP RELEASE

Bring knee back to floor. Slowly sit back on your heels and rest your forehead on the floor. Breathe deeply as you hold this position.

*Come back up onto your hands and knees and repeat movements using the left leg. Then you're ready to do the last body group—the buttocks.*

# Buttocks

*POSITION: Lie on back, knees bent, feet on floor about hip distance apart. Raise hips up a few inches off the floor, putting weight on shoulders and feet. All lifts begin from this lifted position. The movement of the buttocks muscles is very slight. Do not lift so much that you arch your back. Work the muscles by contracting them firmly.*

### 1. HIP RAISES
From the original lifted position, lift hips a few more inches, squeezing the buttocks muscles together. Lower slightly and relax muscles. (Do not lower all the way to the floor.)

### 2. HIP RAISES—FEET AND KNEES OUT
Move feet farther apart. Turn feet toward corners of the room and spread knees. Lift and lower hips as above.

### 3. HIP RAISES—KNEES TOGETHER AND APART

A. Keep feet apart. As you lift hips, bring knees together.

B. Open knees as you lower.

### 4. HIP RAISES—FEET TOGETHER

Bring feet and knees together. Lift and lower hips as before.

### 5. BUTTOCKS RELEASE

Lower hips to floor. Press soles of feet together and let gravity pull your knees toward the floor. Relax the buttocks and leg muscles. Take in a deep breath, and release it as you hold this position the number of seconds indicated in chart.

*Congratulations! You've done a great job. Now you're ready for the cool-down.*

# Cool-Down

## 1. BODY STRETCH

Lie on your back with your legs straight. Reach your arms out over your head. Take in a deep breath as you stretch the length of your body, pulling your arms up and your feet down, and tightening your stomach muscles as you try to make yourself as "long" as you can. Hold a few seconds, then exhale as you relax the stretch. Repeat.

## 2. LEG AND BUTTOCK STRETCH

A. Bend your right knee and raise it toward you. Hold your right leg just behind your knee.

B. Using only your arm muscles, gently bring the knee closer to your chest. Your left leg is lying on the floor, relaxed. Your right leg and foot are relaxed. Only your arm muscles are being used. Hold.

C. Release the leg just enough so that you can straighten your leg. Keep holding it behind the knee. Now, in that same position, point your toe hard and hold.

D. Then flex your foot hard and hold (feel the calf muscle stretch). Point foot again, then flex it once more.

E. Relax foot, then knee. Release the leg and lower it to the floor.

F. Repeat A–C with left leg.

G. Relax foot and knee of left leg and place left foot on floor, knee bent. Bend right knee and place right foot beside left.

### 3. HIP STRETCH
A. Cross the right knee over the left, leaving the left foot on the floor.

B. Use the right leg to push the left inner thigh toward the floor, stretching the left hip. (It is not necessary to reach the floor.) Hold, concentrating on relaxing all muscles. Return to upright position and uncross the knees.

C. Repeat with opposite leg.

### 4. MODIFIED FETAL POSITION
Roll over to right side, bend knees up comfortably, and place head on hands. Close your eyes and relax.

## 5. HAMSTRING STRETCH

A. Use your arms to push yourself up to a sitting position.

B. Straighten left leg in front of you, bend right leg back, and place right foot beside your right hip. (Right knee is down on the floor.)

C. Reach forward toward left foot and hold. Feel the stretch in back of left upper thigh.

D. Repeat movement for opposite leg.

## 6. CROSSED LEGS—BOWED HEAD

Sit up, cross your legs, and bow your head gently, pressing your chin toward your chest. Rest your arms on your knees, close your eyes, and breathe deeply.

## 7. STANDING CROSSED-LEG STRETCH

A. Open your eyes, place your palms on the floor beside you, and, using your hands to push, stand up. Stand with your feet crossed, head and arms hanging down. Feel the stretch up the back of your back leg.

B. Cross your feet the other way and stretch the opposite leg.

## 8. SLOW ROLL-UP

Uncross your legs and balance yourself. Then slowly roll up to a standing position, bringing your hips, back, neck, and head up one at a time.

*Good going! Remember to do this (or a similar) routine three days a week with at least one day's rest between workouts. And remember that you also need to do at least 17½ minutes of aerobic exercise at least five days a week to really improve your fitness level. You're on your way to a stronger, healthier quality of life!*

# Chart of Repetitions

| Level: | I | II | III | Name of Exercise |
|---|---|---|---|---|

## Overall Body Warm-Up

| | I | II | III | |
|---|---|---|---|---|
| Reps | 300 | 300 | 300 | Warm-Up Walk (about 2½ min.) |
| | | | | Walk with Punches (about 4 min. total): |
| Reps | 150 | 150 | 150 | Punch in front |
| Reps | 150 | 150 | 150 | Punch up |
| Reps | 100 | 100 | 100 | Step-Kicks |
| Reps | 300 | 300 | 300 | Gentle Jog (about 2 min.) |

## Arms

| | I | II | III | |
|---|---|---|---|---|
| | | | | Arm Circles (palms up, down; hands flexed up, down): |
| Reps | 8 | 12 | 16 | Circle forward |
| Reps | 8 | 12 | 16 | Circle backward |
| | | | | Back-Cross Shoulder Touch |
| Reps | 16 | 20 | 24 | Right arm |
| Reps | 16 | 20 | 24 | Left arm |
| Reps | 16 | 20 | 24 | Alternating Shoulder Touch |
| Reps | 5 | 7 | 10 | Three-Way Shoulder Touch (1 pattern or 4 counts, 3 ways, counts as 1 repetition) |
| Reps | 8 | 12 | 16 | Straight-Arm Overhead Touch |
| Reps | 8 | 12 | 16 | Butterfly |
| Reps | 16 | 20 | 24 | Lawn-Mower Start (do reps to right side, then repeat to left) |
| Reps | 16 | 20 | 24 | Windmills |

| Level: | I | II | III | Name of Exercise |
|---|---|---|---|---|

## *Waist*

| | | | | |
|---|---|---|---|---|
| Reps | 16 | 20 | 24 | Side Bends—Arms Folded (do reps to right side, then repeat to left) |
| | | | | Three-Way Side Bends (do reps for all 3 to right, then repeat all 3 to left): |
| Reps | 8 | 12 | 16 | Arm over head |
| Reps | 8 | 12 | 16 | Hands behind head |
| Reps | 8 | 12 | 16 | Hands holding wrist |
| Reps | 40 | 48 | 56 | Torso Bends |
| Reps | 3 | 4 | 5 | Waist Twists—Four Each Way (right and left counts as 1 rep) |
| Reps | 6 | 8 | 10 | Waist Twists—Singles |
| Reps | 6 | 8 | 10 | Sitting Stretch (each set of right, left, and center stretches counts as 1 rep) |
| Reps | 8 | 12 | 16 | Sitting Twists (left and right is 1 rep) |
| Reps | 8 | 12 | 16 | Bent-Leg Stretch and Twist (do required number of reps to right, then repeat to left) |
| | | | | Soles of Feet Together: |
| Secs | 10 | 10 | 10 | Stretch |
| Secs | 10 | 10 | 10 | Rounded back |

## *Abdominal Muscles*

| | | | | |
|---|---|---|---|---|
| Reps | 20 | 24 | 28 | Curls with Arms Folded (Levels II and III: arms behind head) |
| Reps | 20 | 24 | 28 | Curls Touching Knees |
| Secs | 10 | 10 | 10 | Knees to Chest |

| Level: | I | II | III | Name of Exercise |
|---|---|---|---|---|
| Reps | 20 | 32 | 44 | Knee Tucks |
| Reps | 8 | 16 | 24 | Knee to Elbow (right and left is 1 rep) |
| Secs | 10 | 10 | 10 | Knees to Chest |
| Reps | 20 | 24 | 28 | Curls with Legs Up |
| Reps | 3 | 3 | 3 | Abdominal Release (right and left is 1 rep) |

# Legs

| | | | | |
|---|---|---|---|---|
| Reps | 16 | 20 | 24 | Side Leg Lifts |
| Reps | 16 | 20 | 24 | Knee Tuck—Straight Leg Back |
| Reps | 16 | 20 | 24 | Knee to Shoulder |
| | | | | Perpendicular Leg Lifts: |
| Reps | 8 | 12 | 12 | Slow |
| Reps | 16 | 20 | 24 | Double time |
| Secs | 15 | 15 | 15 | Hip Release—Cross-Legged Sit |
| Reps | 12 | 16 | 20 | Inner-Thigh Lifts (do required number of reps with pointed toes, then repeat with flexed feet) |
| | | | | Inner-Thigh Circles: |
| Reps | 12 | 16 | 20 | Circle forward |
| Reps | 12 | 16 | 20 | Circle backward |

# Hips

| | | | | |
|---|---|---|---|---|
| Reps | 16 | 20 | 24 | Side Bent-Knee Lifts |
| Reps | 16 | 20 | 24 | Back Leg Lifts |
| Reps | 16 | 20 | 24 | Donkey Kicks |
| Reps | 16 | 20 | 24 | Side Straight-Leg Lifts |
| Secs | 15 | 15 | 15 | Hip Release |

| Level: | I | II | III | Name of Exercise |
|---|---|---|---|---|

# *Buttocks*

| | | | | |
|---|---|---|---|---|
| Reps | 20 | 24 | 28 | Hip Raises |
| Reps | 20 | 24 | 28 | Hip Raises—Feet and Knees Out |
| Reps | 20 | 24 | 28 | Hip Raises—Knees Together and Apart |
| Reps | 20 | 24 | 28 | Hip Raises—Feet Together |
| Secs | 10 | 10 | 10 | Buttocks Release |

# *Cool-Down*

| | | | | |
|---|---|---|---|---|
| Reps | 3 | 3 | 3 | Body Stretch (hold each stretch 5 sec.) |
| | | | | Leg and Buttock Stretch (do entire stretch with right leg, then repeat with left): |
| Reps | 1 | 1 | 1 | Knee to chest (hold 10 sec.) |
| Reps | 2 | 2 | 2 | Point toe and flex foot (hold 5 sec.) |
| Reps | 1 | 1 | 1 | Hip Stretch (right and left—hold 15 sec. on each side) |
| Reps | 1 | 1 | 1 | Modified Fetal Position (hold 30 sec.) |
| Reps | 1 | 1 | 1 | Hamstring Stretch (right and left—hold 15 sec. each side) |
| Reps | 1 | 1 | 1 | Crossed Legs—Bowed Head (hold 30 sec.) |
| Reps | 1 | 1 | 1 | Standing Crossed-Leg Stretch (hold 15 sec.) |

# Part Three

# THE
# BODYCARE
# EATING
# PLAN

*Food-Serving Plans and Food Lists to
Help You Design Your Own Diet for
Successful Weight Maintenance and
Good Health*

# Eating Plans

## *Food-Serving Plans for Weight Loss[1]*

### *1,000 Calories*

    5 oz. fish, poultry, meat, or meat substitutes
    3 servings fat
    2 servings lowfat dairy products
    3 servings grains, breads, and cereals
Unlimited servings nonstarchy vegetables
    1 serving starchy vegetables or soup
    2 servings fruit

### *1,200 Calories*

    6 oz. fish, poultry, meat, or meat substitutes
    3 servings fat
    2 servings lowfat dairy products
    4 servings grains, breads, and cereals
Unlimited servings nonstarchy vegetables
    1 serving starchy vegetables or soup
    3 servings fruit

### *1,500 Calories*

    6 oz. fish, poultry, meat, or meat substitutes
    5 servings fat
    2 servings lowfat dairy products
    6 servings grains, breads, or cereals
Unlimited servings nonstarchy vegetables
    1 serving starchy vegetables or soup
    5 servings fruit

---

1. From *The Houstonian Preventive Medicine Center's Nutritional Advice* booklet, prepared and compiled by Elizabeth Manis, R.D., edited by Mary Pat O'Malley, M.A., R.D., © 1979. Used by permission.

## 1,800 Calories

8 oz. fish, poultry, meat, or meat substitutes
5 servings fat
2 servings lowfat dairy products
6 servings grains, breads, or cereals
Unlimited servings nonstarchy vegetables
1 serving starchy vegetables or soup
6 servings fruit

# Maintenance Plans[2]

## 1,600 Calories

6 oz. fish, poultry, meat, or meat substitutes
5 servings fat
2 servings lowfat dairy products
6 servings grains, breads, or cereals
Unlimited servings nonstarchy vegetables
1 serving starchy vegetables or soup
5 servings fruit
1 serving dessert[3]

## 1,900 Calories

8 oz. fish, poultry, meat, or meat substitutes
6 servings fat
2 servings lowfat dairy products
6 servings grain, breads, or cereals
Unlimited servings nonstarchy vegetables
1 serving starchy vegetables or soup
6 servings fruit
1 serving dessert[3]

---

2. From *The Houstonian Preventive Medicine Center's Nutritional Advice* booklet, prepared and compiled by Elizabeth Manis, R.D., edited by Mary Pat O'Malley, M.A., R.D., © 1979. Used by permission.
3. Or alcohol. See note on following page.

## 2,200 Calories

        8 oz. fish, poultry, meat, or meat substitutes
        9 servings fat
        2 servings lowfat dairy products
        7 servings grains, breads, or cereals
Unlimited servings nonstarchy vegetables
        1 serving starchy vegetables or soup
        6 servings fruit
        2 servings dessert[4]

## 2,600 Calories

Use 2,200-calorie plan, and add 1 serving each of fruit, grain, and fat. Do not increase protein, dairy products, starchy vegetables, or dessert.

# How to Choose a Weight-Loss Eating Plan

## 1,000-Calorie Eating Plan

I suggest this eating plan for women:
- who are 5'2" or shorter,
- whose weight goals are around 95–110 pounds,
- who have fewer than 25 pounds to lose.

---

4. Or alcohol. While I do not recommend that anyone drink, it is recommended that those who choose to do so should limit themselves to only 1 drink in a day. (See detailed description of the health consequences of alcohol on p. 318.) On the 2,200- and 2,600-calorie plans, if you choose not to have alcohol (worth about 100 calories), you may substitute another "dessert" such as jam or jelly on your breakfast toast. Or you may have 1 serving of either a fruit or a grain. Do not increase proteins, fats, dairy products, or starchy vegetables.

## 1,200-Calorie Eating Plan

I suggest a 1,200-calorie reducing plan for women:
- who are between 5'3" and 5'9" tall,
- whose weight goals are 115–145 pounds,
- who have 25 or fewer pounds to lose.

## 1,500-Calorie Eating Plan

I suggest this eating plan for:
- very tall women (5'10" or taller) whose weight goals are 150 pounds or more and who have 25 or fewer pounds to lose,
- shorter women who have more than 25 pounds to lose and whose *first* weight goals are 150–170 pounds,
- men whose height is 5'9"–6'1" and whose weight goals are 154–178 pounds.

## 1,800-Calorie Eating Plan

I suggest this eating plan for:
- men who are 6'2"–6'5" tall,
- men whose weight goals are 185–200 pounds.

# Eating Plan Check Lists[5]

Name: _____ No. Calories chosen: _____

| SERVINGS ALLOWED | TYPE OF FOOD | SERVINGS EATEN |
|---|---|---|
| _____ | Fish, poultry, meat, etc. | _____ |
| _____ | Fat | _____ |
| _____ | Lowfat dairy | _____ |
| _____ | Grains, breads, cereals | _____ |
| _____ | Nonstarchy vegetables | _____ |
| _____ | Starchy vegetables and soups | _____ |
| _____ | Fruit | _____ |

. . . . . . . . . . . . . . . . . . . . . . . . . . . . . . . . . . . . . . . . . . . . . . . . . . . .

Name: _____ No. Calories chosen: _____

| SERVINGS ALLOWED | TYPE OF FOOD | SERVINGS EATEN |
|---|---|---|
| _____ | Fish, poultry, meat, etc. | _____ |
| _____ | Fat | _____ |
| _____ | Lowfat dairy | _____ |
| _____ | Grains, breads, cereals | _____ |
| _____ | Nonstarchy vegetables | _____ |
| _____ | Starchy vegetables and soups | _____ |
| _____ | Fruit | _____ |

---

5. If you are following the eating plan alone, use the top part of the page to check one day's worth of food. Then use the lower part for the next day. If there are two of you following the plan, one person uses the top part of the page and the other uses the lower part. Each person fills in his or her allowed servings on the left, then checks them off on the right. Make up your own copies of this form if you wish.

# Sample Day's Menus for 1,200 Calories

Note: Foods from any food group can be eaten at any meal. This sample day of menus is just an illustration of how to mark off the food groups on your "Eating Plan Check List."

| FOOD<br>(recipes for starred items appear in<br>Part Four of this book) | FOOD GROUP |
|---|---|
| **Breakfast** | |
| Breakfast Smoothie* | 1 lowfat dairy<br>1 fruit |
| 1 BRAN-Bran Muffin* | 1 grain |
| 1 pat margarine | 1 fat |
| 1 cup coffee | |
| **Lunch** | |
| Sandwich made from: | |
|   1 slice whole-wheat bread | 1 grain |
|   2 oz. tuna | 2 oz. fish, poultry, meat |
|   2 tsp. mayo-type salad dress-<br>    ing | 1 fat |
|   1 oz. cheese, melted on sand-<br>    wich | ½ lowfat dairy |
| Raw celery and carrots | 1 nonstarchy vegetable |
| Herbal tea | |
| **Afternoon Snack** | |
| 1 small apple | 1 fruit |
| 3 rye wafers (2″ × 3½″) | 1 grain |

## Dinner

| | |
|---|---|
| 4 oz. Chicken Mexicali* | 4 oz. fish, poultry, meat |
| ½ c. Broccoli Romana* | 1 nonstarchy vegetable |
| 1 small baked potato | 1 starchy vegetable |
| 1 Tbsp. Mock Sour Cream* | ½ lowfat dairy |
| Chives | |
| Tossed salad with No-Oil Dressing* | 1 nonstarchy vegetable |
| 1 whole-wheat roll | 1 grain |
| 1 pat margarine | 1 fat |
| ½ c. Fresh Fruit Aloha* | 1 fruit |

## SUMMARY—1,200 CALORIES

| | Total | Bkfst. | Lnch. | Snk. | Din. |
|---|---|---|---|---|---|
| Fish, poultry, meat, etc. | 6 oz. | | 2 oz. | | 4 oz. |
| Fat | 3 | 1 | 1 | | 1 |
| Lowfat dairy | 2 | 1 | ½ | | ½ |
| Grains | 4 | 1 | 1 | 1 | 1 |
| Nonstarchy Vegs. | 3 | | 1 | | 2 |
| Starchy Vegs. | 1 | | | | 1 |
| Fruit | 3 | 1 | | 1 | 1 |

# Food Lists [1]

## Fruits

Fruits are good sources of fiber, vitamins, sugar, and energy. Raw fruits with skin and membranes still attached are the best sources of fiber, containing about half a gram per serving. A serving of fruit juice, on the other hand, has about a tenth of a gram of fiber. (Prune juice does not contain fiber, but it does have a laxative effect.) An average serving of fruit (see list) contains 40–80 calories.

Frozen, canned, or dried fruits may be eaten raw or cooked. Fruits can be served for dessert, in salads, as snacks, or even as appetizers.

| NAME OF FRUIT | SERVING | NAME OF FRUIT | SERVING |
|---|---|---|---|
| Apple, fresh | 1 small | Honeydew melon | ⅛ |
| Apple juice/cider | ⅓ cup | Mango | ½ |
| Applesauce | ½ cup | Mixed fruit | ½ cup |
| Apricots, fresh | 2 | Nectar (pear, apricot, etc.) | ⅓ cup |
| Apricots, dried | 4 halves | | |
| Banana | ½ small | Nectarine | 1 |
| Blackberries | ½ cup | Orange | 1 |
| Cantaloupe | ¼ | Orange juice | ½ cup |
| Cherries | 10 | Papaya | ¾ cup |
| Cranberries | as desired | Peach | 1 |
| Cranberry juice | | Pear | 1 small |
| low calorie | ¾ cup | Persimmon | 1 |
| regular | ¼ cup | Pineapple | ½ cup |
| Cranberry sauce | 2 Tbsp. | Plums | 2 |
| Dates | 2 | Prunes, dried | 2 |
| Fig, fresh | 1 | Prune juice | ¼ cup |
| Grapefruit | ½ | Raisins | 2 Tbsp. |
| Grapes, tokay | 12 | Raspberries | ½ cup |
| Grapes, green seedless | 18 | Strawberries | 10 |
| | | Tangerine | 1 |
| Grape juice | ¼ cup | Watermelon | 1 cup |

---

1. Unless otherwise indicated, information in the food lists is from *The Houstonian Preventive Medicine Center's Nutritional Advice* booklet, prepared and compiled by Elizabeth Manis, R.D., edited by Mary Pat O'Malley, M.A., R.D., © 1979. Used by permission.

# Vegetables

## List One: Nonstarchy Vegetables

These vegetables are very low in calories and are good sources of many vitamins and minerals. Serve them raw, lightly steamed, or stir-fried. Season with spices and herbs.

Artichokes
Asparagus
Bamboo shoots
Beans: green, wax, lima (green)
Beets
Broccoli
Brussels sprouts
Cabbage
Carrots
Chinese cabbage
Cauliflower
Celery
Chicory
Cucumbers
Escarole
Eggplant
Greens: beet, chard, collard, dandelion, kale, mustard, spinach, turnip

Lettuce: all varieties
Mushrooms
Okra
Onions, shallots, leeks, green onions
Pepper: green and red
Pimento
Radishes
Sauerkraut
Sprouts: alfalfa and bean
Squash, summer (zucchini, yellow)
Tomatoes
Tomato juice
Turnips
Vegetable juice cocktail
Watercress
Water chestnuts

## List Two: Starchy Vegetables and Soups

The vegetables in this list are starchy and have about 60 calories per serving. Serving sizes are: ½ cup of vegetable, 1 cup of soup, or 2 cups of popcorn without added butter, margarine, or oil. (Note: If more than one serving of these foods is desired, eliminate 1 serving of a grain, bread, or cereal product for each additional serving that is eaten.)

| VEGETABLES | SOUP |
|---|---|
| Corn (ear, cream style, etc.) | Chicken gumbo |
| Mixed vegetables | Chicken vegetable |
| Parsnips | Cream of potato (made with |
| Peas, green | water) |
| Popcorn | Minestrone |
| Potato, white or sweet | Onion (plain) |
| Pumpkin | Scotch broth |
| Rutabaga | Tomato |
| Succotash | Vegetable |
| Tomato puree | Vegetable beef |
| Tomato paste | Vegetarian vegetable |
| Winter squash (acorn, etc.) | |

## Not-Recommended Ways of Preparing Vegetables and Soups

The following commercially prepared vegetables are "not recommended" because of high fat content:
- Commercially fried vegetables such as fried potatoes, french fries, onion rings, fried okra, and fried eggplant;
- Dried beans or peas seasoned with bacon fat, salt pork, or ham hocks;
- Commercial vegetables—frozen or canned—packaged with sauce or butter.

Cream soups or soups containing meat fat or cheese are not recommended. Also, adding cream or cheese sauces, breading, or lots of fat can make a low-calorie vegetable very high in calories.

# Grains, Breads, and Cereals

Grains and grain products give us fiber and many B vitamins and minerals. One serving of a grain, bread, or cereal product contains approximately 70 calories, little or no cholesterol, and very little fat.

The wheat bran found in the outer layer of cereal grain seeds is one of the most concentrated and effective forms of fiber. Although the human requirement for fiber is not yet known, 7–10 grams of crude fiber (roughly double the average American intake) is currently recommended. The foods on this list are divided into three groups. Group 1 consists of foods that are very high in fiber; group 2 is made up of foods that are good sources of fiber; and group 3 contains foods that, while they are low in fat and cholesterol, are poor sources of fiber.

| *NAME OF FOOD* | *SERVING SIZE* |
|---|---|
| **Group I: Best Sources of Fiber (2 Grams per Serving)** | |
| Unprocessed wheat bran | 1–2 Tbsp.[2] |
| High-fiber bran cereal, cold or cooked | ⅓ cup |
| 100% bran flakes | ½ cup |
| Bran muffin made with unprocessed wheat bran (not bran cereal) | 1 small |
| **Group II: Good Sources of Fiber (.4 to 2.0 Grams per Serving)** | |
| Pumpernickel bread | 1 slice |
| Pumpernickel bagel | ½ |
| Pumpernickel roll | 1 small |
| High-fiber biscuit | 1 (omit 1 serving fat) |

---

2. Since calorie content is so low, do not count as a bread serving. Eat as desired.

| | |
|---|---|
| Bran bread | 1 slice |
| Whole-wheat bread | 1 slice |
| English muffin, bran | ½ |
| English muffin, whole wheat | ½ |
| Hamburger bun, whole wheat | ½ |
| Pancakes, whole wheat | 1 (5″ diameter, omit 1 serving fat) |
| Waffle, whole-wheat | 1 (5″ diameter, omit 1 serving fat) |
| Wheat germ | 2 Tbsp. |
| Whole-grain ready-to-eat cereal | ¾ cup |
| Shredded wheat | 1 biscuit |
| 40% bran flakes | ¾ cup |
| Raisin bran | ½ cup |
| Whole-wheat roll or muffin | 1 |
| Bran muffin made with prepared bran cereal | 1 |
| Whole-grain pasta and noodles | ½ cup |

## Group III: Poor Sources of Fiber (.3 Grams or Less per Serving)

### BREADS

| | |
|---|---|
| Bagel, plain | 1 (2–3″ diameter) |
| Biscuit, plain | 1 (2″ diameter, omit 1 serving fat) |
| Bread | |
|   French | 1 slice |
|   Cracked Wheat | 1 slice |
|   Italian | 1 slice |
|   Roman Meal | 1 slice |
|   Oatmeal | 1 slice |
|   Rye | 1 slice |
|   Raisin | 1 slice |
|   White | 1 slice |
| English muffin, plain | ½ |
| Hamburger bun, plain | ½ |
| Pita Bread | ½ pocket |
| Rolls | |
|   French | 1 small |
| Tortilla | |
|   Corn | 1 (6″ diameter) |
|   Flour | 1 (6″ diameter) |

| | |
|---|---|
| Boston brown bread | 1 slice (3″ diameter, 1″ thick) |
| Bread crumbs | 3 tsp. |

### QUICKBREADS

| | |
|---|---|
| Cornbread | 1 square (2″ x 1″, omit 1 serving fat) |
| Muffin, cornbread | 1 (omit 1 serving fat) |
| Muffin, plain | 1 (omit 1 serving fat) |
| Pancakes made from white flour | 1 (5″ diameter, omit 1 serving fat) |
| Waffles made from white flour | ½ (7″ diameter, omit 1 serving fat) |

### CRACKERS

| | |
|---|---|
| Bread sticks | 5 (7″ long, ⅜″ diameter) |
| Graham crackers | 2 (2½″ squares) |
| Matzoth | 1 (6″ square) |
| Oyster crackers | 20 |
| Pretzels | |
|   Dutch | 1 (3″ long, ½″ diameter) |
|   Logs | 3 (3⅛″ × ⅛″) |
|   Sticks | 30 |
|   Large Rings | 6 (2″ diameter) |
| Rye wafers | 3 (2″ × 3½″) |
| Saltines | 6 small squares |
| Soda crackers | 3 (2½″ diameter) |

### CEREALS AND GRAINS

| | |
|---|---|
| Barley, uncooked | 2 Tbsp. |
| Cereal | |
|   Concentrated ready-to-eat (Grape-nuts) | 3 Tbsp. |
|   Cooked (Cream of Wheat, oatmeal) | ½ cup |
|   Puffed (unfrosted) | 1 cup |
|   Ready to eat (unsweetened) | ¾ cup |
| Grits, cooked | ½ cup |
| Rice, white and brown, cooked | ½ cup |
| Pasta, such as spaghetti, lasagna, noodles, macaroni, cooked | ½ cup |
| Egg noodles, cooked (a serving contains approx. 20 mg. cholesterol) | ⅓ cup |
| Rice noodles (Chinese), cooked | ⅓ cup |

*FLOUR AND MEAL*

| | |
|---|---|
| Flour, all kinds | 3 Tbsp. |
| Cornmeal | 2 Tbsp. |
| Cornstarch | 2 Tbsp. |

## Not-Recommended Breads, Crackers, and Cereals

Due to high amounts of saturated fat and/or sugars, the following are not recommended:

Butter rolls
Croissants
Biscuits
Cheese breads
Commercial muffins
Egg breads
Commercial doughnuts
Sweet rolls
Commercial mixes containing dried eggs and whole milk

"Party" crackers
Potato chips
Corn chips
Tortilla chips
Cheese- and bacon-flavored crackers
Cereals containing coconut
Commercial cakes, pies, cookies, fried pies, and cupcakes

# Fish, Poultry, and Meats

On the average, one ounce of meat, fish, or poultry has about: 60 calories, 8 grams protein, 3 grams fat, 0 grams carbohydrate, 0 grams fiber, and about 25 mg. cholesterol (except for organ meats, shrimp, crayfish, and eggs—these high-cholesterol foods should be limited to 1 serving a month). Fish and poultry have about 30–50 calories per ounce; lean red meat has about 60–80 calories per ounce.

Meat, poultry and fish shrink 25% during cooking, in addition to weight loss due to bone and fat removal. Therefore, 8 oz. of raw meat is equal to 6 oz. cooked. Weigh your food-serving portions on a food scale *after* cooking. (Some good, lowfat methods of cooking fish, poultry, and meats appear on p. 306.)

## Fish and Shellfish

| | |
|---|---|
| Clams, 4–5 | 1 oz. |
| Crabmeat, ⅓ cup | 1 oz. |
| Fish, all fresh-water and salt-water varieties, 3″ × 3″ × ¾″ fillet | 3 oz. |
| Fish, chopped, 1 cup | 4 oz. |
| Lobster, ⅓ cup | 1 oz. |
| Oysters, 3 medium or 4 small | 1 oz. |
| Salmon (drain the oil), ¼ cup | 1 oz. |
| Scallops, 2 medium | 1 oz. |
| Shrimp, 5 large, 10 medium, or 20 small (limit to 3 oz. per month due to high cholesterol content) | 1 oz. |
| Tuna (drain the oil), ¼ cup | 1 oz. |

## Poultry (Remove the Skin)

| | |
|---|---|
| Chicken | |
| ½ large breast | 3 oz. |
| 1 drumstick | 1 oz. |
| 1 thigh | 2 oz. |
| Chopped poultry, 1 cup | 4 oz. |
| Rock cornish game hen (½) | 4 oz. |
| Turkey, 3″ × 3″ × ¾″ slice | 3 oz. |

## Beef (Choice or Good Grade—Well Trimmed)

| | |
|---|---|
| Chipped or dried beef, half of 6-oz. pkg. | 3 oz. |
| Chopped cooked beef, 1 cup | 4 oz. |
| Chuck | Weigh after cooking |
| Flank | Weigh after cooking |
| Ground beef, very lean | Weigh after cooking |
| Loin (porterhouse, T-bone, sirloin, tenderloin) | Weigh after cooking |
| Round | Weigh after cooking |
| Rump | Weigh after cooking |
| Sliced roast beef, 3″ × 3″ × ¾″ slice | 3 oz. |

## Pork (Fresh, Well Trimmed)

| | |
|---|---|
| Cubed pork steak, 1 cup | 4 oz. |
| Leg (fresh ham), 3″ × 3¾″ slice | 3 oz. |
| Loin, 3″ × 3″ × ¾″ slice | 3 oz. |
| Shank, 3″ × 3″ × ¾″ slice | 3 oz. |

## Pork (Cured or Smoked, Well Trimmed)

| | |
|---|---|
| Canadian bacon, 3″ × 3″ × ¾″ piece | 3 oz. |
| Ham—center slice, rump or shank, 3″ × 3″ × ¾″ slice | 3 oz. |
| Loin | 3 oz. |

## Lamb (Well Trimmed)

| | |
|---|---|
| Leg | Weigh after cooking |
| Loin | Weigh after cooking |
| Rib | Weigh after cooking |
| Shank shoulder | Weigh after cooking |

## Veal

| | |
|---|---|
| All well trimmed cuts | Weigh after cooking |

## Luncheon Meats

| | |
|---|---|
| Boiled ham | Weight shown on package |
| Precooked lowfat luncheon meats | Weight shown on package |

| | |
|---|---|
| Roast beef, lean 3″ × 3″ × ¾″ slice | 3 oz. |
| Turkey pastrami | Weight shown on package |
| Turkey ham | Weight shown on package |
| Turkey breast | Weight shown on package |

## Game

| | |
|---|---|
| Dove | Weigh after cooking |
| Pheasant | Weigh after cooking |
| Quail | Weigh after cooking |
| Rabbit | Weigh after cooking |
| Squirrel | Weigh after cooking |
| Venison | Weigh after cooking |

## High-Cholesterol Foods

The following foods are good sources of protein but are also very high in cholesterol. They are recommended only in the following amounts:

Egg yolks—limit to 2 per week, including those used in cooking
Caviar—limit to 2 Tbsp. per week
Organ meats (all kinds of liver, heart, kidney, sweetbreads, brains)— limit to 3 oz. per month
Shrimp and crayfish—limit to 3 oz. per month

## Lowfat Cooking Methods for Meats

Before cooking:
  • Select "good" or "choice" grades instead of "prime."
  • Trim all visible fat from meat.
  • Remove all poultry skin.
Cooking methods:
  • Broiling
  • Boiling—skim the fat off the broth.
  • Roasting—set meat or poultry on a rack.
  • Charcoaling.
  • Braising—drain off fat used for browning.
  • Stewing and slow-cooker method—skim fat off the broth.

- Stir-frying—use a recommended oil.
- Frying—use a recommended oil.
- Stocks and gravies—skim the fat off the broth by chilling the stock overnight, adding ice cubes to harden the fat more quickly, or using a gravy skimmer or paper towel to absorb the fat.

## Not Recommended Fish, Poultry, and Meats

Due to high levels of saturated fats, the following are not recommended:

### FISH AND SHELLFISH

Commercially breaded and fried fish

### POULTRY

Duck
Goose

### BEEF

All "prime" graded meats
All untrimmed cuts
Brisket
Hamburger meat
Pastrami
Prime rib (40% fat)
Rib eye
Ribs—short or spare
Sausage, beef

### PORK (FRESH)

All untrimmed cuts
Loin back ribs
Ground pork
Picnic ham, fresh
Shoulder blade
Spare ribs

### PORK (CURED OR SMOKED)

All untrimmed cuts
Bacon (52% fat)
Country-style ham
Deviled ham (canned)
Neckbones
Ham hock (44% fat)
Picnic ham, smoked
Pig's feet and jowls
Salt pork
Sausage, pork

### VEAL

All untrimmed cuts
Breast riblets
Summer sausage

### LUNCHEON MEAT

Bologna (23% fat)
Canned luncheon meat
Frankfurters (28% fat)
Headcheese
Liverwurst
Salami

### GAME

Sausage, venison

## Not-Recommended High-Cholesterol Foods

Egg yolks—more than the 2 allowed per week
Caviar—more than 2 Tbsp. per week

Eggnog
Hollandaise sauce
Organ meats (liver, heart, kidneys, sweetbreads, brains)—more than
    3 oz. per month
Shrimp and crayfish—more than 3 oz. per month

# Protein from Vegetable Sources

Protein is made up of 22 amino acids. All but nine of these can be manufactured by our bodies. These nine are called "essential amino acids." Meats, fish, poultry, milk, and eggs contain all nine of these, and are called "complete" proteins. There are other foods, however, which contain some of these acids, and are called "incomplete proteins." When these foods are combined with other foods that have the missing amino acids, the foods together form good quality protein.

A one-cup serving of cooked legumes (such as peas or beans) served with 1 serving of a grain product, a small amount of animal protein, or a lowfat dairy product, provides the same amount of complete protein as you'd get from a 3 oz. piece of meat, fish, or poultry. You can use this kind of food combination in place of meats on a weight-loss plan, and in place of or in addition to meat on a maintenance plan.

The following lists show possible combinations of legumes with grains or lowfat dairy products. After the lists is a chart from *Jane Brody's Nutrition Book* showing how to combine various vegetable proteins to get complete protein. The reading lists in Part Five of this book suggest some books and cookbooks that give even more information about how to combine proteins.

## Legumes

(For serving sizes, see list for Starchy Vegetables and Soups.)

Black-eyed peas
Garbanzo beans (chickpeas)
Kidney beans
Lentils
Lima beans, mature
Navy beans

Peanuts
Pinto beans
Soybeans (highest-quality protein in the legume family)
Soybean meat substitutes
Split peas

## Foods to Combine with Legumes

(For serving sizes, see list for Grains, Breads, and Cereals.)

| | |
|---|---|
| Cornbread | Tortilla |
| Rice | Whole-wheat bread |

(For serving sizes, see list for Dairy Products.)

| | |
|---|---|
| Cheese | Lowfat milk |
| Cottage cheese | Lowfat yogurt |

## Complementary Vegetable Proteins: Possible Combinations[3]

If you combine vegetable proteins in the same meal in any of the ways suggested below, you will obtain complete protein equivalent to the protein in meat and other animal food:

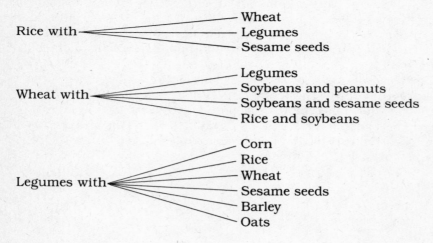

Rice with — Wheat, Legumes, Sesame seeds

Wheat with — Legumes, Soybeans and peanuts, Soybeans and sesame seeds, Rice and soybeans

Legumes with — Corn, Rice, Wheat, Sesame seeds, Barley, Oats

3. Reprinted from JANE BRODY'S NUTRITION BOOK by permission of W. W. Norton & Company, Inc. Copyright © 1981 by Jane E. Brody.

# Dairy Products

Dairy products contain calcium, protein, and riboflavin (a B vitamin). Adults need 900 mg. of calcium a day (the amount in about 2 cups of milk). Teenagers and pregnant or nursing women need about 1200 mg.

But dairy products also contain saturated fat (animal fat). The fat content of dairy products ranges from ½% to 80%. The products listed below are relatively low in saturated fat. One serving of each of these lowfat dairy products contains: 90—100 calories, 8 mg. cholesterol, and 2 grams of fat.

## Lowfat Dairy Products

| FOOD | SERVING SIZE |
|---|---|
| Cheese | |
| Creamed and lowfat cottage cheese | ½ cup |
| Low cholesterol cheese made with vegetable oil | 1½ oz. |
| Lowfat hard or soft cheese containing less than 10% butterfat | 2 oz. |
| Milk | |
| Buttermilk made from skim milk | 1 cup |
| ½% lowfat milk | 1 cup |
| 1% lowfat milk | 1 cup |
| Nonfat dry milk, reconstituted | 1 cup |
| Skim milk (nonfat) | 1 cup |
| Yogurt, lowfat (made with skim milk), plain | ⅔ cup |

## Not Recommended Dairy Products

Due to the high fat content of the following dairy products, they are not recommended. (Note: If you do choose to eat "regular," high-fat cheese such as cheddar or Swiss, limit consumption to no more than 1–2 oz. per week.)

Butter (80% fat)
Cheese
  American cheese
  Cheddar cheese
  Cream cheese
  Cheese made from whole milk
    or containing 10% or more
    butterfat
  Natural cheeses (up to 50%
    fat)

Chocolate milk
Condensed milk
Evaporated milk
Half-and-half (12% fat)
Ice cream (10–20% fat)
2% lowfat milk
Mellorine
Sour cream (20% fat)
Whipping cream (20% fat)
Whole milk

# Fats

The amount and kind of fat a person eats plays an important role in maintaining the health of his or her cardiovascular system. Eating lots of saturated fats raises the level of serum cholesterol, while eating polyunsaturated fats helps lower the serum cholesterol. Monounsaturated fats are considered neutral because they do not raise or lower the serum cholesterol.

In order to lower your cholesterol level, you will need to choose polyunsaturated fats to make up your daily fat allowance. The oils highest in polyunsaturated fats are called "Best Oils" and contain a P.S. ratio of 5 or greater (see p. 195 for explanation of P.S. ratio). The oils, margarines, and nuts in the list entitled "Recommended fats" contain less polyunsaturated fat and have a P.S. ratio of 1–5. They cannot be substituted for "Best Oils," but can be used in addition to them, as long as the total amount of fat still falls within the daily guidelines of your eating plan.

The fats listed in this section contain 45 calories and about .5 grams of fat per serving. Oils and margarines contain little or no carbohydrates or protein. Nuts, avocados, olives, and peanut butter are all very high in fat, but they do also contain carbohydrates and protein.

| FAT | SERVING |
|---|---|

### Best Oils (P.S. Ratio of 5 or Greater)

| | |
|---|---|
| Safflower oil | 1 tsp. |
| Safflower oil blend | 1 tsp. |
| Corn oil | 1 tsp. |
| Sunflower oil | 1 tsp. |
| Walnut oil | 1 tsp. |
| Black walnuts | 4 halves (1 Tbsp.) |
| English walnuts | 4 halves (1 Tbsp.) |
| Homemade or commercial oil- and-vinegar salad dressing made with "Best Oils" | 2 tsp. |

## Recommended Fats (P.S. Ratio of 1–5)

### MARGARINES

| | |
|---|---|
| Tub margarines listing liquid safflower, sunflower, corn, or soybean oil as first ingredient | 1 tsp. |
| Diet tub margarines listing *liquid* oil as main ingredient | 2 tsp. |

### SALAD DRESSINGS

| | |
|---|---|
| Commercial mayonnaise | 1 tsp. |
| Commercial mayonnaise-type salad dressing | 2 tsp. |
| Commercial salad dressings | |
|   French dressing | 2 tsp. |
|   Oil-and-vinegar dressing | 2 tsp. |
|   Italian dressing | 2 tsp. |
|   Russian dressing | 2 tsp. |
|   Thousand Island dressing | 2 tsp. |
| Commercial low-calorie salad dressing | 1–2 Tbsp. |

### OILS

| | |
|---|---|
| Cottonseed oil | 1 tsp. |
| Cottonseed/soybean oil blend | 1 tsp. |
| Olive oil | 1 tsp. |
| Peanut oil | 1 tsp. |
| Sesame oil | 1 tsp. |
| Soybean oil | 1 tsp. |

### NUTS AND SEEDS

| | |
|---|---|
| Almonds | 7 |
| Brazil nuts | 2 |
| Cashews | 3 medium |
| Chestnuts | 5 small |
| Filberts (hazelnuts) | 5 |
| Hickory nuts | 7 small |
| Peanuts | |
|   Spanish | 20 |
|   Virginia | 10 |
| Pecans | 6 halves |
| Pine nuts | 1 Tbsp. |
| Pistachios | 15 |

| | |
|---|---|
| Pumpkin seeds, hulled | 1 Tbsp. |
| Soynuts | 1 Tbsp. |
| Sunflower seeds, hulled | 1 Tbsp. |

**OTHER**

| | |
|---|---|
| Avocado | ⅛ |
| Olives, green | 10 |
| Olives, ripe | 5 |
| Peanut butter | 2 tsp. |

## *Not-Recommended Fats*

Bacon
Bacon fat
Butter
Chocolate
Coconut
Coconut oil
Cream sauces
Gravy made with meat
    drippings
Ham hocks
Hydrogenated vegetable oils
Lard
Macadamia nuts
Meat drippings
Meat fat

Palm kernel oil
Salad dressings
    Bleu cheese
    Green goddess (made with
      sour cream)
    Roquefort
    Sour-cream-based dressings
    Cheese-based dressings
Salt pork
Solid shortening
Stick margarine
Tub margarine not listing liquid
    oil as first ingredient

## *"Hidden" Fats*

To compensate for "hidden" fats in certain foods, omit the amount of fat specified below from your daily servings:

| | |
|---|---|
| Vegetables seasoned with margarine or stir-fried | ½ tsp. per ½-cup serving |
| Vegetables, breaded and fried | 1 tsp. per ½-cup serving |
| French fries | 1 tsp. per 10 small fries |
| Fried or scrambled eggs | 1 tsp. per egg |
| Pan-fried or basted fish, poultry, or meat | 1 tsp. per oz. |
| Salads: potato, noodle, tuna, salmon, chicken, or egg | 1 Tbsp. per ½-cup serving |
| Coleslaw | 2 tsp. per ½-cup serving |
| Tossed salad with dressing | 1 Tbsp. per 1-cup serving |

# Desserts and Sweets

These foods, high in sugar and calories and low in nutrients, are not recommended for anyone who is trying to lose weight. If you are following a maintenance plan, here are some suggested desserts, and some others which are not recommended. One serving of dessert contains approximately 100 calories.

| RECOMMENDED DESSERTS | SERVING |
| --- | --- |
| Angel food cake | 1″ slice (1/16th cake) |
| Cake[4] | 1 piece (1″ × 2″ × 2″) |
| Cupcakes[4] | 1 (not iced) |
| Candy, hard | 1 oz. |
| Carbonated beverages | 8 oz. |
| Cookies (fig bars, gingersnaps and other lowfat varieties[4]) | 2–3 |
| Fruit-flavored drinks | 6 oz. |
| Fruit ices | ½ cup |
| Fruit whips | ½ cup |
| Fudgesicles, Popsicles | 1 |
| Gelatin dessert | ⅔ cup |
| Honey | 2 Tbsp. |
| Ice milk | ½ cup |
| Jellies, jams, preserves, marmalade | 2 Tbsp. |
| Molasses | 2 Tbsp. |
| Pie[4] | 1″ slice |
| Pudding[4] | ⅓ cup |
| Sherbet | ⅓ cup |
| Sugar, syrup | 2 Tbsp. |
| Yogurt, fruit flavored | ⅓ cup |
| Yogurt, frozen | ⅓ cup |

---

4. Prepared with allowed ingredients, such as lowfat milk, vegetable oil, etc.

## *Not-Recommended Desserts and Sweets (too high in saturated fat)*

Commercial cakes, cookies, pies, pastries, cupcakes, and cheese-cakes

Commercial mixes containing dried eggs, whole milk, coconut oil, or shortening

Fried pies

Homemade cakes, cookies, pies, pastries, cupcakes, and cheesecakes made with eggs, shortening, butter, sour cream, or other saturated fats

Ice cream

Mellorine

Puddings made with whole milk

# What about Alcohol?

In different quantities for different individuals, alcohol is a toxic drug and a major cause of nutritional deficiencies. As the incidence of alcoholism has soared in the United States, so has the incidence of liver cirrhosis, which now ranks as a leading cause of death among Americans. The rate of fatal liver disease is increasing more rapidly than the rate of coronary heart fatalities. Alcoholism is also a major cause of auto accidents and broken homes.

A great deal of evidence has accumulated during the last twenty years indicating that alcohol produces pathological changes in liver tissue. Even an optimum diet cannot prevent the liver degeneration which results from prolonged and heavy alcohol intake.

Alcohol has a high caloric value (7.1 calories per gram), and these are "empty" calories, providing few, if any, nutrients. When alcoholic beverages are substituted for food on a regular basis, nutritional deficiencies are inevitable. Regular alcohol consumption can cause malnutrition by interfering with normal digestion and absorption of food.

If you do choose to drink, follow the guidelines listed on the maintenance eating plans, which recommend a maximum of only one drink per day of alcoholic beverages. One serving of alcohol contains approximately 100 calories.

| *ALCOHOL* | *SERVING* |
|---|---|
| Liquor (gin, rum, scotch, vodka, whiskey, bourbon, etc.) | 1½ oz. (1 jigger) |
| Table wine (red or white) | 4 oz. |
| Dessert wine (sherry, etc.) | 2½ oz. |
| Beer | |
|    Regular | 8 oz. |
|    Lite | 12 oz. |

# Part Four

# BODYCARE
# RECIPES

*Healthful Cooking That
Tastes Great, Too!*

*Except where indicated, the recipes in this section were developed by Nancy Lew Fong, Nutritionist, and Deborah Rae Davis, Chef, for The Phoenix. The Phoenix is a health and fitness spa for women and men and is located at 111 North Post Oak Lane, Houston, TX 77024.*

*NANCY LEW FONG, R.D. is nutritionist for the renowned Houstonian Preventive Medicine Center and consultant to The Phoenix, where she has helped develop creative and tasty menu ideas for the guests. Prior to that time she served as a clinical and research dietitian at M.D. Anderson Hospital in Houston, as well as nutrition instructor at the University of Texas School of Allied Health.*

*DEBORAH RAE DAVIS has been the full-time chef for The Phoenix since its opening in June of 1980. Debbie received her formal training in the art of culinary preparation from Houston's chapter of the Educational Institute of the American Culinary Federation. Afterward, Debbie was employed by the Marriott Hotel. But after working at the Marriott a few months, she began to feel as though her artistry and experimental abilities were being stifled. She heard about The Phoenix, agreed with its philosophies on healthful eating, and applied for the position of Executive Chef.*

# Breakfast

## *Breakfast Smoothie*

2 oranges, peeled and cubed
2 bananas, peeled and cubed
1 pint strawberries, hulled
2 Tbsp. honey

½ cup plain lowfat yogurt
2 eggs
2 cups ice cubes

Blend fruit, honey, yogurt, and eggs until smooth. Add ice cubes. Blend until smooth.

Yield: 4 servings
Calories: 165 per serving

## *Low-Calorie Danish*

1 pkg. Equal (aspartame)
2 Tbsp. lowfat cottage cheese
1 Tbsp. plain lowfat yogurt
¼ tsp. vanilla or lemon extract

½ raisin English muffin, cut
    into 2 thin slices
¼ cup fresh peaches or other
    fresh fruit, sliced
⅛ tsp. cinnamon

Combine cottage cheese, yogurt, extract, and Equal. Mash together until fairly smooth (this can be done in a food processor).

Spread mixture on each slice of the half of the English muffin. Arrange fruit on top. Sprinkle with cinnamon.

Place in a toaster oven or under broiler for 3–4 minutes until heated through, being careful not to burn.

Yield: 1 serving
Calories: 130 per serving

# Strawberry-Egg Pancakes

¾ cup creamed lowfat cottage cheese
¼ cup flour
⅓ cup nonfat dry milk
¼ cup lowfat (½% or 1%) milk
½ tsp. cinnamon
¼ tsp. nutmeg

3 eggs, separated
1 cup strawberries, thinly sliced
1 cup strawberries, pureed
½ cup plain lowfat yogurt
Artificial sweetener to taste

Combine cottage cheese, flour, milks, and spices. Add egg yolks and beat until smooth.

Beat egg whites until stiff peaks form. Gently fold egg whites into cottage-cheese mixture.

Drop by spoonfuls onto a hot, *lightly* greased nonstick skillet. Stud with sliced strawberries. Cook slowly so pancakes can cook through. Turn once.

Make sauce by combining pureed strawberries, yogurt, and Sweet 'n' Low to taste. Serve pancakes immediately with sauce.

Yield: 4 servings
Calories: 190 calories

# Appetizers

## Gazpacho

1 small cucumber, peeled and
    seeded
3 medium tomatoes, peeled
Juice of 1 lemon

1 small clove garlic, finely diced
Dash of Worchestershire sauce
⅓ cup celery, diced
⅓ cup cucumber, diced

Combine 1 cucumber, tomatoes, lemon juice, garlic and Worchestershire sauce in a blender and blend until smooth. Refrigerate until ice cold. Serve topped with diced celery and cucumber.

Yield: 6 ½-cup servings
Calories: Negligible

## Herbed Neufchâtel Cheese Rounds

1 8-oz. pkg. Neufchâtel cheese,
    softened
1 tsp. Italian herbs

⅛ tsp. black pepper
½ tsp. garlic powder
Melba rounds, whole wheat

Beat cheese with herbs, pepper and garlic until well mixed. Spread or pipe onto melba rounds.

Yield: Many
Calories: 1 tsp. cheese mixture on 1 melba round is 33 calories.

## Pickled Shrimp

½ cup cider vinegar
½ cup water
1 tsp. Creole seasoning

1 bay leaf
4 white peppercorns
1 dozen large shrimp, peeled
    and deveined

Mix liquids with other ingredients; place in saucepan and bring to a boil. Cook shrimp until done. Refrigerate in liquid at least 3 hours—6 hours or more is ideal.

Yield: 12 servings
Calories: 20 per serving

# Yogurt Dip for Raw Vegetables

1 cup plain lowfat yogurt
1 tsp. Spike (a blend of herbs. I find it in health food stores.)
1 Tbsp. Dijon mustard

Blend together. Chill and serve with raw vegetables.

Yield: 1 cup
Calories: 1 Tbsp. is about 10 calories.

## Baked Fish Fillets (Rule of Thumb)

Fish fillets (sole, trout, etc.)          Juice of ½ lemon
Pam or other spray-on nonstick           Lite salt
    coating                                   Pepper

    Arrange fillets in shallow baking pan sprayed with Pam. Sprinkle with lemon juice, lite salt, and pepper.

    Bake at 500° for about 5 minutes per inch of thickness. Watch closely, since some fillets are only ½″ thick and only need to be baked for 2–3 minutes.

    When done, fish will be white and flaky when pricked with a fork. If fish is baked too long, it will be tough.

Yield: 4-oz. serving is 200 calories.

## Succulent Fish

2 lb. sea bass or other fish fillets       Lite salt
½ cup unsweetened pineapple               Pepper
    juice                                          Pam or other spray-on nonstick
¼ cup steak sauce                                 coating

    Cut fillets into serving-size pieces. Place fish in single layer in shallow baking dish. Combine remaining ingredients and pour over fish. Refrigerate, covered, for 30 minutes, turning once. Remove fish, reserving marinade.

    Place fish on a broiler pan sprayed with Pam. Broil about 4 inches from heat source for 4–6 minutes. Turn carefully and brush with reserved marinade. Broil 4–6 minutes longer, or until fish flakes easily with a fork. (Note: if fish fillets are small, less broiling time may be required.)

Yield: 8 servings
Calories: 120 calories per serving

*ess Breast of Chicken*

1 pineapple juice
ed chicken breasts

n baking dish and make enough pineapple-soy sauce mixture to cover chicken.* Bake at 350° for about 25 minutes, or until done. Chicken may be marinated overnight, if desired, prior to cooking.

(Note: For two of us, I use three chicken breasts and make 1 cup of the mixture, or ⅓ cup soy sauce and ⅔ cup unsweetened pineapple juice. I eat one chicken breast, and Keith gets two!)

Calories: 180 per serving (one chicken breast is a serving.)

## Chicken Mexicali
### (by Elizabeth Manis)

2 frying chicken breasts, split*
¼ cup low-calorie Italian salad dressing
⅓ cup plain or seasoned tomato juice
Chili powder or pepper sauce to taste

Marinate chicken in remaining ingredients several hours in the refrigerator; turn occasionally. Drain and reserve marinade.

Arrange chicken skin-side up on a shallow nonstick pan. Broil 4 inches from heat source, turning often, until done—about 35 minutes. Baste frequently with reserved marinade. Chicken can be cooked on charcoal grill if preferred. Remove skin before eating.

Yield: 4 servings
Calories: 210 per serving

*I use other chicken parts, like thighs and drumsticks, and they taste great, too.

# Turkey Breast Singapore

| | |
|---|---|
| 1 4–6 lb. turkey breast, thawed | 1 onion |
| 1 Tbsp. curry powder | 1 carrot |
| 1 Tbsp. fines herbes | 1 stalk celery |
| 1 Tbsp. lite salt | ½ orange, unpeeled |
| 1 tsp. paprika | 1 cup water |
| | 1 cup gin (optional) |

Wash and dry turkey breast. Mix curry powder, fines herbes, lite salt, and paprika. Rub turkey with this mixture. Place in pan with vegetables and orange. Roast uncovered at 350° for 3 hours or until tender (until internal temperature reaches 185°). Baste often with water (mixed with gin, if desired).

When done, spoon off all the fat from juices. Serve turkey sliced thin with unthickened pan juices.

Calories: 2-oz. serving is 100 calories.

# Meatless Main Dishes

## Frijoles (Beans)[1]

2 cups pinto, black, or red
    kidney beans
2 onions, finely chopped
2 cloves garlic, chopped
1 bay leaf (or sprig of *epazote*)
2 or more *serrano* chilies,
    chopped (or 1 tsp. dried
    *pequin* chilies, crumbled)

3 Tbsp. vegetable oil
Salt
Freshly ground pepper
1 tomato, peeled, seeded, and
    chopped

Wash the beans and place in a saucepan (without soaking), with enough cold water to cover: 1 of the chopped onions, 1 of the garlic cloves, the bay leaf (or *epazote*), and the chilies. Cover; bring to a boil; reduce heat; then simmer gently, adding more boiling water as it boils away. When the beans begin to wrinkle, add 1 Tbsp. of the oil. Continue cooking until the beans are soft. At this point, stir in enough salt and ground pepper to taste. Cook for another 30 minutes over the same heat, but *do not add water*, as there should not be a great deal of liquid when the beans are done.

Heat the remaining oil in a skillet and sauté the remaining onion and garlic until limp. Add the tomato and cook for about 2 minutes over medium heat; add 3 Tbsp. of beans, bit by bit, with some of the liquid from the pot, and mash until you have a smooth, fairly heavy paste. Return this to the bean pot and stir into the beans over low heat to thicken the remaining liquid.

Yield: 6 1-cup servings
Calories: 325 per serving

---

1. From THE COMPLETE BOOK OF MEXICAN COOKING by Elisabeth Lambert Ortiz. Copyright © 1967 by Elisabeth Lambert Ortiz. Reprinted by permission of the publisher, M. Evans and Company, Inc. New York, New York 10017.

# Herbed Lentils and Rice
### (*by Elizabeth Manis*)

2⅔ cups chicken broth
¾ cup dry lentils
¾ cup onion, chopped
½ cup uncooked brown rice
¼ cup dry wine (optional)
½ tsp. basil
¼ tsp. lite salt

¼ tsp. thyme
⅛ tsp. garlic
⅛ tsp. ginger
⅛ tsp. pepper
¼ tsp. oregano
4 oz. lowfat white cheese (optional)

Soak lentils overnight, or at least 4–6 hours. Combine broth, drained lentils, onion, rice, wine, and spices with 2 oz. cheese. Bake at 375° in 1½ quart casserole for 1–2 hours, stirring occasionally. Top with remainder of cheese, return to oven to melt cheese, and serve.

Yield: 8 servings
Calories: ½ cup is 100 calories without cheese.
    ½ cup is 140 calories with cheese.

# Marinated Tofu with Vegetables
### (*adapted by Andrea Wells Miller*)

1 lb. tofu, cubed
1 eggplant, cubed and steamed
(can substitute zucchini)
Cherry tomatoes
1 small onion, sliced
Whole mushrooms
1 green pepper, sliced

*Marinade:*
⅓ cup tamari soy sauce (or regular soy sauce)
⅓ cup vegetable oil
1 Tbsp. lemon juice
1½ Tbsp. wine vinegar
1 clove garlic, minced and
sauteed
⅛ tsp. black pepper

To press tofu, place cubes of tofu on towel on counter. Place another towel on top of tofu. Then place a cookie sheet or cutting board over covered tofu. Put about 3 pounds of weight (heavy cookbooks, jars, etc.), evenly distributed, on top of cookie sheet. Let stand 15–20 minutes. This removes the water from the tofu.

Marinate pressed tofu for 5 hours (1 hour is sufficient). Place tofu and vegetables in a shallow pan. Broil about 4 inches below the heat. Baste with marinade and turn twice. When tofu appears crisp (in about 10–15 minutes), it's done.

# Mexican-Style Quiche

4 6″ flour tortillas
Pam or other spray-on nonstick coating
2 oz. Monterey Jack cheese
   (Lite Line—4 slices)
1 medium onion, sliced and
   separated into rings
2 Tbsp. unprocessed bran

2 chili peppers, diced
2 cups skim milk
2 beaten eggs
½ tsp. lite salt
½ tsp. chili powder
¼ tsp. dry mustard
A few parsley sprigs, optional
Pickled peppers, optional

    Gently press one flour tortilla in each of four individual au-gratin casseroles sprayed with Pam. Top with cheese slices. Place onion rings, chili peppers, and bran on cheese slices. Hold back one onion ring per casserole.

    In saucepan, heat milk until almost boiling, but do not allow to boil. Gradually add the milk to the 2 beaten eggs, blending well; stir in lite salt, chili powder, and mustard. Place casseroles into shallow baking pan; place on oven rack. Divide egg mixture evenly among casseroles. Top each with a reserved onion ring.

    Bake in 350° oven about 30 minutes or until knife comes out clean. Let stand 5 minutes before serving. Hold at room temperature. If desired, garnish with parsley sprigs and pickled peppers.

Yield: 4 servings
Calories: 225 per serving

# Hearty Minestrone

½ cup Great Northern beans,
   soaked overnight in water
   and drained
1 Tbsp. olive (or safflower) oil
1 clove garlic, minced
1 cup onions, thinly sliced
1 cup carrots, diced
1 cup celery, diced
½ cup potatoes, peeled and
   diced
2 cups zucchini, diced
1 cup green beans, diced

3 cups cabbage, shredded
1½ qts. low-sodium beef stock
4 Italian plum tomatoes, peeled,
   or 1 8-oz. can low-sodium
   tomatoes with their liquid
1 tsp. dried basil
½ cup elbow macaroni
¼ cup freshly grated parmesan
   cheese (optional)

Put beans in a saucepan and add water to cover by 2 inches. Bring to a moderate boil, cover, and cook until beans are tender, about 40 minutes. Let stand in cooking liquid until ready to use.

While beans are cooking, heat oil in a large kettle. Add garlic and onions and cook over medium heat until the onions are tender and golden but not browned. Add the carrots and cook, stirring frequently, for 3 minutes. Repeat this procedure with the celery, potato, zucchini, and green beans, cooking each vegetable for 3 minutes. Add the cabbage. Cook, stirring occasionally, about 5 minutes. Add stock, tomatoes with their liquid, and basil. Cover and simmer for at least 3 hours.

About 15 minutes before the soup is done, drain beans and add with macaroni to soup. Just before removing from heat, swirl in parmesan cheese, if desired.

Yield: 5 servings
Calories: 112 per serving

# Vegetables

## Broccoli Romana

1 Tbsp. safflower oil
1 tsp. finely chopped garlic
3 cups broccoli florets

Pepper to taste
Juice of 1 lemon

Heat oil in a skillet or wok. Add garlic and cook for 30 seconds. Add broccoli florets and toss until tender but still crisp (about 7 minutes). With a slotted spoon, transfer florets to a heated bowl and sprinkle with pepper and lemon juice.

Yield: 6 servings
Calories: 40 per serving

## Hawaiian Carrots

2 cups carrots, sliced
1 cup chicken broth
¼ cup onion, minced
¼ cup green pepper, chopped

8 oz. can juice-packed pineapple chunks, drained (reserve juice)
2 tsp. cornstarch
Lite salt and pepper to taste

Place carrots and chicken broth in saucepan. Simmer, covered, 10 minutes or until carrots are nearly tender. Add onions and green pepper. Cook uncovered 2 minutes.

Drain liquid from saucepan. Add pineapple. Cook 1 minute. Mix cornstarch with reserved pineapple juice until well blended; stir into simmering vegetables. Cook and stir until mixture simmers and thickens. Sprinkle with lite salt and pepper.

Yield: 6 servings
Calories: 51 per serving

# Ratatouille

This can be served as a lunch dish with crackers. The cheese combines with the grain in the crackers to increase the protein content.

1 medium eggplant, peeled and
    diced
2 tomatoes, diced
1 large onion, diced
1 green pepper, diced
3 green onions, diced
2 zucchini (optional), diced
4 yellow squash (optional)

1 Tbsp. safflower oil
1 Tbsp. lemon juice
1 tsp. Italian herbs
Lite salt
⅛ tsp. white pepper
3 oz. lowfat Monterey Jack
    cheese, grated

Mix oil, lemon juice, herbs, lite salt, and pepper. Place with diced vegetables in casserole dish and bake at 350° for 45 minutes. Place cheese on top. Serve hot.

Yield: 6–8 servings
Calories: 50 per serving

# Dilled Vegetable Medley

1½ cups cucumbers, thinly
    sliced
½ cup radishes, sliced
¼ cup green onion, sliced
¼ cup plain lowfat yogurt
2 Tbsp. dairy sour cream

2 Tbsp. tarragon vinegar
2 tsp. snipped fresh dill or ½
    tsp. dried dill
Dash lite salt
4 leaves leaf lettuce

Combine cucumber, radishes, and onion. In small bowl combine yogurt, sour cream, tarragon vinegar, dill, and lite salt; add to vegetable mixture and toss to coat. Chill thoroughly. Serve on individual lettuce-lined plates.

Yield: 4 servings
Calories: 33 per serving

# *Coleslaw*

½ head of green cabbage,
   shredded
3 carrots, grated
2—3 McIntosh apples, chopped

Juice of 1 lemon
1½ tsp. Creole seasoning with
   cayenne (adjust to taste)

Toss together and serve.

Yield: 6—8 servings
Calories: Negligible

# Breads (Mostly Muffins)

## BRAN-Bran Muffins
### (by Andrea Wells Miller)

3 cups unprocessed bran
1 cup boiling water
1 stick margarine
½ cup honey
½ cup molasses
2 eggs

1 tsp. vanilla
2 cups buttermilk
2¼ cups unbleached white flour
1½ tsp. baking soda
1 tsp. salt

In the main mixing bowl, combine 1 cup bran and the boiling water. Stir well and allow to stand for 5 minutes.

Meanwhile, in a small bowl, cream margarine. Add honey and molasses slowly, beating until creamy. Beat in eggs, then add vanilla and buttermilk. Stir well. Add this to bran mixture.

In a third bowl (medium size), combine dry ingredients: flour, soda, salt, and remaining two cups of bran. Add dry ingredients to wet bran mixture, stirring only until flour is moistened.

Spoon into greased or paper-lined muffin cups, filling ⅔ full. Bake at 375° for 20–25 minutes, or until toothpick comes out clean.

OR spoon batter into plastic container and cover tightly. This will keep in the refrigerator about 6 weeks. Bake muffins as above when needed.

Yield: 1½ quarts batter (about 4 dozen regular-sized muffins)

Calories: 50 calories each for regular-sized muffins
          20 calories each for miniature muffins

# Three-Grain Muffins

⅓ cup stone ground cornmeal
⅓ cup soy flour
1 cup whole-wheat flour
⅓ cup brown sugar
½ tsp. salt
1 tsp. baking soda

1 large egg, lightly beaten
1 cup plain lowfat yogurt
⅓ cup diet margarine, melted

In a bowl, combine cornmeal, flours, brown sugar, salt, and baking soda.

In a separate bowl, mix the egg and yogurt together lightly. Stir into the dry ingredients. Then stir margarine into the mixture.

Fill muffin tins ⅔ full and bake at 350° for 20–25 minutes, or until toothpick comes out clean.

Yield: 20 regular-sized muffins, 48 miniature muffins
Calories: 50 calories each for regular-sized muffins
        20 calories each for miniature muffins

# Zucchini Muffins (or Bread)

2 cups grated zucchini
3 eggs
1 cup safflower oil
2 tsp. vanilla
1 cup molasses
2 cups unbleached flour

1½ cups graham flour
1 tsp. baking soda
¼ tsp. baking powder
2 tsp. ground cinnamon
½ cup chopped nuts

Peel and grate zucchini and put into strainer to drain until later.

Beat eggs at medium speed for 1 minute. Stir in oil, vanilla, and molasses. In a separate bowl, stir flour, soda, baking powder, cinnamon, and nuts together. Add to batter; mix at low speed only until flour is moistened. Stir in zucchini.

Spoon batter into greased muffin tins or loaf pan. Bake in a preheated oven at 325° for 20–25 minutes for muffins, 50 minutes for bread, or until toothpick comes out clean.

Yield: 25 regular-sized muffins, 60 miniature muffins, 1 loaf
Calories: 60 each for regular-sized muffins
        30 each for miniature muffins
        60 for each ½″ slice of loaf

# Miscellaneous

## Mock Sour Cream
*(from The Houstonian Preventive Medicine Center's*
*Nutritional Advice Booklet)*

1 cup lowfat cottage cheese
1–2 tsp. lemon juice
1–2 tsp. skim milk

Blend until smooth. Add more liquid if consistency is not satisfactory. Chill and use as dip base or in recipes.

Yield: 1 cup
Calories: 1 Tbsp. is 12 calories.

## No-Oil Dressing
*(by Andrea Wells Miller)*

½ cup red wine vinegar
¼ cup water
1 Tbsp. Dijon mustard

3–4 sprigs fresh parsley
½ clove garlic, chopped

Place all ingredients in blender and blend.*

Yield: About ¾ cup dressing
Calories: Negligible

*To help get this no-oil dressing on the salad evenly, try placing it in a plastic "zip"-type bag. Add salad, seal bag, shake and turn until dressing has coated salad. (I have found that this is a great way of getting the small amounts allowed of other dressings evenly on salads.)

# *Vinaigrette Dressing*

⅓ cup water  
⅔ cup red wine vinegar  
⅓ cup safflower oil  

1 tsp. Dijon mustard  
1 clove garlic, minced  
2 Tbsp. chopped parsley  

    Mix all ingredients thoroughly and chill. Recommended portion is 1 Tbsp.

Yield: 1⅓ cup dressing  
Calories: 1 Tbsp. is 115 calories.

# Desserts

## *Fresh Fruit Aloha*

1 cup fresh pineapple chunks*
1 papaya, peeled, seeded, and
    cubed*

½ cup fresh strawberries, sliced
1 tsp. lime juice
2 Tbsp. honey

Combine fruits, lime juice, and honey. Chill thoroughly.

*Peaches, bananas, or nectarines may be substituted if papaya or pineapple are not available in your area.

Yield: 4 servings
Calories: 80 per serving

## *Pineapple-Orange Sherbet*

2 cups plain lowfat yogurt*
1 cup fresh pineapple (or
    drained crushed pineapple
    canned in its own juice)
1 tsp. finely grated orange peel

½ cup frozen orange juice
    concentrate
½ tsp. coconut (or vanilla) ex-
    tract

Stir all ingredients together and freeze until mushy. Beat thoroughly and return to freezer. Serve within 1 hour, or freeze until firm and let stand 10–15 minutes before serving. Garnish with grated orange peel.

Yield: 1 quart
Calories: 52 per 2-oz. serving

*The resulting taste of this sherbet is delicious, but quite tart. I found that adding some artificial sweetener can tone down this tartness. But if you like the tart flavor of plain yogurt, you might like the recipe just as it is.

# California Cheesecake

1 16-oz. pkg. part skim ricotta cheese, or 16-oz. carton lowfat cottage cheese
2 eggs
¼ cup fructose
¼ cup lowfat vanilla yogurt
1¼ tsp. grated lemon peel
1 tsp. fresh lemon juice
½ tsp. imitation butter (an extract)
3 egg whites
¼ tsp. cream of tartar
Graham cracker crust (see recipe below)
Lemon topping (see recipe below)

Combine cheese, eggs, fructose, vanilla yogurt, lemon peel and juice, and imitation butter in a mixing bowl. Beat at low speed with an electric mixer until blended, then increase speed and blend until smooth. In a small bowl, beat egg whites with cream of tartar until stiff but not dry. Gently fold egg-white mixture into cheese mixture. Turn into Graham Cracker Crumb Crust and bake at 325° for 35 minutes, or until set. Remove from oven and cool on wire rack. Spread Lemon Topping over pie after cooled. Chill at least 12 hours or overnight before serving.

Yield: 12 servings
Calories: 126 per serving

# Graham Cracker Crumb Crust

1 cup fine graham cracker crumbs (7–10 crackers)
¼ tsp. ground cinnamon
Dash ground nutmeg
2 Tbsp. diet margarine, melted
Pam or other spray-on nonstick coating (optional)

Combine crumbs, cinnamon, and nutmeg in a bowl. Work in melted margarine until evenly distributed. With your fingertips, press crumb mixture evenly over the bottom and sides of a nonstick 9″ springform pan. (Spray pan with Pam, if desired.) Bake at 425° for 5–7 minutes, or until crumb mixture browns slightly around edges.

# Lemon Topping

2 Tbsp. fructose
1½ tsp. cornstarch
⅓ cup water
2 Tbsp. fresh lemon juice
1 Tbsp. egg substitute, or 1 drop egg yolk

In a small saucepan, combine fructose, cornstarch, water, and lemon juice. Cook over low heat until thickened. Remove from heat and let cool. Stir in egg substitute or egg yolk for color.

# Sharing Healthful Recipes

If you have created an original recipe following the guidelines outlined in *BodyCare* and would like to share it with others who are on the *BodyCare* adventure, send your recipe to me at this address:

*BodyCare*
P. O. Box 234
Port Aransas, TX 78373

If your recipe meets the standards and passes the "taste test," it might be included in a cookbook (with your name). In addition, you'll receive a free copy of the book. Send a self-addressed, stamped envelope for a summary of the guidelines.

All recipes submitted must be original, typed on 8½" x 11" paper, and must not be published under copyright.

# Part Five

# RESOURCES FOR BODYCARE LIVING

*Recommended Reading, Charts, and Worksheets to Help You Make BodyCare a Way of Life*

# Reading Lists

## Fitness and Exercise Books

There are many resource books available on the subject of fitness and exercise. Here are a few I've found to be especially helpful to me.

Bailey, Covert. *Fit or Fat?* Boston: Houghton Mifflin Company, 1977. A guide to health and fitness through nutrition and aerobic exercise.

Bennett, William, M.D., and Joel Gurin. *The Dieter's Dilemma: Eating Less and Weighing More.* New York: Basic Books, 1982. A doctor (Bennett) and a writer (Gurin) discuss some new findings on how human bodies resist weight-loss attempts, and discuss ways of overcoming the body's resistance.

Cooper, Kenneth H., M.D., M.P.H. *Aerobics.* New York: M. Evans & Co., 1968. (The copy I have is a paperback published by Bantam Books, New York, 1968.) A thorough description of what aerobic exercise is and how it improves health, with scientific research to illustrate findings. Also includes detailed descriptions of various kinds of aerobic exercise programs.

Cooper, Kenneth H., M.D., M.P.H. *The New Aerobics.* New York: M. Evans & Co., 1970. (The copy I have is a paperback published by Bantam Books, New York, 1970.) A book suited for the general public with detailed descriptions about how to safely and effectively begin an age-adjusted exercise program. It includes information about a special kind of physical examination and about fitness testing and categories, tips and safeguards, and a chapter handling many questions women ask about the Aerobics program. There are exercise programs for walking, running, cycling, swimming, stationary running, handball, basketball, and squash.

Cooper, Kenneth H., M.D., M.P.H. *The Aerobics Way: New Data on the World's Most Popular Exercise Program.* New York: M. Evans

& Co., 1977. (The copy I have is a paperback published by Bantam Books, New York, 1978.) More data on the positive connection between aerobics and weight loss, with a specially developed point system showing how each person can design her own aerobic program.

Edwards, Ted L., Jr., M.D. *From Weight Loss to Super Wellness.* Austin, TX: The Hills Medical/Sports Complex, 1983. A step-by-step program you can use to gradually and naturally reduce your weight and tone up your body. Good details included for "Aqua Aerobics"—both exercises in the water and lap swimming.

Fixx, James F. *The Complete Book of Running.* New York: Random House, 1977. If you choose to be a runner, everything you need to know about how to begin and what's likely to happen to you along the way—mentally, emotionally, and physically—is in this book. And a good factor to me is that Jim Fixx is not a medical person, but a journalist. He approaches this subject with a combination of good writing, thorough research, and personal experience. The appendix also gives many helpful lists of books about running, shoes, shoe repair by mail, mail-order running gear, organizations which encourage running, and running periodicals.

Fixx, James F. *Jim Fixx's Second Book of Running.* New York: Random House, 1980. In the three years between the publication of Jim Fixx's first book and the publication of this one, new scientific discoveries about the health benefits and hazards of running came to light. This companion book deals with many of these issues, looking realistically at what running can really promise, where to find help for foot problems, how to train for a race, and what to eat to stay both healthy and thin. Lists of major magazines and books about running are also included.

Sheehan, George A., M.D. *Dr. Sheehan on Running.* Mountain View, CA: Anderson World, 1975. (The copy I have is a paperback published by Bantam Books, New York, 1978.) Written when Dr. Sheehan was 57 years old, this book deals with practical aspects of running—physical effects, the importance of rest, mental attitudes. He says, "Success rests with having the courage and endurance and, above all, the will to become the person you are, however peculiar that may be. Then you will be able to say, 'I have found my hero and he [she] is me.'"

Sheehan, George A., M.D. *Running & Being: The Total Experience.* New York: Warner Books, 1978. This book is an inspirational, philosophical, and "popular" medical discussion of running. Dr. Sheehan's idea of running is "mostly the idea of play. Of bringing back your body, of becoming yourself," a total person.

# Nutrition Books

The bookstores are full of books about how to manage food, and many good ones have not come to my attention. However, the following is a list of books I have studied over the past three years—books which have helped teach me a more proper way to cook, eat, and view food. Many of them contain great recipes, too.

Berger, Stuart, M.D., and Marcia Cohn. *The Southampton Diet.* New York: Simon & Schuster, 1982. A description—by a man who is a medical doctor, psychiatrist, and has lost 210 pounds himself—of the physiological effects foods have on our moods and energy levels. His way of combining foods while dieting helps ensure an even level of blood sugar throughout the day, eliminating the "ups and downs" that often lead to food binges, feelings of failure, and energy drops—things which cause many people to abandon their diets. The book includes recipes.

Brody, Jane. *Jane Brody's Nutrition Book: A Lifetime Guide to Good Eating for Better Health and Weight Control by the Personal Health Columnist of the New York Times.* New York: W. W. Norton & Company, 1981. (The copy I have is a paperback published by Bantam Books, New York, 1982.) Jane Brody is the nutrition editor for the *New York Times* and has studied this subject in depth for years. Her book is an easy-to-understand, well-organized reference for learning about food. In my opinion, it's the book to start with.

Claiborne, Craig, and Pierre Franey. *Craig Claiborne's Gourmet Diet.* New York: Times Books, 1980. The *New York Times* food editor and a gourmet cook, Craig Claiborne developed hypertension. As a result, he revised his cooking methods to save his life and improve his health without losing the superb flavors and consistencies of the foods. After six months on the diet he was off medication for controlling his hypertension and cholesterol and was taking only one vitamin pill. You don't have to wait until your doctor tells you it's life or death. Now you can eat interesting, well-flavored gourmet foods, using the recipes found in this great book.

Goldbeck, Nikki, and David Goldbeck. *The Supermarket Handbook: Access to Whole Foods.* New York: Plume Books, div. New American Library, 1976. (The copy I have is the expanded, revised edition published by Signet Books, div. New American Library, 1976.) A guide to a better understanding of foods available in the supermarket, what the various additives are, and their potential dangers to the body. Be advised that this book was first published ten years ago, and the F.D.A. has done a lot to eliminate harmful additives in our foods since then.

Lappe, Frances Moore. *Diet for a Small Planet.* Rev. ed. New York: Ballantine Books, div. Random House, 1975. Information about ways to save money and still eat a high-quality, nutritious diet with meatless meals. This book explains what foods to put together to make delicious, protein-rich meals without heavy use of meats, tells why you must have protein and how much, and gives a cost comparison of non-meat proteins. This book contains recipes, and there is also a companion volume entitled *Recipes for a Small Planet,* which gives many more excellent recipes for meatless cooking.

Prince, Francine. *Diet for Life.* New York: Cornerstone Library, div. Simon & Schuster, 1981. A best-selling author's husband was told by a cardiologist that, because of heart disease, he would die if he walked a single city block. Through the Princes' study of nutritional literature and the application of what they learned, Mr. Prince, seven years later, is in perfect health—slim and brimming with energy. He has even climbed a mountain! The food approach presented in this book is built around a no-sugar, no-salt cuisine, low in fat and cholesterol and supplemented with the right amount of vitamins and the right kind of exercise. The guidelines are approved by the American Medical Association, the American Heart Association, and the U.S. Department of Agriculture. Recipes are included.

Robertson, Laurel, Carol Flinders, and Bronwen Godfrey. *Laurel's Kitchen: A Handbook for Vegetarian Cookery and Nutrition.* Petaluma, CA: Nilgiri Press, 1976. (The copy I have is a paperback published by Bantam Books, New York, 1978.) A handbook for vegetarian cookery and nutrition, written by a writer in conjunction with a nurse and a fabulous cook who taught the other two her arts. Especially good are the descriptions of whole grains and instructions on how to make marvelous breads that turn out well every time. Recipes are included.

# Cookbooks

Many, many cookbooks are available. A few have found their way to my home and I have enjoyed them immensely. Here is a little list.

El Molino Mills. *The El Molino Cookbook.* City of Industry, CA: El Molino Mills, 1976. The El Molino grain products have become part of my standard pantry contents, and I have learned much from this cookbook. There is a section describing grains, seeds, legumes, and carob, and another about how to bake with, store, measure, grind, sprout, and select them. The recipes for breads, cereals, pancakes, snacks, soups and salads, meat, poultry, fish, stuffing, meatless dishes, beverages, and desserts provide interesting wholesome alternatives to less healthy but more traditional recipes. Recipes include sugar and whole dairy products and are not low calorie. Use judgment with these. For information about obtaining this book, write to El Molino Mills, Box 2250, City of Industry, CA 91746.

Eshleman, Ruthe, and Mary Winston. *The American Heart Association Cookbook.* 3rd rev. ed. New York: David McKay, 1979. (The copy I have is a paperback published by Ballantine Books, New York, 1980.) This book was recommended to me by the nutritionist at the preventive medicine center where I have my annual physical exam. It is an excellent source of lowfat, low-cholesterol recipes and includes calorie counts per serving on each recipe. There are recipes for every food category, menus for holidays and special occasions, a chapter on how to adapt your own recipes, tips for when you eat out or pack a lunchbox, and some charts showing fat/cholesterol contents and conversion tables to convert measurements into metric units.

Fong, Nancy Lew and Deborah Rae Davis. *The Phoenix Spa Cookbook.* Houston, TX: Living Well, 1984. Lowfat, low-sugar, delectable recipes prepared by Nancy Fong, nutritionist, and Deborah Davis, chef, for The Phoenix Spa. Includes 60 recipes divided into eight chapters: Breakfasts; Lunches; Dinners; Hors D'Oeuvres;

Beverages; Desserts; Soups, Salads, and Side Dishes; and Breads. Also includes one week's worth of sample menus at 1,000 calories a day, using the recipes in the book. Can be ordered through The Phoenix Spa Boutique, 111 North Post Oak Lane, Houston, TX 77024.

Ford, Marjorie Winn, Susan Hillyard, and Mary Faulk Koock. *The Deaf Smith Country Cookbook.* New York: Collier Books, div. Macmillan Publishing Company, 1973. A vegetarian cookbook which offers delicious alternatives to meat. Copyrighted by Arrowhead Mills, a leading company in whole-foods products, the book treats the handling of natural foods with a sincere and reverent attitude:

> In these days, the Holy Spirit is truly being poured out upon all those who seek, and the right relationship with God, which begins with faith, can logically be extended to the methods used in farming and food preparation as well as our relationships with each other. It may become an exciting adventure for you and your family, and you will be in good company (p. xi, Preface).

Recipes are included for every time of day, plus baby foods, children's foods, lunchbox recipes, and comprehensive information for storage and care of natural foods. All recipes emphasize whole grains and natural seasonings and use no refined sugar, white flour, or other refined foods.

Knox, Gerald M., editor. *The Dieter's Cook Book.* Des Moines, IA: Better Homes & Gardens Books, div. Meredith Corporation, 1982. This book is another excellent source of recipes, guides to weight loss, calorie information, and so on. It includes a chapter each on meatless meals, exercise, and a weight-loss diet based on food exchanges. Calorie content per serving is included with each recipe.

Jones, Jeanne. *The Calculating Cook: A Gourmet Cookbook for Diabetics & Dieters.* San Francisco: 101 Productions, 1972. Jeanne Jones approaches food preparation through the need to control her own health problem—diabetes. But, realizing that her diabetic diet is also beneficial to other people trying to cut down on fat, sugar, cholesterol, and calories, she wrote this cookbook. It is full of wonderful recipes and invaluable cooking tips and provides calorie counts and nutritional information for each recipe.

It also contains an easy-to-follow version of the diabetic diet, a balanced food-serving diet, and gives information about how to fit each recipe into the diet.

Jones, Jeanne. *Diet for a Happy Heart: A Low-Cholesterol, Low-Saturated-Fat, Low-Calorie Cookbook.* Rev. ed. San Francisco: 101 Productions, 1981. A lowfat, low-cholesterol, low-calorie cookbook that gives not only the calories per serving, but cholesterol and fat content, too. There is information about the difference in saturated and polyunsaturated fats, and about a "happy heart" diet program. This book began when Jeanne Jones realized that her diabetic diet was beneficial to her husband's cholesterol problems. (Jeanne is active with the American Diabetes Association and a member of the board of directors of the San Diego County Heart Association.) In this book, she shows how to cook tasty broths, soups, sauces and gravies, salad dressings, vegetables, eggs, fish, poultry, meat, bread, desserts, and beverages while cutting down on fats and cholesterol. There is also a section on menu planning, some time-saving hints, and some information on equivalents for measuring purposes.

Martinsen, Charlene S. *Cooking with Gourmet Grains.* Bloomington, MN: Stone-Buhr Milling Co., 1971. I found this collection educational and also full of delicious recipes for using barley, buckwheat, corn, millet, oats, rice, rye, soybeans, sunflower seeds, and wheat. Also included is information about other forms of grains, including bran flakes, cracked wheat, golden farina, wheat germ, and wheat flakes. There are also a number of recipes included for people with allergies. The book is divided into sections: morning grains (cereals), vegetables and salads, main dishes, breads, pies, and desserts. Recipes call for whole dairy products and sugar at times, so judgment must be used in selecting recipes to fit your needs. For information about ordering, write to Stone-Buhr Milling Co., 2201 Killebrew Drive, Suite 122, Bloomington, MN 55420.

Prince, Francine. *The Dieter's Gourmet Cookbook.* New York: Cornerstone Library, div. Simon & Schuster, 1979. Francine Prince is the author of *Diet for Life*, in which she described her husband's diagnosis of hypertension and heart disease, and the steps she took to learn to cook properly. (See reading list for nutrition for more details on that book.) This is a cookbook full of delicious lowfat, low-cholesterol cooking and baking recipes using no sugar or salt! Prince also gives ideas about where to shop for the ingredients you need and about the utensils she uses, as well as sharing some money-saving hints.

Renwick, Ethel H. *The Real Food Cookbook.* Grand Rapids, MI: Zondervan Publishing House, 1978. This book is full of recipes that represent years of pleasure in cooking and experimenting with natural foods. A Christian writer and homemaker, Ethel Renwick explains about natural foods and about how to add nutrition to meals. Recipes are included for breakfast, lunch, dinner; breads, soups, salads and dressings, vegetables, desserts and drinks, snacks and refreshments. The recipes are not low-calorie or low-cholesterol, however. A list of source books and recommended reading is also included. This is a companion volume to Mrs. Renwick's book, *Let's Try Real Food,* also published by Zondervan.

Weight Watchers International, Inc., eds. *Weight Watchers 365-Day Menu Cookbook.* New York: New American Library, 1981. Based on the Weight Watchers full-choice food plan, this cookbook tells you what to eat every day of the year. If you're in a fast-paced lifestyle in which there is little time to calculate food servings and plan your own menus, this book can save you all that bother. And the variety, freedom, and flexibility help keep the menus interesting.

# Other Resources

## *Recommended Exercise Recordings*

There are many good exercise records and tapes on the market. The following are some I have enjoyed. They all feature Christian music but vary in the kinds of exercise they offer and the degree of difficulty. These recordings are available as record albums or cassettes and may be ordered from Word Inc., Waco, TX 76796:

Hanson, Vickie. *Aerobic Glow: Fitness in Action.* Waco, TX: DaySpring Records, div. Word Inc., 1982. This advanced, high-energy aerobic dance program is set to vibrant Christian music. A booklet with photographs and instructions provides details of the movements and steps. Album: 7-01-411101-9. Cassette: 7-01-411157-4.

Moser, Judy and Bobbie Wolgemuth. *Firm Believer: A Complete Exercise Program Featuring Today's Christian Music.* Waco, TX: DaySpring Records, div. Word Inc., 1982. A good program to begin getting muscles in shape. *Firm Believer* works on each muscle group (arms, waist, stomach, etc.) in sequence. The routines consist of easy-to-understand exercises which are done to lively Christian music. The instruction booklet clearly explains each exercise with photographs and directions. Album: 7-01-410501-9. Cassette: 7-01-410557-4.

Moser, Judy and Bobbie Wolgemuth. *Firm Believer Advanced: A Challenging Workout to Stretch and Strengthen You.* Waco, TX: DaySpring Records, div. Word Inc., 1983. While easy to understand, these exercises call for more strength and flexibility than the original *Firm Believer* program. This advanced tape also builds muscle tone by working on each muscle group separately. The instruction booklet provides complete directions with photographs. Album: 7-01-411601-0. Cassette: 7-01-411657-6.

Stout, Cathi. *Believercise: Choreographed Exercise to Contemporary Gospel Music.* Waco, TX: DaySpring Records, div. Word Inc., 1982. This program provides aerobic exercise while continuing to build muscle tone. Each song includes a simple series of three to five movements for an enjoyable workout. A large, easy-to-follow poster outlines movements for each song. Album: 7-01-410801-8. Cassette: 7-01-410857-3.

Warren, Jaime. *AerobiRhythms.* Waco, TX: DaySpring Records, div. Word Inc., 1983. A collection of aerobic dances with timely verbal cues make this recording fun to follow. The more energy applied to these exercise, the more effective the cardiovascular workout will be. Details of movements are given on a handy two-sided poster. Album: 7-01-411501-4. Cassette: 7-01-411557-x.

# A Study Course for Exercise Groups

Miller, Andrea Wells. *BodyCare: Studies in Nutrition and Exercise for God's Body of Believers.* Waco, TX: Educational Products, div. of Word Publishing, 1984. A set of 12 tapes: five exercise tapes (described above) and seven leadership tapes. The ten-week (three times a week) course features a 12-minute "talk" on tape by Andrea Wells Miller which includes a scripture, meditation, and prayer, followed by a short lesson about fitness or nutrition. After this, the group exercises together using the exercise tapes, changing tapes each two weeks. The exercise program begins with a beginning muscle-tone tape, progresses through aerobic activity tapes, and ends with an advanced muscle-tone tape. The course also includes worksheets for handout in class and helpful guidelines for the class leader, along with ideas for how to continue the group after the initial ten weeks are over and ideas for church suppers. A copy of this book is also included. 12-cassette kit: 2-01-071800-3.

# Materials I Have Ordered at No Cost

| Name of Information | Address from Which to Order |
|---|---|
| *The Prudent Diet* (booklet)<br>*Prudent International Recipes*<br>*Prudent Entertaining* | Bureau of Nutrition<br>New York City Dept. of Health<br>93 Worth Street, Room 714<br>New York, NY 10013 |
| *Recipes* (for fat-controlled and low-cholesterol diets) | American Heart Association<br>7320 Greenville Avenue<br>Dallas, TX 75231 |
| *Cook with Love, Cook with Corn Oil* | Consumer Service Dept.<br>Best Foods<br>A Division of CPC International, Inc.<br>International Plaza<br>Englewood Cliffs, NJ 07632 |
| *Dietary Control of Cholesterol— Cooking with Egg Beaters* | Fleischmann's Margarines<br>625 Madison Avenue<br>New York, NY 10022 |
| New "Ideal Weight" charts (self-addressed, stamped envelope requested) | Metropolitan Life Insurance Co.<br>Corporate Communications Dept.<br>One Madison Avenue<br>New York, NY 10010 |
| *Seasoning with Angostura Bitters* | A-W Brands, Inc.<br>1200 Milk Street<br>Cartaret, NJ 07008 |

# Weekly Time Map

| | MONDAY | TUESDAY | WEDNES-DAY | THURS-DAY | FRIDAY | SATUR-DAY | SUNDAY |
|---|---|---|---|---|---|---|---|
| 6:30 | | | | | | | |
| 7:00 | | | | | | | |
| 7:30 | | | | | | | |
| 8:00 | | | | | | | |
| 8:30 | | | | | | | |
| 9:00 | | | | | | | |
| 9:30 | | | | | | | |
| 10:00 | | | | | | | |
| 10:30 | | | | | | | |
| 11:00 | | | | | | | |
| 11:30 | | | | | | | |
| 12:00 | | | | | | | |
| 12:30 | | | | | | | |
| 1:00 | | | | | | | |
| 1:30 | | | | | | | |
| 2:00 | | | | | | | |
| 2:30 | | | | | | | |
| 3:00 | | | | | | | |
| 3:30 | | | | | | | |
| 4:00 | | | | | | | |
| 4:30 | | | | | | | |
| 5:00 | | | | | | | |
| 5:30 | | | | | | | |
| 6:00 | | | | | | | |
| 6:30 | | | | | | | |
| 7:00 | | | | | | | |
| 7:30 | | | | | | | |
| 8:00 | | | | | | | |
| 8:30 | | | | | | | |
| 9:00 | | | | | | | |
| 9:30 | | | | | | | |
| 10:00 | | | | | | | |
| 10:30 | | | | | | | |

# Worksheets

## *Pulse Rate*

Resting heart rate at beginning of exercise
commitment: _____

Date taken: _____

Resting heart rate after _____ months: _____

Date taken: _____


MAXIMUM HEART RATE: _____
                                    *(subtract your age from 220)*


WORKING HEART RATE RANGE:

    (1) .70 × _____ = _____ (lower)

    (2) .85 × _____ = _____ (upper)

    (3) Working heart rate range is: _____ to _____$^2$
                                            *(lower)*   *(upper)*

---

2. After aerobic exercise, pulse rate should be between the upper and lower figures.

# My Ideal Weight

Height: _____

Frame Size: _____(S, M, L)


First 5', allow 100 pounds:                         100

Add 5 pounds per inch over 5':                    ____

Add or subtract 5 pounds if L or S frame:      ____

                                        TOTAL: ____

Ideal range is: _____ to _____
                *(total minus 5)*              *(total plus 5)*

# My Eating and Exercise Plan

MY WEIGHT GOAL: _____


No. cal. needed for *new* weight: _____ $\times$ 15 = _____
                                     *(new wt.)*

Exercise bonus (_____ miles x _____ cal.):     _____
                      *(use chart on p. 147)*

                        (1) TOTAL:       _____


No. cal. I choose for diet:              _____

Exercise bonus (less than above):       _____

                        (2) TOTAL:       _____


Deficit in calories: (1) _____ − (2) _____ = _____


$\dfrac{3{,}500}{\textit{(cal. per lb.)}}$ ÷ _____ = _____ days per pound
                           *(deficit)*


To lose _____ pounds will take:
       *(desired no.)*

_____ $\times$ _____ or _____ days.
*[desired no.]*         *[days per lb.]*


With this information, my weight loss plan would be to:
(1) Eat _____ calories per day;
(2) Run _____ miles per day or equivalent exercise;
(3) Stick to this for _____ days.

From THE COMPLETE BOOK OF RUNNING, by James F. Fixx. Cpyright © 1977 by James F. Fixx. Reprinted by permission of Random House, Inc.

# About the Author

Andrea Wells Miller is a professional writer, speaker, consultant, and health enthusiast who has made the long journey from being overweight, unwell, and apathetic to a state of fitness, health, and vitality. She shares her life-changing discoveries in this book as well as in a study course, also called *BodyCare*. Both grew out of her studies and experiments with information about exercise and healthy eating, along with her application of Bible study and prayer to the process.

Andrea began her career as a writer in 1980 with the release of a 12-cassette study course, *Faith, Intimacy, and Risk in the Single Life*, co-written with her husband, Keith Miller. She and Keith also co-authored a popular book entitled *The Single Experience*.

In addition, Andrea compiled and edited *A Choir Director's Handbook* and has written articles for *Christian Bookseller* and *Solo* magazine. She also wrote a discussion/study guide for the Keith Miller film series, *New Wine: Evangelism As a Biblical Way of Living*.

Prior to becoming a full-time writer, Andrea was director of marketing for the music division of Word, Incorporated. She has also been active as a speaker, and in 1978 she addressed a national singles conference in Green Lake, Wisconsin. Subsequently, she spoke and led workshops at *Solo* magazine's first annual singles conference, SALT I, and has spoken and led workshops at other conferences during the past seven years.

Andrea received a bachelor's degree in music from Furman University and has done post-graduate study at Baylor University in music theory, commercial art, and photography. She is now working on a master's degree in business administration at Corpus Christi State Univerity.

Raised in Tennessee, Andrea now lives in a small fishing town on an island in the Gulf of Mexico, near Corpus Christi, and remains active as a speaker, consultant, photographer, and writer. She welcomes your comments and questions about *BodyCare*. Address correspondence to P.O. Box 234, Port Aransas, Texas 78373.